The Naked Pilgrim

D1500871

The Naked Pilgrim

Keith Manton

Best wishes

Kith 2014

for Jeff.

VANTAGE PRESS
New York

Cover design by Susan Thomas

FIRST EDITION

All rights reserved, including the right of
reproduction in whole or in part in any form.

Copyright © 2009 by Keith Manton

Published by Vantage Press, Inc.
419 Park Ave. South, New York, NY 10016

Manufactured in the United States of America
ISBN: 978-0-533-15989-5

Library of Congress Catalog Card No: 2008901037

0 9 8 7 6 5 4 3 2 1

Contents

The Naked Pilgrim

1

Beginnings

"Fall in, fall in. Come on, what's the facking problem?" Drops of spit liberally sprinkled several of us on the front row as the uniformed officer began to go red in the face, screaming at our blank faces with arms pinned to his side like they were bolted in place. His stance leaning forward at an angle that would make most people fall flat on their faces. He continued to stare right at me as if I were some deserter who had run off with the rum fanny. (I was yet to learn what a rum fanny was, or what delights it was able to provide.)

I had been unfortunate enough to position myself right in the middle of the group after we had scrambled off the blue busses that brought us from the railway station. Now I was in the direct line of fire of the saliva that emanated from his flapping mouth with every word. Within seconds we were all rigid and silent trying to emulate his stance like rows of comical tin soldiers. Only we were not soldiers, we were sailors. Well, for the last four minutes and thirty seconds we were.

I was one of a group of fifteen- and sixteen-year-olds who had, for a multitude of reasons that were as yet unknown to me, volunteered to join Her Majesty's Royal Navy. The day was October 3rd, the year 1962, not long after the Bay of Pigs, before the Beatles' first number one and only days before the Cuban missile crisis.

1

I was fifteen years, eight months old and eight stones (112 lbs) dripping wet. Like the other forty or so lads in this group I had signed on at a local recruiting office (mine being in Lincoln) for what would have been almost twelve years of active service.

In those days, to join as a boy, one committed to a nine-year service period but time did not start until you had turned eighteen.

Thus, at fifteen my scheduled departure age would have been twenty-seven. I say would have because much was to happen that eventually changed that; but at the onset I had signed on for the full term.

The place was HMS Ganges at Shotley Point just south of Ipswich and it was the Royal navy's premier junior sailors training establishment that had been in existence in one form or another since before the 20th century began.

I was soon to discover that the mentality and methods of the instructors was also established before the 20th century began. CPO Hutchins, as I quickly discovered, was just one of a number of noncommissioned offices that would make my life an absolute misery for the next twelve months.

I might add that at the same time, in the most opposite of ways, he was also responsible for saving me from a very different and possibly wasted life. To explain that I had better go back a bit and explain how I got here.

Where does any story begin? Well, like everyone else, I guess, at birth. "Come on, Daisy, push, push, here he comes, yes well done, it's a boy, oh that's disappointing my God he's ugly."

I have no knowledge of what my father was doing at the moment of my birth but back then he probably was not at the bedside whispering encouragement in my mother's ear. My guess is that he was at his regular spot at the Chequers Inn in

Weston where he would have been raising a glass to my impending arrival. (It is not insignificant that he had actually been born himself in that very pub some fifty years before.) That is assuming he had actually remembered where mother had gone.

Don't get me wrong, I am not suggesting he did not care about his family but he did have an unusual way of appearing to be inside a cocoon that protected him from the real world around him.

Of course I have no memory of the actual happenings but I can sort of guess the sequence of events. It took about four years on this earth before I actually had any recollection of anything.

This momentous event took place at Wyberton West Hospital in Boston Lincolnshire on February 1st 1947. It would be many years before I had any understanding of how Boston and the county of Lincolnshire played a role in the eventual establishment of the United States of America as the place from where the Puritans first tried and then fled to Holland in 1608. Of course John Smith was already over there checking things out beforehand. This was twelve years before the *Mayflower* eventually carried them to the new world and 354 years before I made it to the US myself.

Our journey from Boston was a little shorter, and this all happened during the worst snowstorm of the 20th century. My mother, once ejected from the warmth of the hospital and onto the local bus to take us home, had observed that the snowdrifts were higher than the bus.

You could say that I was born in interesting times. This year proved to be a year of great importance when remembering some of the major events that were unfolding at the time. The establishment of the state of Israel and the independence of India are just two worthy of note. I think I preferred Gandhi's tactics on behalf of India in his quest for independence to those of the other lot but I guess they both achieved their objectives in the end.

So, much of the British Empire was being lost before I would even have time to make my mark, and as I had no influence on any of these events perhaps we should go back to my first days on earth.

I am not sure if the snowstorm was some kind of sign that my early life was to involve some tough times but I like to think it was a toughening up experience for both of us. Not that Mother needed any more hardship to hone her resolve. From what I know it had already been a rough ride for her and would not get any easier for many years. This was apart from my father's knack of remaining totally aloof to all but the most interesting events such as the 3 o'clock race at Newmarket or the price of grain at the Spalding corn exchange.

I had been fourth down the chute for Mother, and she was to have my little sister Sandy three years later before being able to retire the reproductive equipment at the grand old age of thirty-six.

By the time I have any memory of anything, the 2nd World War had been over for five years and for those who had lived through it, there were constant reminders like the many old army lorries, now put to service as farm vehicles, or the still ever present rationing. It's almost impossible for me to imagine how life was just after the war. Everyone had lost loved ones, friends or just folks they knew.

Food and petrol rationing was still in force and some buildings still lay in ruins. Many servicemen, home from their respective duties, were still suffering from extreme mental anguish along with their physical scars. As for me, I was totally oblivious to any of this post war trauma. I was all right Jack, thank you very much. Well, all right until I was old enough to figure out what was going on around me.

We were living in a little bungalow in the quaint village of Weston, just a couple of miles from Spalding in Lincolnshire. My father, by the time I was born, was already fifty years old. He owned a smallholding growing vegetables and fruit for the local markets. Just down the road lived an old gentleman who I knew as Uncle Arthur; the connection I will go into in a while.

Of course only five years after the end of the second war Britain had little time to forget before we were plunged into the Korean War, which had got going in 1950. As we all know now, hostilities eventually ended with a cease-fire in July 1953.

I, of course, was totally unaware of any of this, but then we did not have embedded reporters and twenty-four-hour CNN. I wonder if today do five-year-olds actually comprehend what they see on the hourly news, day after day, and if they do, will they remember it in fifty years time.

I thought of the idea for writing about my life and seven years afore the mast in 2001 whilst sitting on a Delta Airlines flight in Atlanta, Georgia. Consumed by abject boredom I was looking at the back of the head in the seat in front. Atlanta, of course, is the home of the Braves and a curiously high number of quite strange people. Well, strange to me perhaps as I adjusted to the cultural delights of the South.

Mind you, I did wonder why anyone would want to read about some bloke who was totally unknown, never invented anything, can't run fast or play football and has no other redeeming features to his name. However, I put that small impediment behind me and decided to give it a shot anyway.

Little did I know that within months of me deciding to write a book, one of the most significant events of a whole lifetime was to occur on September 11th that same year. Fortunately for me I was on vacation on a Greek island on 9.11

and was totally unaware until some twenty hours after it all began, seeing it on CNN in a bar on the island.

The flight home from Greece was just three days after air travel was resumed, coming through the UK and Amsterdam, which took on an unusually somber mood. In previous years I had made several aborted attempts to write a book, but was trying to write fiction using a notebook and pencil.

Now it dawned on me that there's nothing as strange as the truth so I switched my thinking to things that had actually happened to see if that made more sense. Anyway, after digging out several very poor earlier attempts I realized I couldn't read my own writing. It was only after I had become computer literate that the very concept became feasible.

"Welcome 'bord ya'll, this is Mary-Beth Traminski, your flight leader for today's flight to Las Vegas.

"For those not familiar with the Braves, ya'll, that's the Atlanta baseball team. In baseball parlance, the Braves had been pretty successful over the years. I only know this from local news as I have never watched a game and still do not profess to have any understanding of the rules."

I think points are awarded for how far the pitcher (bowler) can actually spit tobacco juice. Or maybe it's the iron stare contest.

Whenever the subject came up amongst my American work colleagues I would always tell them that in England the girls play rounders (which is the same as baseball) but the men play rugby and cricket. It makes me wonder, if the Americans are so smart, why did they make their cricket bat round?

It's a bit like the Chinese with all that intellect and they designed pointed sticks to eat rice with!

Braves aside, while sitting on this plane waiting out a delayed take-off time, I was reading through the current issue of *Sky Flight*, or whatever it's called, for the third time that month. Having exhausted the bits that actually have some writing, I had moved on to the section where you can view maps of the many terminal buildings at the airports where Delta flies the most. Atlanta Hartsfield (the one I was trying to get away from), Cincinnati, Salt Lake City, Boston's Logan and so on, when it hit me like a brick.

Every single airport I had been through; some many times, others only passing through and never setting foot on the soil outside. It occurred to me that I was a very well-traveled person; in fact, not just well-traveled but an absolute bloody world explorer in the true spirit of the greats, Cortez, Raleigh, Pissarro, Columbus, and Michael Palin, etc. Now I admit that they experienced a higher degree of difficulty than I did (except Palin) and they did get to places before me.

Nevertheless I suddenly felt some kind of connection. After all here I was sitting in Atlanta, Georgia USA, an American citizen, and only yesterday I was sitting on Uncle Arthur's lap in the little village of Weston in Lincolnshire.

That's in England, UK, listening to stories about the voyage of Her Majesty's Ship *Ajax*. The springboard for all of this world travel, which continued long after my time in the navy, was prompted by that early experience of discovering the world outside the UK from a gray painted luxury warship.

So why not write about the experience that had triggered it all off?

I mention the UK and England bit because in America they don't all know that Britain is made up of several entities. My wife (#2) and I were making one of our first visits to a supermarket in Fresno, California in 1992 when this flaw in the American education system came to light. We had just moved to this rather strange hot desert town from our home in Southern England on one of those company transfers that does not always equip one for what is in store.

We had just discovered that unless you don't actually need to borrow money, you can't. Borrowing money in the States requires you to first establish some kind of credit record or you are unable to get a credit rating.

So, we had deposited some meager funds in our brand new bank account in an effort to begin the credit building process and were doing some shopping. Now we were at the checkout to pay for our stuff and I gingerly produced my brand spanking new checkbook.

"Drivers license," mumbled the teenager, scratching bits of metal attached to parts of her face. I produced my license issued by the British Motor Vehicle Licensing office. "There's no photo," retorted the metal-infested teenager without raising her eyes to look at me. "I need a photo ID for you to write a check."

My wife Julie, after just a few days in Fresno and already highly suspicious of this "lucrative" company transfer deal, delved into her handbag and produced her passport. She promptly plonked it in front of metal face.

After a long pause and several looks up and down there followed, "Wow, are you guys from Briddish." I can only assume that the teenager had absolutely no concept of the subtle difference between England, the United Kingdom or Britain as names that are used in reference to the British Isles.

Julie responded in a very calm but firm manner, "No, my dear, we *are* BriTish."

"Oh wow," squawked the awestruck teenager, as if we had literally stepped out of a silver spaceship from Mars.

She was so impressed that the bubble gum that frequently came into view as she merrily slopped and talked at the same time, almost fell out of her mouth.

8

Anyway not to digress, I was going to explain who Arthur was. "Was" because he passed away in 1978.

Arthur Mears was actually my half brother Ray's uncle on his mother's side but when you are four that doesn't seem to matter. Mum was so busy doing the million things Mums do with four kids at home and a husband who knows a woman's place (this was the 1950s), that any attention was welcome.

Add to that, three siblings who only want to poke you with a stick and make sure you take all the blame for anything that happened that parents get revenge for. "Mum, Mum he did it, he caused the Holocaust, he got up last night and went to Germany and got in charge and, and, well he did it . . . hit him, Mum."

It's funny how your closest family can want you dead or severely maimed when you have done absolutely nothing to provoke any kind of retribution. As my sister Sandy got older she realized very quickly that a claim that I had kicked her in the stomach could bring great benefits to her and awful spankings for me.

I cannot remember one occasion when the accusation was true but I did suffer many slaps on the back of the legs with Mum's slipper. At a recent family gathering I got Sister Sandy to actually admit in front of witnesses that she did falsely accuse me of these crimes, unfortunately some fifteen years after our mother had passed away. So Mum, if you can see what's going on down here, "I TRIED TO TELL YOU SHE WAS LYING."

Mind you, I used to scare the shit out of her by creeping up behind her in the dark and shouting "Tiger." This was promoted by a film that was showing in the '50s called *Harry Black and the Tiger,* which we had been taken to see, and Sandy had a morbid fear of big cats (and small ones if it was Kitty, who will be featured a bit later.)

Anyway, back to Arthur. Arthur, distant uncle, was also a close neighbor in Weston and one of those great people of a bygone age who never questioned their responsibility to die if the government said you had to.

He was one of millions who believed that for Britain to remain great, she needed people like him to help suppress the natives and make them toe the line. To take our huge warships and roam the world looking for the slightest bit of a punch-up ready to put down any dissent that the British government considered to be not allowed.

I have in my possession a handmade map that Uncle Arthur drew while serving on HMS *Ajax* in the Persian Gulf in 1920–21. It's ironic that this region, and the influence that Britain had on its destiny during that period, is now so much in the news in the 21st century. The map provides a pictorial record of the voyage of the *Ajax* and shows all the places they visited during that commission.

It was much later in life when I started to read political history, that I realized how incredibly naïve I have been for most of my life about events and people that have shaped world history. Perhaps if I had taken an earlier interest I might have been Prime Minister or head of the UN by now, and thinking about it, I could probably do a better job than some recent efforts.

I remembered sitting listening to all the stories about strange people that had cloths on their heads who didn't eat Yorkshire pudding before they could have their meat, and about huge waves that tossed the mighty ship around like a cork in the bath and a sun that was so hot it actually melted the steel decks under the sailors' feet.

I suppose life was so one-dimensional in rural Lincolnshire in the '50s that *anything* else seemed exciting. It was probably those early stories of the sea that made me pay more attention to geography and history when I finally made it to the secondary modern school in Sleaford.

These were the only subjects that I had any hope learning at a passable level. I was one of those kids that got caught up in the educational postwar revolution. This was supposed to be a time when every child was to be given the same opportunity and the system was fair to all, regardless of wealth or status. I quickly learned that there is nothing fair about anything in this life.

Before I could get school over with I had to make it through the first dangerous years as a target for my older brother and two sisters, one older, one younger. My older half brother Ray had moved out to work before I came along and my half sister Nova had never lived at home with us and it would be some time before I even figured out who they were.

2

School and the Early Years

My recollection of my first home in Weston is very vague. Apart from Uncle Arthur's stories I can only really remember just one incident as a four-year-old falling off my tricycle into the ditch by the front gate at the tiny one-story house that was home to six of us.

My mother used to tell everyone about the time my father reversed his old pickup truck over my foot when I ran outside to see where he was going. (The damage inflicted by the truck paled into insignificance to the damage that winkle pickers would do some twelve years later.) This should have been a sign to my parents that I was going to be a bit accident-prone in later life, which even now is still true. I am the only man I know that can injure himself with about every tool in the toolbox.

The next ten years, till I was fifteen, were spent at Beacon Hill. We moved to this farm at the side of a little hill that, according to local legend, was so named because it actually was used to light a beacon hundreds of years previously.

This was to warn folks of some marauding band of savages coming to rape and pillage the locals. This subtle piece of information never actually connected with me till long after I had fled the area to do my own raping and pillaging. (In a manner of speaking.)

Life on a farm for an accident-prone, skinny, and frightened-of-his-own-shadow kid, could be downright danger-ous. Tall trees to climb, barns to fall off, tractors to play with, wells to fall in and all kinds of implements with spikes, blades and cutters to get feet and hands caught in.

Farming in the fifties was still waiting to move into the technologic age and much of the equipment on this estab-lishment was either pre-war or at least of that pre-war era. Safety guards were still a thing of the future. If you got wound 'round a tractor tire, spiked with a pitchfork, burned on an overheating engine, or poisoned by toxic chemicals, it was your own damn fault.

I remember one day hanging underneath a straw eleva-tor (like you would a bar in the gym), where the bed had been wound down to its lowest position to be towed down the road to its next place of duty.

This machine had a set of six-inch-long metal spikes spaced out along its belt to carry the sheaves of corn up the elevator to the top of the stack. The spikes alternated with three on one bar and two on the next. With the bed wound down in this position I could just jump high enough to reach the cross bar between two spikes and hang on.

In its lowest horizontal position it was highly unstable at the end furthest from the wheels and towing hitch (that was the end where I was hanging), so much so that even a fifty-pound weakling with heavy boots could break the equi-librium.

This brought the end crashing down to earth. Fortu-nately for the fifty-pound weakling the spikes were far enough apart for the skinny chest to pass between them and the spikes to sink into the soil either side without more than a light bruise.

I let go with a scream and the bed shot back up once the weight was released. Then it bounced back down again a split second after I rolled out of the way. This was just one of the many occasions when either luck or divine intervention saved me from a very early demise.

One of the most vivid memories I have of the early years at Beacon Hill is the sound of a racing car engine screaming round a track early on a Sunday morning. Beacon Hill was about ten miles as the fast sports car flies, from the little town of Bourne.

Motor racing enthusiasts will know that this little town is synonymous with one of the most famous of all early British racers and racing legacies.

Raymond Mays and the E.R.A. (English Racing Association) and B.R.M. (British Racing Motors) were based in Bourne. Mays was a racing fanatic who hailed from a wealthy family who made their money in the wool trade.

After the First World War young Raymond took up all kinds of racing in the '20s and '30s, however, his real interest was in the rapidly developing technology of more and more sophisticated racing machines and more powerful engines.

During the 1930s, along with his friend and partner Peter Berthon, they had designed, at least on paper, a revolutionary 16-cylinder supercharged engine that had the potential of over 300-horse power.

Unfortunately Hitler took a hand in slowing the project down and it was not until 1949 that the object of their fascination finally took on life embedded in a grand prix racing car. The engine and car they designed around it were very complex and fraught with mechanical problems but Mays and Berthon painstakingly persevered with it to the point where it achieved some success around Europe's racetracks.

It survived long enough for me to hear it at age five or six in the early '50s, being put through its paces on the war-time airfield at Folkingham just three miles across the fields from my home. Because the engine was so different to any other at that time, the sound was very distinctive.

Imagine 16 cylinders screaming in an engine that was only 1.5 liters. That sound conditioned me to want to race cars and even now in my advanced stage of age and physical dilapidation, I still do.

On the farm, the wheat was cut by a binder. The binder was a machine that was developed many years before the combine harvester and originally horse drawn. It was a fearsome little machine that now trailed behind a tractor with its cutting blade out to one side. As the blade chattered away cutting about six inches above the ground the wheat would trundle up a canvas belt and be bound in a bundle with binder twine and dropped off the back of the machine.

Several men would follow up on foot and "stouk" these sheaves in little clusters of three or four on their ends, with the grain at the top. Some weeks later when it was dry it was loaded onto trailers and brought to the stack yard and then piled into neat stacks around the place.

Some time later the threshing contractor with his ancient tractors and wooden threshing machines would arrive to process the stacks of wheat.

Grain, chaff and straw would miraculously separate from the chaos as the old Field Marshal tractor chugged away driving the huge canvas belt that turned the threshing machine cogs.

I was fascinated by the method that started the tractor engine. A cartridge was placed in a cavity in a flywheel on the front of the engine and fired, causing the flywheel to turn, thus cranking over the engine.

It would gradually gain revs until a steady thump, thump, thump set in as it ticked over. Then a large handle on the side of the tractor would be pulled over, tightening the belts to the threshing machine and the whole setup would be underway.

Upwards of a dozen laborers would then scurry around the various tasks, throwing the sheaves into the top of the machine and the stack would gradually descend to the ground level.

This was the point when all the kids came into play. The stacks had been in place for sometimes several months and during that time, being a rich source of food, they had become home to hundreds of rats. Now I'm not kidding when I tell you these rats were huge. Some were over a foot long without the tail, and probably weighing a couple of pounds.

The kid's job was to kill the rats with thatching pegs. These were hefty pieces of wood about five feet long that were used at the top of each stack to pin the sheaves, laid flat on the top to waterproof the whole structure.

As many as a dozen kids, mostly belonging to the laborers, ranging from tots and up to the teens, would be positioned around the base of the work area waiting for the rats to break.

This would happen when the last couple of layers were being taken up for threshing. The excitement built as we waited for the onslaught.

Once the rats appeared in their hundreds all hell broke loose with kids flailing thatching pegs like crazed warriors in a hand-to-hand battle. On one occasion my sister Elizabeth had the misfortune to be too close behind me as I tried to make my third or fourth kill. I swung the stick back, ready to strike another fat rat and hit her firmly across her teeth, drawing blood.

Other, less dangerous, jobs around the farm included collecting the eggs. Now you might think that was quite easy until you consider that the chickens were free range. That is to say they laid their eggs where the hell they liked.

The trick was to wait in a quiet spot for a while and watch as the hens scratched around in the dirt. When the hens thought no one was looking they would scurry off to a hidden nest in the undergrowth or the side of a haystack and settle on the nest. I could mosey up with my little basket and shoo them off and take the eggs.

It was common to be attacked by the damn things as they took great exception to me pinching their kids. It was also necessary to remember where each nest was to ensure we got the eggs before they were past the eat by date.

As there was a rooster around we also needed to make sure we got them before they hatched! It was not unusual to suddenly see a little collection of chicks wandering around behind a mother hen. Bugger, I missed that one!

Picking potatoes, singling sugar beet, chopping sticks, feeding pigs and shelling peas, all made up the daily chores that fell to the kids. It seems there was never any time to just sit around and be bored.

Along with psychopathic chickens we had another animal that required careful handling called Kitty the cat. Sounds quite safe but kitty was a Ferrell cat that came from a litter we found on the farm one day. Kitty had a reputation of being extremely vicious and woe-betide anyone who crossed her. Another cat we had was called Fluff and she was the complete opposite.

The problem was, whilst being farm cats they also had the run of the house. Fluff would wander in and sit on someone's lap and lie down purring. We would be in fear of Kitty coming in because she too would hop on someone's lap and dig her claws in the recipient's knees. It was not wise to try to push her off as she would hiss and spit and just as likely sink her teeth into the hand doing the pushing.

So if you were the unfortunate duffer to have her on your knee you sat rigid and silent until Kitty decided your knees had bled enough and she would suddenly leap off with one final gouge with her back claws. Needless to say we became skilled at whipping a magazine or comic book on our knee if Kitty appeared at the door with those beady eyes looking for a warm spot.

Physical hazards and farm chores aside my biggest problem was to become school. School began just after we had relocated from Weston to Beacon Hill where my Dad had secured employment as a stockman for gentleman farmer Mr. Philip Proctor. My dad, Harry Manton, was born in 1896 and had been fifty when I was born to my mother some eighteen years his junior.

He was one of ten children of my grandfather, who was a butcher and presumably champion fornicator. During the '20s Dad had owned a haulage business with several Thornycroft Lorries. He often talked about five-day round-trip journeys to Bristol carting four tons of produce on a vehicle with solid rubber tires.

Such a trip today could be achieved in a lorry carrying five times the weight in less than thirty-six hours. That is unless the council are digging up the road. Actually, thinking about it, it was probably quicker in 1920!

During the thirties and the Great Depression this enterprise went bankrupt and Dad switched his remaining resources to a smallholding in the village of Weston. He grew vegetables and fruit for the local community.

The little bungalow on the property was called Dandy and this is where I first lived. Dad's first wife and mother to my half brother Ray had died in the '30s from breast cancer. It was nearly forty years later that I discovered the truth about her demise from my sister Liz. Dad had always told me she died having her teeth out.

I guess in those days it was not done to talk to kids about things like breasts.

Consequently I had gone through most of my adult life still believing that to be the case. It had never occurred to me to question what my Dad had told me many years before. On a similar note I always believed my mother's first husband had gone missing in action on some wartime secret operation only to find out, again from Sister Liz, that they had separated very soon after getting married and Mother had moved to Lincolnshire where she met Father.

Mum had a daughter from this first liaison—my half sister Nova who was brought up by her father's family in the southeast of England.

I must have been eleven or twelve before I really figured out who Nova and Ray actually were although they appeared from time to time with their respective spouses and kids at family gatherings on the farm.

When we moved from Weston to Beacon Hill in 1951 I was just four years old, about the time that I have my earliest memories. The trip over in the back of an old army lorry had been fairly uneventful but I had been given an orange to eat as we bounced along the country roads for over an hour or so on a set of springs that seemed to do anything other than provide spring.

At four I had probably never seen an orange before nor knew that you are supposed to take the peel off before eating it. All had seemed well till we got to the old farm cottage that was to be home for the next ten years. Mother and Father were busy carting their modest possessions into the house and had just laid the vinyl floor in the bedroom. The orange was now beginning to percolate in my stomach as I lurched into the room for Mum to perform her soothing magic.

As I ran into the room I let forth a mighty multicolored stream of vomit across the floor, as the orange, the peel and probably several other foreign objects splattered over the shiny floor covering. I don't remember exactly what my father said but I'm sure the words came in very handy over ten years later when I took my turn to scour the world for trouble in her Majesty's behalf, as Able Seaman Manton.

This was to be the mighty aircraft carrier *Ark Royal*, a sailor, just like Uncle Arthur.

It was quite exciting learning about the new place where we were to live.

The farm had around three hundred and fifty acres at this location, a great deal of which was dedicated to rearing beef cattle. Other than a few fields of fodder crops most of the land was pasture for grazing. Even at the age of four or five I was able to explore the grounds with my sisters without fear of anyone bothering us.

Brother Pete, being six years older than me, always seemed to be doing more grown-up stuff and didn't really play with me. Of course we were blissfully unaware of bad people that preyed on children so we basically had a three hundred and fifty acre playground. One day Liz and me were in one of the fields about half a mile from the house when we decided to climb over a fence to paddle in the stream that ran through the property. As usual I was first over the top of the fence but having underestimated the height I fell head first down the other side.

I landed on my head with both hands stretched out to break the fall. Liz dutifully came over and helped me back to the house where Mum was again engaged in trying to figure out how badly I was really hurt.

For several days I complained about my arm and my head hurting until she finally gave in and took me down to the surgery in Billingborough to see Dr. Henderson. He was a Scot and just a great family doctor of the old school.

After some poking and twisting followed by a short discussion it was decided that I needed an X ray on my arm. On closer inspection of my head he discovered that I had a very large thorn buried deep in the middle that proved very painful to remove.

The next day we went off to Grantham Hospital, some fifteen miles on the bus to have my arm x-rayed. Because I was a cute little boy with curly hair the nurses and staff made a big fuss over me. After several encounters with various members of the staff we were informed that I had fractured my wrist.

Now the next thing that happened provided my mother with one of the best stories she used to tell at family gatherings.

We were ushered into the casualty room where the nurse asked me to hold out my arm so that she could begin to wrap it with the first layer of bandage that went on before the plaster of paris.

I dutifully held out my arm and the nurse began to wrap my wrist. After a few layers she asked me if it still hurt. Because of all the fuss and attention I had actually not taken much notice of the pain that was really not that bad at that point.

Without thinking I held up my other arm and said that it didn't hurt. The nurse looked at me a bit strange and then turned to the desk behind her and picked up the X ray.

Looking up at me she started to laugh out loud. Mother, by now wondering what was going on, suddenly realized that they have been wrapping the wrong arm. I swear to this day I did not do this purposely but Mother always told the story about how I deliberately fooled the nurse.

Over the years I was to visit Grantham Hospital on a number of other occasions, some funny, some not.

On that visit to Grantham Hospital I was totally unaware that literally just half a mile away resided a lady who was to become one of the twentieth century's most influential politicians and leaders of the free world, and in my wife's terminology my Hero. (At this point, whenever Dame Margaret Thatcher is mentioned I stand and salute.)

So now, just a few weeks after arriving at Beacon Hill, I was climbing out of that Austin Ten school taxi for my first of many miserable and unfulfilling days as a scholar. The school was about two miles from the farm and the local authority provided transport by way of a taxi as no school bus came in our direction.

Pointon, like many small rural Church of England schools in the early fifties had only two classrooms and two teachers, Mrs. Spriggs and Miss Darby.

Spriggy, as she was known, was a battleaxe of a woman who ruled the place with a rod of iron. Miss Darby on the other hand was a quiet spoken lady with ample breasts and always wore big fluffy jumpers which made them look even bigger.

She spoke in soothing tones and seemed to want to mother everyone. Spriggy was the exact opposite; any deviation from the rules would bring a screeching rebuke and several long minutes in the corner facing the wall until one could behave like a human being. I spent so much time facing the wall that I wondered if I would ever be able to join the human race for more than a few days at a time.

I really don't remember very much about the educational part of the six years that I spent at Pointon although the buildings and the coke stoves used to heat the place are still very clear. In those days it was usual to stay at infant and junior school till your eleventh year when the dreaded eleven plus exam came into focus.

One thing I remember very well were the heavy boots that I was required to wear, which could have been the medium that nearly took my life under the elevator before I was even ten.

I had weak ankles. It took me some time to come to

terms with the remedy that my mother provided to combat this insidious affliction, big, heavy lace up boots. I hated those rotten boots with a passion. Many years later I was the only one that cried in the movies when the young Forrest Gump was fitted with his leg irons. I knew how that kid felt.

"Na, na, you've got clod hoppers on." "What's wrong with your feet, Manton?" "You're stupid cos you ain't got no shoes." I was taunted in the playground so much that I would hide behind the coke shed around the back of the schoolhouse till the bell went and I could scurry back inside and listen to miss Darby's soothing tones.

Of course, if it was Spriggy's lesson it was less safe but at least if I kept my head down I could stay out of trouble till the end of the day. Playground time was usually pretty scary; if it wasn't the boot taunts it would be something else.

I don't know why they picked on me; maybe it was because I was from outside the village or I was skinny or perhaps everyone had their turn. Whatever, it just felt like me. My two sisters, who were at the same school for part of the time, made futile attempts to protect me but they were not always around at the right time. Maybe they thought it was a good time to work on ways when they would get their chance to have a go at me when we were at home.

It's funny how certain kids stay in your mind forever and others who were just as much part of the past are totally forgotten. I wonder if any of them that I have not seen or heard of for fifty years remember me.

One kid who was much bigger than me made a habit of always trying to push me over. This was not such a difficult task until you took into account the boots. Despite my intense dislike of those boots they did provide me unusually good anchor when given a sharp push in the back by the offending Peter Bristow.

Pete was a huge kid for his age—no doubt growing up

on a dairy farm had its advantages—and although I was normal height I was very light for my age. One day, after several unprovoked pushes, I must have snapped.

I staggered forward but didn't fall. Instead I turned round and lunged back at the now somewhat startled Pete. With all my might I swung my hand in a great arc and slapped him hard across the face. He just stood rigid and silent with a complete look of disbelief on his rapidly reddening face.

Just for a second I thought I would have to flee to the safety of Miss Darby's breasts, but no, he suddenly let out a bloodcurdling yelp and began to sob uncontrollably. At that moment I thought I would press home my now dominant position. So, with reckless abandon, I lunged forward again, arms outstretched, and pushed him hard in the chest. He toppled over like a felled tree.

However, unbeknown to me, the yelling gaggle of other kids who were witness to this David and Goliath conflict had attracted the attention of none other than Spriggy on playground duty. She scurried across the yard toward me with those piercing eyes fixed on mine.

Miss Darby appeared right behind her and immediately dropped down on one knee beside the still sobbing carcass of the defeated Goliath. Spriggy grabbed me by my ear and promptly marched me into the classroom.

Standing in the corner facing the wall all I could think about was the injustice of me (sore ear and all) getting all the blame, and Pete with Miss Darby's breasts pressed against him as she gently led him into the building for lots of TLC and a glass of warm milk. Lesson number thirty-four in life's not fair.

Infant school continued much the same for the next few years. As I got older I started to get a little more body weight but even by the standards of the day I was still pretty skinny. On the weekends I discovered that the farm, though dangerous, did provide lots of things to do.

For instance hurling bricks at the huge glass bottles known as carboys that from time to time appeared at the back of the farm by the potato fields. Now if I had known that they contained a solution of sulfuric acid used to burn off the tops of the potato vines I might have been a little more careful.

Many years later I was to fall foul of the dreaded potato acid again where, in addition to my duties as a pesticide salesman for a farm supplies distributor, I also managed the activities of a spraying contractor who applied acid to potatoes for my company.

One day I was visiting the field he was spraying and as usual pulled right into the gateway to see how things were going. Unfortunately he was just making his end of field turn and the spray boom trailed right over the bonnet (hood to you yanks) of my shiny new yellow Ford Cortina.

The contractor stopped and jumped off the tractor to have a chat. As we talked, standing at the side of my car, I noticed the paint on the bonnet was looking a little bumpy. Within about two minutes the paint started to bubble and began flaking right off as I frantically tried to wipe the acid off with a towel. Mr. Paul was not going to be happy.

In fact Mr. Paul, WWII veteran and senior director of the company, never actually found out. He was another one of the generation like Uncle Arthur who went off to war and came back sort of different.

Different era but the effect seemed to be the same. Mr. Paul had actually been a prisoner of the Japanese in Burma and that had certainly made its mark. A passionate motorist, his function seemed to be mainly trying to stop the twenty or so sales reps like me from wrecking our company cars.

Because of his wartime experience he was violently opposed to any product that came from Japan. One hapless sales rep, blissfully oblivious to this fact, had gone into Mr. Paul's office one day to request a deviation from the car policy.

British Leyland, Ford or Vauxhall were the choices carefully administered by Mr. Paul. At that time the Japanese Nissan Company had just introduced a very fast "Datsun" middle-size car that was priced about the right level for the basic rep mobile that we were all allowed.

Unfortunately this rep had the misfortune to not be aware of the war history of the man he was asking for a Japanese product. I don't think the conversation lasted very long. This same rep, later equipped with a Ford Escort, was out one afternoon looking for a particular farmer's field where he was to walk about to inspect the weeds. This was before prescribing the weed killer remedy that was the mainstay of the business we were in. As usual, like the rest of us who thought the rural roads of Lincolnshire made a great rally circuit, he was screaming at full throttle in third gear down a narrow road when he came upon a sharp right turn. No chance of making the turn at 60 mph plus, he went straight on through the hedgerow and came to rest several yards into a field of winter wheat. After collecting his thoughts and surveying the surprisingly modest damage to the front end of his Ford he realized he was in the field he was looking for.

So, before calling out the farmer to tow him out of the field, he did his inspection and wrote out the field report.

It's a surprise to me that so few of us actually came to any real harm when I recall how we would tear around the county lanes at breakneck speeds. I remember one Vauxhall I had that would actually go faster in third gear than in fourth. Consequently, for most of its life, this unfortunate car spent its time at maximum revs in third gear with all four tires at their limit of adhesion.

I often wonder how long it lasted after being sold to some unsuspecting pensioner, the car with 100,000 miles on the clock. One owner used locally and very clean!

Anyway, this was all to come later, much later. It's so easy to digress from the topic when you are afflicted with an untidy mind, like a filing cabinet where the dividing sections have been removed and all the files get jumbled up.

Most football fans will remember the tragic events surrounding the air crash in Munich of the Manchester United football team. Returning from a successful trip to play Red Star Belgrade in February 1958 they had touched down in Munich to refuel.

On the third attempt to take off in heavy snow, the plane crashed through a fence eventually killing twenty-three people on board.

In my class there were the Smalley twins, Colin and Michael. These kids were fanatical Manchester United supporters.

They had come to school the day after the crash having heard the bad news about many of their heroes dying. During the lesson they were both so distraught that they couldn't stop crying. Spriggy, in her usual style, was trying to console them with little success. In the end she blurted out that it was only a stupid football team and they had to get on with their sums. With today's softly, softly approach I wonder if she might have used a little more compassion?

At about the same time period, another boy, Alan Nicholson, who was a little older, got into a big scuffle with Spriggy which caused her to chase him round the classroom. All the other kids were dumbfounded at Nicky's bravado, as no one went up against Spriggy. He ran around, jumping over chairs and benches as the aging teacher tried to catch him. He then tried to jump and slide along a wooden bench in his hurry to escape.

He suddenly let out a mighty scream and fell to the floor holding his hand close to his chest. The bench had a frayed edge and Nicky had impaled himself with a huge splinter that looked about the size of a broom handle but was probably only two or three inches long. Nevertheless, the sight of that bit of wood sticking out of his hand with blood all over the place was enough to make me faint.

I had managed to survive the majority of my years at Pointon but during my eleventh year I began to have more problems with bullying and I was moved to another school at Billingborough.

This was a couple of miles away and it was where it was thought I could get through the 11 plus exam. Not so, despite three attempts, which were not allowed by the rules; I still failed. This created a problem as I had now passed the age that I should have transferred to the secondary school.

The problem was compounded by the fact that we had replaced a couple of medium-size bullies with one very big one. Darren just didn't understand his own strength and getting a whack in the back of the head as he barreled by in the playground could be near terminal for a wimp like me.

This was a boy who at twelve years old was already six feet tall and twice my weight. It's ironic that, some fifteen years later, he was involved in a street fight where a man died and he was tried for murder. He was acquitted, and Darren, if you read this, I knew you were innocent all along, mate.

On my first day at Billingborough one of the lessons was gardening. We were all marched down to the plots over the road from the school to dig and weed and learn how to manage our allotments. This was to equip us once we secured employment as a mechanic or lorry driver, got married to the girl next door, had four kids and finally secured our council house with, yes you got it, an allotment.

For those not familiar with the allotment program, it was a scheme that dates back to the 1790s when landowners would allow the peasants to have a little plot of the owners' land to grow their own food and thus not need wages.

In 1908 actual laws were passed to formalize this ancient system where the local authority could own a block of land in the village or small town. The land was divided up into blocks of about one eighth of an acre and allocated to local residents on some kind of first come first served system.

The lucky tenants would then grow whatever they liked on the plots to feed the family or compete in mind-numbing "grow the biggest marrow" contests.

In 1945 there were about 1.5 million allotments in the UK which had been immensely significant during the war in helping to feed the nation in its darkest hour. These plots became a refuge for many a henpecked bloke who got fed up with being pushed around at home. "Got to do the allotment, dear" became a rallying call to all the men in the village to get down there and weed.

Some of the most innovative construction projects could be seen on allotments, usually including an old bedstead in the framework somewhere. Beer, whisky, darts, dominos and cards were more prevalent in these works of architectural brilliance than hoes and seeds but they did perform a wonderful service to mankind.

During that first gardening session I managed to stick the fork into my right leg and was taken under the wing of a rather large tubby lad called Irvin Lang. He helped me remove the fork with a sharp tug and then came across the road with me to Dr. Henderson's surgery, which was conveniently nearby, to get medical assistance.

The hole wasn't too bad but I made a big fuss about it to ensure I did not have to go back to the plots that day.

"Och the laddy's hurt himself again" was Doc Henderson's now familiar response whenever I turned up bleeding or broken.

The next few months were spent trying to stay out of the way of Darren and another boy, Ken "Mush" Banner, who also liked to knock over wimps for fun.

After the headmaster's valiant, but failed attempt to help me pass the eleven plus I was finally moved to the secondary modern in Sleaford. Fortunately for me Darren and Mush ended up going to a different school in Bourne where the General Certificate of Education (GCE) option had not yet been established.

The educational system was undergoing changes to reduce the fallout at the age of eleven. Those kids that failed the eleven plus exam were previously doomed to finish school with no chance of any academic qualification. All that was left were several more years of compulsory education that remained, if you had failed that test.

However, if you passed, off you went to some of the finest educational institutions in the land. Schools like Carr's Grammar School in Sleaford, where my older brother Peter excelled.

Top student, cross-country team and many other accolades, accolades that I came to be so intimidated by as I realized that, even at an early age, I exhibited very few of the qualities that shape successful people.

Carr's was just down the hill from the secondary modern school where I would eventually end up, but a world away in academic expectation.

Carr's and other great old schools were the seats of learning that produced the material for doctors, scientists,

30

architects and the like who went on to universities to learn their skills in preparation to become leaders. However, if you missed the shot at eleven it was car mechanic, coal miner, farm worker or lorry driver for you, mate, a fate that I seemed destined for as the time came closer.

So changes to the system were very necessary and they did indeed change for the better during that period. Unfortunately for me I got caught in the middle and that resulted in me missing the first year in the secondary system. This was now where, if bright enough, you could upgrade to the GCE level and still have a shot at the academic results that could take you on to higher goals.

Unfortunately for me, when I finally transferred in 1959, I was already a year behind all the other kids in my class. Missing a year of basic chemistry, algebra, French, etc., handicapped me to the extent that, for the most part, I was a troubled passenger at the back of the class. My main contribution to the educational day was entertaining the rest of the kids with my disruptive behavior. Incidents like the water-filled glove throwing, just as Mr. Hollingsworth, the history teacher, turned round to see Manton's arm, still in the cricketer's over arm bowling position.

The glove burst against the blackboard drenching Mr. Hollingsworth. The snotty girl, whose glove it was, had a father who was a Squadron Leader at RAF Cranwell, an Air Force base just three miles from the school. She and others like her were transit kids who often moved around as their parents were transferred from base to base.

Daddy had this and Daddy had that and my Dad just seemed to work seven days a week and had very little. This had already started to get on my nerves so I suppose it was childish jealousy that prompted me to use her fancy leather glove for the crime. The six across the fingers in the headmaster's office still make me cringe and I often wonder if the stiffness I feel in my hands today could have resulted from those brutal canings. I guess now I could sue for millions but the statute of limitations may have passed on child abuse in the '50s.

While I was getting used to the cane, General Batista was making a rapid exit from Cuba with Fidel Castro's boot up his backside. Buddy Holly was just a few weeks ahead of Billie Holiday dying from very different causes. Eamon de Valera was elected President of Eire and Sir Alec Issignosis gave us the mini. All this as Harold Macmillan was telling us, "You've never had it so good."

Getting to school was the first hurdle. The school was about twelve miles from the farm where we lived but the bus that picked me up passed by over a mile away. I had to ride my bike in all weathers, down the lane to where the bus passed by, throw my bike in the hedgerow and then pick it back up on my way home.

In the three years I did this, my bike never once went missing. This two-part journey made for a rather long school day as I would leave home about 7:30 A.M. and get back at about 5:30 P.M.

My class teacher for my first year in 2 GCE was Miss Chambers. Although much younger she had all the makings of a Spriggy in waiting. I have only a vague memory of most of the kids in my class, the majority of which progressed through the three years of two, three and four GCE along with me.

One boy I remember very well was John Harris. He was the class bighead (sorry John). John knew everything and was indeed a very bright lad who came from a small farm near to Sleaford. For a brief period in my career in the pesticide industry as a field salesman, John was my boss. Later on

32

he became a customer of mine for other companies I worked for.

Another lad in the class became my best buddy at school. His name was Keith "Rooker" Boyfield.

Rooker came from a large family and he and I seemed to hit it off right away. We were usually involved in some misdemeanor at the back of the class. On one occasion we were in religious studies, a subject that neither of us had an interest in, when the teacher focused his attention on us as we casually chattered away on the back row.

Now this teacher unfortunately had a speech impediment that caused his words to sound muffled and elongated. "Bwoyfield and Mwanton dob talking, dob talking." I was, and still am, very prone to uncontrollable giggling and so was Rooker.

The more we rolled about laughing the more excited the teacher got. Finally we were marched out to the headmaster's office, still shuddering from top to bottom.

The giggling stopped at the first strike of the cane, a weapon I was to encounter several more times before I ended three unfulfilling years coming to terms with the fact that academia was not my thing.

The giggling tendency very nearly caused an international incident many years later on a business trip to Japan.

My next encounter with headmaster Speachly's cane came after I had quadrupled the ingredients of the chemistry class "let's make hydrogen" lesson. The chemistry teacher was a fat miserable bloke, typical of the introverted scientific loner that ended up teaching idiots like me how to make dangerous gasses. I just thought half an ounce of zinc chips and two drops of conc. sulfuric acid didn't seem enough to make much of a pop at the top for my flask.

When the word came down from Fatty to wave the Bunsen burner over the top of the flask I wanted to make sure I heard the pop. My increased concentration certainly taught me that chemistry could be rather risky. There was a very loud bang and splintering sound as my flask exploded into a million pieces. Kids near me suddenly demonstrated an instinct to dive under tables and behind solid objects as if trained by the army on war maneuvers. Several, like me, had little bits of glass peppered in their faces and hands but no one seemed to be seriously hurt. That is other than me after my next trip to the headmaster's office. Fatty screamed some obscenities at me from a safe distance and pronounced my permanent exclusion from any further chemistry lessons.

Making hydrogen gas is still about the only bit of chemistry I can remember to this day.

Despite some of the problems previously touched upon there were a few things that went well outside classes. I loved to play football and cricket. Although I was not that good at it, it provided some measure of enjoyment in an otherwise miserable day.

On sports day time seemed to fly by and there were some happy moments, like scoring the only goal, where I thought my head would be too big to get on the bus. Irvin, my savior in the gardening crisis, had also moved to Sleaford and on one end of term sporting event managed to throw a cricket ball out of the school grounds.

This was an actual event but no one had ever thrown it that far. I remember the headmaster's words at the prize giving: "Well done, lad. I have no idea what good throwing a ball two hundred yards will do for you but well done anyway." "Sir, Sir, maybe he could play cricket for England, Sir, Sir, Sir."

Another highlight was woodwork with Mr. Taylor, where I constructed my first set of bookends. Only problem was my rather clumsy use of chisels and other sharp objects. When my daughter Anna attended the same school many years later Mr. Taylor, still at the bench, remembered me as being the most accident-prone child he had ever taught.

Whilst school continued to be a daunting experience (I now had another bully who was a year younger than me to deal with), evenings and weekends became more fun as I made friends mostly from Pointon Village. Kevin "Lobby" Harris, Gilbert "Jack" Wesley, Mervin "Tiny" Chessum, Phil Taylor, Martin "Barney" Wesley (Jack's cousin) and a few others became the lads I spent most of my spare time with whenever I could ride my bike the two miles down to the village.

We all seemed to have nicknames that either were carried over from our fathers or evolved from something unique about us at the time. Tiny Chessum was so called after his dad Tiny; Senior who was a huge six foot six farm worker.

Tiny Junior was heading for the same physical stature. Lobby Harris played wing at football like his Dad before him and "lobbed" the ball in to the centers so the mid field players could shoot for goals. My nickname at that time was usually Manty but evolved to "Minge" at some point; why, I have no idea.

Bikes were sort of essential in those days, as most of our families did not have cars. We were no exception until my Mum won 240 pounds on the football pools (quite a lot of money in the '50s) and bought an Austin A30. However, this did not improve my personal mobility as my parents had far better things to do than taxi me around. So, if I wanted to go anywhere it was the bike.

This would often be up to fifteen or twenty miles away depending on how serious the need to be somewhere else was.

Bike riding became an art, like driving cars later on, where the vehicle was put to its absolute limits. When I think back to how fast we would race around the village footpaths, screeching round blind corners and frightening old ladies it's a wonder any of us made it to fifteen.

Talking of old ladies, there were some other things we did to lighten the moment. Pointon had its share of council houses and a feature of these homes in the '50s was the outside chemical toilet fitted in lieu (no pun intended) of an underground sewer system. These comprised of a row of brick buildings at the back of the houses equipped with a small trap door at the back to facilitate the "dilly" cart's access to the chemical bucket that was emptied once a week. Dilly cart was the nickname given to the council sanitary collection vehicle. (Based on what concept I have no idea.) The trap door made for a perfect wheeze.

We would get a bunch of nettles or better still thistles if we could find them, select one of us to actually do the deed, and wait till one of the ladies visited the facility. We would have previously unlatched the trap to enable a totally silent assault knowing the ladies were familiar with the stunt, and wham!

One of us would swing the door open and the other would ram the nettles up inside between the bucket and the underside of the toilet seat. "You little bastards, I know who you are, you wait till I tell your Dad what you just did."

It took the ladies a couple of minutes to pull up their drawers so we could always get a head start in retreat.

However, it was very difficult to run at forty miles an hour whilst being completely creased up with laughter. I was usually immune to retribution because I lived outside the village and the old dears were not sure who I belonged to.

This was one of the few benefits of being a farm kid as I

could melt into the greenery like an SAS soldier after blowing up an enemy fuel dump.

Sometimes the local bobby would come round on his bike asking questions of who had done the terrible deed. Honor was paramount between kids and no one would squeal on his mates so we tended to get away with it most of the time. Looking back we may have been responsible for several heart attacks for which I am very sorry, really.

During this period we were still living in the little semi-detached cottage that belonged to the farm where my father worked. The adjoining cottage had been briefly occupied a few years earlier but was vacated when the farm suffered the dreaded foot and mouth disease and all the stock had been slaughtered. The only time I ever saw my father cry was when they buried his cattle in huge trenches dug in the fields.

Our neighbors had moved on because the man was a horse handler and the farm no longer used horses. My father's duties had changed from feeding a herd of beef cattle to general laboring around the place.

The farm was now dedicated to arable crops like wheat, barley, sugar beet and potatoes. Across the road on the other side was the farm itself with a stone built farmhouse dating back some three hundred years.

Here lived George Clarkson with his wife Francis and two sons. The younger boy, also Peter, was my brother Pete's age, six years my senior and his brother Jack was a couple of years older than that. Peter was nothing short of a psychopath. He would follow my sisters Liz and Sandy and I around the farm when we were playing some kind of game and throw large rocks as close as he could without actually hitting us. On many occasions the rocks would be so large that had they hit us they could have been fatal.

When we had first moved to the cottage we did not have

electricity or a bathroom. The toilet was out the back and like the council facilities in the village it was emptied once a week by the dilly cart. Light came from oil lamps and bath time was Friday night for everyone in front of the fire in a tin bath.

We had a radio where the "Goon Show," the "Navy Lark" and Billy Cotton's band show, among others, would keep us entertained. The radio had an enormous battery pack called an accumulator that also was changed every week by the man in a passing delivery van.

I discovered that the outside toilet itself could prove to be a hazard if I was determined enough to let it.

One day I was playing hide and seek with my little sister Sandy and it was my turn to hide. As she was three years younger than me it was easy to fool her for hours. I decided that I would sneak into the toilet and stand on the flat scrubbed seat by the wall. Therefore, if Sandy were to peek in she may not see me in there. Mother spent a lot of time scrubbing the wooden seat so I was careful not to have mud on my Wellington boots. After what seemed like hours I could still hear Sandy running about in the garden calling my name. By now I was getting bored so I decided to give her a clue. I began to whistle so she could get a fix on where I might be. Trouble was while I was whistling I allowed my foot to edge toward the round hole in the middle of the seat. Sure enough my boot dropped right down into a week's worth of . . . well you know what I mean.

Horrified, I pulled my boot out of the mire and brought with it a fair amount of the contents which spread all over Mum's clean seat. Oh shit, I thought. Sandy still hadn't cottoned on my location so I ran out of the toilet and across the road to the drainage ditch on the other side. I jumped down into the muddy water that was about a foot deep and made sure it filled up both Wellies. This will fool Mother, I thought.

Not so. When I finally sauntered up to the back door to tell her I had slipped in the dyke, she sat me down on the doorstep and pulled off my boots.

The smell was awful and my cover story did not fool Mother for one minute as toilet paper and turds appeared from my boot. She grabbed me by the collar and dragged me to the toilet. One look inside was enough to evoke the hardest arse slapping I had experienced that month. To follow I spent some time with a bucket and scrubbing brush cleaning the seat.

Soon after that the owner finally decided that we should enjoy the luxury of inside plumbing and organized the building of an extension to both cottages adding bathrooms and inside toilets. Finally, we were wired up for mains electricity, completely transforming our level of comfort.

I used to love Sundays, the "Navy Lark" was on the radio in the morning and at 11:30 A.M. precisely Dad would mount his trusty old bike and head off up the hill past the Bell Ground field to the Robin Hood pub, usually referred to by him as the church where the hymn books have handles.

This was at the village of Acelby about two miles away. (Everywhere was about two miles away from this farm.) On Sunday the pub opened at 12 noon and his departure was timed perfectly for his arrival for his customary two pints of black and tan and a game of dominos.

One of the things that I thought must be the most wonderful thing in the world is when I got to eighteen and could go to the pub for a pint. All the kids, other than Pete, who by now was too old for such childish pleasures, would be kneeling on the chairs looking out of the two front windows, keeping an eye on the Bell Ground field watching for signs of

did more damage to my thrum than any wild life I targeted from time to time.

However, the most voluminous effort involved rearing a pig for Christmas. Pig rearing was very common in these rural areas and many of the tied cottages that farm laborers occupied had a pig sty at the bottom of the garden. Our home was no exception. Early in the year Dad would acquire a little piglet from one of his coworkers or friends and the process of fattening him up would begin.

It was not a good idea to get too attached to the little blighter as you knew full well that come about December 15th this little piggy would not be wee, wee, wee'ing all the way home. Rather, he would have grown to about 300 pounds and be stretched out on a "cratch" (a wooden two wheeled cart made for butchering animals) and having its throat cut to drain the blood that would eventually be used to make blood sausage as one of the many meat items this food factory was to produce.

All year we would watch the pig grow and there was much skill involved in the kind of food that was used as this would have a huge bearing on the way the meat would eventually turn out. I have no idea what the right nutritional balance for a pig was, but my father knew exactly what to do to get the result he was looking for.

The fact that I cannot remember one time naming the animal nor feeling any remorse as he was eventually shot in the head with a humane gun (by a licensed operator) and then hung up on the cratch, is testament to the fact that we grew up knowing the realities of country life in the raw.

The day of execution would be quite something as Jack Wesley Senior would arrive with his humane killer. This was a hand gun that had a charge inserted. The gun had a bolt about six or eight inches long that was forced out of the barrel by the charge and into the head (and brain) of the receiving animal, causing instant death.

The pig, seemingly totally unaware that he was about to be shot in the head, was ushered out of the pen having had a strong leash put around his neck and was tied to a stout post nearby. The men always seemed to have a sense of urgency at this point as I think the longer it took the more likely the pig was going to cotton on to what was about to happen. A 300-pound pig, if spooked, could inflict quite a lot of damage with those four-inch teeth and I sensed the tension in the air as the men went about this delicate part of the proceedings.

Once secured to the post, Mr. Wesley would hold the gun to the center of the large head and bang! A pitiful squeal and it was all over as piggy flopped to the ground, like, well a dead pig. It would then require the men to manhandle the dead animal up onto the cratch as it was positioned in a horizontal manner. Once the animal had been successfully mounted and strapped in place with the head at the wheeled end, the cart would be raised to about a seventy-five degree angle. A large bucket would be placed under the now hanging head and its throat cut to allow the blood to drain. It all sounds quite grotesque now but as a kid to me it seemed perfectly normal and I watched with keen interest as the whole process unfolded.

Once the blood-letting had been done the cart would be wheeled up into the concrete yard at the back of the house and the next part of the process would begin. This was washing down the animal with buckets of boiling hot water that Mother had been heating up over a fire in the outside washhouse for several hours, in anticipation of the next step.

After a good wash the gutting came next (that part I did not watch as it was incredibly unpleasant and very smelly) till the animal was properly cleaned out and ready for butcher-

43

ing. One part that was critical at this stage was for the intestinal tubes to be recovered and thoroughly cleaned as they would eventually be used to make the sausages. Nothing was wasted as each part of this beast had a use in one form or another.

Prior to slaughter day we would have had several large slabs of salt delivered to the house. Eventually the animal was cut up into all kinds of different joints. There were hams, slabs of pork to be salted down to preserve it for later consumption and of course the part my father loved best, thick slabs of fat bacon. We did not have sufficient refrigeration or any freezers for the various cuts, so much of it was preserved with salt or hung and dried.

Once all the larger cuts had been sorted out, salted where necessary and laid on shelves in the pantry or hung on hooks in the kitchen, there would be lots of small pieces of meat left. The better parts of this would be minced up and used to make sausages. The rest, which was not really fit for that would be boiled up and mixed with gelatin to make brawn. This would then be poured into large bowls and left to set into domed shaped mounds that were almost clear in appearance. Once, formed you could see it contained little slivers of meat and bacon. This was often served at lunch times and eaten between big slices of bread and smeared with Daddy's brown sauce.

Once all the other stuff had been taken care of the sausage making would begin. The meat pieces would be pushed down into the sausage machine and the now cleaned intestinal tubes held over the spout to be filled into long sausages. They would be twisted and formed but kept in long strings with each individual sausage about four inches long. Once formed, they would be hung on ceiling hooks in strings and left to mature for sometimes several months. Mold would grow on the skins and this would be washed off just prior to cooking. I have never ever found a sausage since then that had such a wonderful flavor as those that hung around in our house for months on end. I wonder if our children today have so many ailments because they were not exposed to, and built immunity to, the natural bacteria that in my day were commonplace in most homes.

My father would eat a couple of thick slices of cold fat bacon at lunchtime along with a hearty piece of Gorgonzola cheese. God knows what the calories from fat were in that little bundle but he never had any heart-related problems that we knew about for the whole of his eighty years.

At the time I hated the smell of Gorgonzola cheese, now I love the stuff and preferably wash it down with a nice vintage port. How times change?

A simple life but for me it all seemed perfectly normal. The empty house next door made a great place to hide stuff and play when the weather was bad.

My brother utilized the outside washhouse to build a car. He bought a 1930s Austin Seven and stripped it down to the chassis.

He then built a wooden frame and fabricated an aluminum body that was eventually screwed to the frame. Finally it was painted bright red. It was fantastic—a little open sports car that turned heads anywhere it went.

Pete got all the DIY skills and over time has built all manner of things including his own house. I, on the other hand, have had very few construction projects that would pass close scrutiny although there have been a couple where I even surprised myself.

Another of Pete's projects was a strange motorized bicycle called a Cycle Master. This beast was a heavy duty man's peddle cycle with a little two-stroke engine actually mounted in the center of the back wheel.

The idea was motorized assistance, not designed to do all the work just to help with the peddling. I was fascinated by anything with an engine and this obsession got me into a number of scrapes over the years.

One day when Pete was away from the house I decided to give the Cycle Master a run. Now this was of course taboo as Pete had made it quite clear if I went within a hundred yards of his stuff he would remove my head from my shoulders and pour liquid shit down my neck hole.

Firmly believing that he would never find out I gingerly wheeled Cycle Master out of the gate and onto the graveled road in front of the house. It was quite tall and I wasn't, so the first problem was figuring out how to get it going and then how to climb on. There was a fuel tap on the top of the engine for the tiny fuel tank sitting above. I knew enough to do that and gave it a twist.

Then I pulled the little throttle lever on the handlebar round to full on. I had watched Pete from a distance get up on the bike and pedal like mad till the engine coughed and sputtered into life but I was too short to reach the pedals.

So my strategy was to run alongside pushing the bike until it fired up and then quickly jump on and away we would go. With all systems go, as if this was the space shuttle's first mission, I started to push and run.

The bike seemed to require very little effort to push and there was no noise coming from the engine that should by now be turning over. Then it dawned on me: the gear, it wasn't in gear. On the other side of the handlebars was another lever that engaged the engine. Now, running at full speed, I grabbed the gear lever and pulled it round.

There was an immediate pull from the bike that slowed me down and the engine started to cough and emit blue smoke.

By now I was almost exhausted and nearly at a standstill

when suddenly the engine burst into life and the machine took off with an enormous jerk. Too stupefied to let go I was dragged along, hopping and trying to swing my leg up to get on the seat.

Alas not to be, instead I lost my footing and dropped to my knees still clutching the handlebars like grim death. My knees bit into the gravel road and ripped my jeans to shreds, very quickly followed by most of the skin. The pain was excruciating but I couldn't let the bike go because if I let it crash I was in for a neck hole full of liquid shit.

In what seemed like a lifetime I managed to drop the bike over onto the grass roadside and fall away from it. Cycle Master lay in the mud with the engine puttering away and the back wheel spinning around till it finally coughed and spluttered to silence.

I lay on my back on the road screaming in agony as my profusely bleeding knees throbbed as if they would explode.

After a few seconds I realized that I might still avoid the removal of my head if I could get the beast back to the shed and cleaned up before Pete got back.

I hobbled back to the house pushing the muddied bike. The house seemed a lot further away than it should after only running for about half a minute.

I managed to get Cycle Master wiped down and placed exactly as it had been. For now the pain in my knees seemed to have abated as I concentrated on not leaving any evidence of my crime. However, once I thought I had done enough to disguise the dirty deed the pain returned with a vengeance.

I limped into the house to find my mother and proceeded to tell her some cock and bull story about falling off my own bike. Dr. Henderson was to expect yet another visit soon. My cover was blown the minute Pete returned, going straight to the shed to check his prized machine. "You little bugger, you've been in my Cycle Master, the throttle's wide open and the fuel tap's on." Pete lunged across the room trying to take swipes at my head but fortunately for me Mum would not let him near me as she determined that I had suffered enough.

Getting injured seemed to be an almost daily hazard for me; this obsession with wheels and engines was always too much of a draw for me to exercise caution.

One other form of wheeled transport was a truck, as we would call it. A truck was a homemade device, mostly a wooden structure with wheels fixed under a flat platform designed to sit on and coast down hills. Some of them were quite sophisticated with a proper steering wheel connected to the front axle with string or wire, others with just string tied directly to the ends of the front axle to pull it either way for direction.

One in particular had quite a unique feature. Instead of the usual pram wheels all round I had secured a set of iron sack wheels on a heavy metal axle that I had nailed in place at the back.

Our house was halfway down a shallow valley in between two hills. The nearest high point was less than a quarter mile to the summit. This was the steepest slope so off I went pulling my truck to the top. Once there I carefully checked the opposite hill to make sure no traffic was coming up toward me and sat on board.

Because the iron sack wheels were small and heavy, progress started slowly, gathering momentum as I jiggled about trying to get maximum velocity on the short run. Now I was going faster, much faster, in fact very fast. Also I observed a car approaching from down in the valley which had escaped my previous scan and likely to be upon me before I reached the farm gate where I intended to turn in.

Well, maybe I could make the gate in time if I didn't apply the crude wood block brake attached to a lever nailed on the side of the frame. Now at breakneck speed I was rapidly approaching the turn as the car, whose driver seemed oblivious to the speeding object in the middle of his path, got nearer and nearer. Just in time I yanked the string steering to make the turn.

Of course, iron wheels on a metallic road surface did not provide much grip, in fact, no grip at all. I went into a 360° spin and was hurled off the machine into the ditch by the farm gateway. The car carried on by without so much as a glance in my direction. I can only speculate that the driver had not even seen me coming, and I survived by pure chance. Bruised and stung by nettles I climbed out of the ditch and surveyed the wooden wreck that was now propped against the gatepost near where I had been thrown off. The sack wheels were missing and the front pram wheels were buckled and bent. Other than that with a lick of paint she would be ready to go again in no time!

Another feature of this farm was an old, kerosene Ford-Son tractor that had been converted to run on diesel fuel; furthermore it was equipped with a starter motor rather than the crank handle that used to be a feature of many of the machines still around at the time.

One Friday, when Dad was taking his weekly bath, I decided it was time for me to try out the tractor for real. I was about nine or ten at the time so the tractor was huge to me. I snuck off over the road to the farm and checked in the garage next to the barn to see if Mr. Clarkson's Hillman Minx was out.

Sure enough it was gone so I knew the coast was clear for the inaugural run. I gingerly climbed up the back of the Ford-Son that was parked in an open fronted "Dutch" barn, facing in.

After fiddling around with switches and knobs for a couple of minutes I hit on the action button. The mighty beast burst into life and to my horror started to chug forward as the engine throbbed at low revs. In the front of the tractor was a huge fuel tank and now the tractor was butting up against it, banging forward and rolling back. Starting it was one thing but stopping it was quite another.

Unbeknown to me to stop this kind of diesel engine you had to pull out a long knob that cut the fuel supply to the engine. After several frantic minutes of pulling, pushing, twisting and screaming I concluded that my only hope of stopping this monster from destroying the barn and bursting the fuel tank was to run for Dad.

I ran like a maniac the two hundred yards down the road to the cottage and burst into the kitchen as my Dad was standing in his long john underwear toweling his hair. His instinct that something was amiss was right on the mark as I blurted out the awful truth of the tractor still bouncing off the fuel tank in the barn.

It's almost impossible to describe my Dad in a state of high anxiety as he rarely showed any emotion. However, this time he flared up like a spooked stallion and after plunging his feet into his Wellington boots he literally ran out of the door to deal with the pending disaster. It didn't help that in his haste he got the boots on the wrong feet. Five minutes later he was back with a scowl as wide as the barn that fortunately had suffered no lasting harm.

"You little bugger, I'm going to belt your arse till it bleeds," he screamed at me as I cowered behind my mum.

"Don't you dare lay a finger on that boy, Harry, or you will have me to deal with." I think my mother overcompensated for me, as I always seemed to be in trouble with one family member or another.

Dad had no stomach to go up against Daisy, so on this occasion I escaped without too much retribution.

Anyway, the tractor incident passed and I learned another valuable lesson in mechanical engineering: never start something you don't know how to stop. I guess you could apply the same logic to life itself.

One other distraction on the farm was a mysterious little wooded area known locally as the Ossuary Beds. I had no idea why the wood was so named until I looked up the word in the dictionary. Ossuaries are vessels or vaults that hold corpses but you knew that, right?

That's interesting because at the far end of the wood was the 12th century Sempringham Abbey which had a graveyard with headstones dating back to that time. I believe at one time that the woods were part of the Abbey grounds and were used to produce all manner of things for the monks in residence.

I would often go across the fields to the Ossuary Beds and always felt a strange sense of fear when stepping out of the light into the dense undergrowth. Once inside the wood it was dark, damp and cold and always silent and creepy. There were no pathways and many of the old trees were rotted and fallen, making it very difficult to move around. The whole area was probably only four or five acres but to me, as a child, it seemed huge and endless. I would creep further into the middle, stopping to listen to every creak or sound until I had completely convinced myself that the place was haunted.

Now I believe it was.

Thinking back, regardless of how warm it was in the open, it was always cold inside the wood; it was always silent and I always sensed someone was watching me. At the same time I felt a strange peace, like the worries of school and the bullies didn't seem to matter when I was in the wood.

Despite the fact that we were as poor as church mice I don't ever remember feeling that we were disadvantaged in any way. Our parents had an uncanny ability to make everything seem OK regardless of living on the poverty line. What we could not buy we improvised. Much of what we ate came from the land.

Our own home grown vegetables and eggs, chickens and home-raised pork were just a few of the things we took for granted. We had little money but we lived very well in that respect. I don't ever remember going to bed hungry, other than the few times when crimes against humanity were punished by starvation.

This was usually well compensated for, by eating two breakfasts the next morning. It was only at certain times of the year when the lack of liquid funds became more apparent. Christmas was the most obvious when presents were expected.

Children nowadays expect very expensive gifts like computer games, bikes, TVs, audio equipment, etc. We felt very lucky if we got a Beano album that had the inside cover page missing thus removing any evidence of the kid who had received the book a few years ago, and then for it to languish in the attic with twenty others before my mother acquired it at a humble sale. It was one of my quests to try to find the hiding place for these gifts as Mum would secrete them around the house before the day came to hand them over.

3
Guns, Cars, Booze, Ciggies and Girls

One other area of keen interest for me was guns—not that we had one or that I had ever been around a real gun. Toys I had, quite sophisticated revolvers that banged little rolls of caps as fast as I could pull the trigger.

Whilst toys satisfied the general interest I was always longing for the time I could handle a real one. Occasionally a pheasant shoot would be held on the farm when Mr. Proctor, gentleman farmer and Dad's boss, would host a group of his "plus four"-wearing pals from around the farming community.

I always loved it when the boss came by because he was a car nut and usually had an exotic motorcar. One was a vintage Bentley from the '20s that was a magnificent open wheel monster. Later on he had a little two seat Alfa Romeo that was probably the first one in the county.

On the shooting days I would hang around the farm as the Land Rovers and Jaguars would start to roll in. I would try to get a look at all the shiny shotguns and imagine I could take the cars out for a drive while the men went to shoot. The guns were mostly twelve-bore weapons, and looked very expensive.

A crowd of older boys and some of the farm laborers would serve as beaters to drive the birds out of the kale or sugar beet to fly across the stand where the guns would be positioned.

I was not allowed to go near the action but I could hear the cacophony of sound as the guns opened up on the first wave of birds to be flushed out of their refuge.

A couple of weeks after one of these shoots when my interest was at its peak, I was down at the village messing around with Gilbert "Jack" Wesley on his dad's dairy farm with another lad, Phil Taylor. Climbing on top of some bales in a barn we discovered a rusty old side-by-side twelve-bore shotgun with hammerlocks, lying across a beam in the roof. All of a sudden we had this real gun in our hands.

After a few whispered discussions we decided that I would take it home and try to clean it up and free off the triggers that were rusted and immobilized. I already had a bit of a reputation amongst my mates as being able to fix things, which underlines how bad they must have been at the time.

We wrapped the gun in an old sack and I carefully mounted my bike and headed the two miles home. As I peddled along I was shaking with fear in case the gun might go off or someone might discover me with the thing. Once home I hid it in the back of the coalhouse where it could lay undiscovered until I had an opportunity to get to the workbench in Pete's outhouse next door and get it fixed.

That chance came a few days later on a Saturday and I carefully unwrapped the prize as if it were made of glass. After staring at it for a couple of minutes I decided to squirt some WD 40 on the little lever that enabled the barrels to break from the stock for loading. Sure enough, after a few tries, the lever moved and the gun opened.

I was relieved to see that both barrels were empty and at this point my confidence increased so I started to unscrew screws, poke cleaning cloths down the barrels and try to figure out how to free off the frozen hammers and trigger mechanism.

Maybe an hour later I had one side trigger working and the safety catch would slide up and down quite easily. I gave up on the other side in my haste to get down to the village and show Jack and Phil the now shiny operating weapon.

Phil's older brother was already into shooting and owned his own twelve-bore gun. More importantly he had ammunition. Phil, in anticipation of our gun being made to work, had already secured a few shells and had hidden them at Jack's place ready for the big day. I arrived out of breath at Jack's and after a few hurried exchanges we hid the gun in the barn and both mounted up to go find Phil. We were all about thirteen at the time so we really should have known better but the draw of firing this fearsome weapon at a bird or rabbit was overwhelming.

Back at Jack's, now with an excited Phil in tow, we checked to see no adults were around and then we cycled out of the village to a green lane about half a mile away. This lane was lined with trees and bushes and was bordered by fields on both sides. Leaving our bikes at the bottom we started to walk up the lane in pursuit of the first furry or feathered victim that might come into view.

Because Phil had got the ammunition we had agreed that he should get the first shot. Phil was walking a few yards ahead swinging the gun about, now with one shell loaded into the working barrel. Jack and I were walking side by side a couple of feet apart behind. The excitement was mounting as we anticipated the first bit of action.

Phil kept turning around and pretending to aim the gun at various objects in the hedgerow or up in a tree. I was somewhat apprehensive about this rather casual handling of the gun but not wanting to seem like cowardly custard I kept my mouth shut.

"Don't worry, the safety catch is on," Phil called, anticipating my discomfort. "See," he retorted, turning to face us with the gun at hip level and pointing at the ground in front of Jack and me.

BOOM . . . there was the most deafening bang and flash of flame as the gun fired. I felt the rush of air as the pellets ripped into the ground between our feet and a tug on my baggy jeans. All three of us stood rooted to the spot, silent and shaking in fear. After what seemed like an eternity I looked down at my legs expecting to see two blooded stumps. There were several little holes in the left leg of my jeans but no blood.

A hole about six or eight inches wide and several inches deep had been blown into the dirt roadway within inches of my left foot. Jack uttered several mumbled expletives and Phil dropped the gun and burst into a loud wail staring at the sky as if the lord was on his way down to take him away.

"Fuck, fuck, bloody fuck, you fucking idiot." I just screamed at Phil thinking the worse the language the more it would hurt his feelings. Jack still stood motionless and I do not know to this day if he shit his pants but there was an unusual smell drifting about that lane and there was no livestock in sight.

Finally I grabbed the gun and threw it into the ditch at the side of the lane. Jack who was now back in the land of the living, picked up a large rock and from above his head smashed it down on the gun. After several hits the once magnificent trophy was bent and broken and above all safe.

We had probably destroyed a valuable antique shotgun.

In total silence we walked back to our bikes. Jack and Phil went left back to the village and I went right heading home to the safety of Beacon Hill. Once there I slowly pulled up the leg of my jeans to see if there was any damage. Miraculously there was no sign of anything on my leg, so all I had to do now was convince my mother that moths were very active in Pointon village.

I don't believe any of us ever mentioned the gun incident again but it taught me another very valuable lesson: If a gun is going to fire, make sure you're behind it. This lesson would come in very handy some time later on a small-arms training course at HMS Raleigh in Cornwall about a year into my naval career.

Gilbert was one of those lads who allowed himself to be led a bit by the nose. Because of this he had been roped in to pump the mighty wind organ that was in Sempringham Abbey whenever it was used for church services or weddings.

My brother Peter was married at this Abbey in 1964 and it was rumored that the vicar had his cricket pads on under his robes so that he could make it to the game as soon as the ceremony was over. Gilbert had a habit of losing concentration as he sat on the bench hidden behind the organ at the bellows.

He would often have a fag as he was out of sight. His job was to pump the bellows at a fairly constant pressure to retain an even pressure in the system.

At that time the organ player was an 80+ year-old lady who used to drive around in a vintage Austin 7, usually in the middle of the road at about fifteen miles per hour. On several occasions Gilbert would doze off or forget to pump altogether and as the organ tones began to drone off in some awful off-key melody, Miss Brocket would be heard to whisper as loud as she dare, "more wind, Gilbert, more wind."

The gun incident had lowered my interest in guns so I concentrated more on wheeled entertainment. At every opportunity I would sit in Pete's car and pretend to be driving at breakneck speed. This passion had been fuelled by the sixteen-cylinder BRM racing car I mentioned earlier, that had so captivated me when I was younger.

As the airfield was jut a few miles across the field, occasionally, just on the off chance they might be there, I would bike over and hide in the bushes by the old runway.

I never got to actually see the cars as by the time I had heard the sound it took me over an hour to get there. Kicking around in the bushes to pass the time I did discover some old artillery shells that could well have still been explosive.

When I did my gunnery training several years later I recognized the ammunition I had kicked over in the bushes as Bofor's anti-aircraft shells.

As I got older my skill at building bikes improved. It was unheard of at our level of income to buy a bike; most of the parts came from the local refuse tip or were acquired a piece at a time from a local bike shop.

The owner, Gandy Curtis, had abandoned his former occupation of producing poultry and had converted his deep litter house into a bike warehouse. My brother Pete had worked for him in the past, after school hours, and was probably Gandy's best customer for bike bits so he would always help me out with secondhand parts.

In the end, and mainly with Pete's help, we managed to build a fairly good racing bike that lasted me out till I left home at the tender age of fifteen to join the navy.

Before then I began to take an interest in girls, although now I realize I was well behind many of my contemporaries in that regard.

At school there was one young lady, Sondra, who was a year younger than me but we seemed to hit it off very well and when I was around here I felt very happy. She lived in Cranwell a couple of miles north of Sleaford and I lived south some twelve miles. For that reason our only opportunity to be together was at school. Now Sondra had the most perfect breasts and I swear the biggest in second year.

Our relationship was limited to quiet conversations and holding hands as we walked through the town center to the bus stop where we went our separate ways at the end of the school day. I think I actually kissed her a couple of times but I'm not even sure of that. The conversation was usually about fairly mundane things but that didn't seem to matter as long as we were together.

My feeling of tranquil harmony was shattered one Monday morning when another boy who lived in Cranwell told me that at the weekends Sondra was spending her time with another lad in her class. Furthermore they weren't limiting their relationship to holding hands and the odd kiss. I thought the world had come to an end and refused to speak to her again.

That was my first lesson in dealing with the opposite sex and it should have been a warning that the words that are spoken do not in anyway resemble the actual desires of the female in question.

Most of the lads that I spent time with were smoking cigarettes or at least had tried them out. I decided at the age of thirteen that it was time for me to demonstrate that I could hang out with the lads and smoke fags. In today's vernacular one needs to be careful with the term fag as it has an entirely different connotation to what it had then.

Fags were ciggies right! My Mum was an avid forty-a-day smoker at that time, unfortunately an affliction that took her life at age seventy-one. So it was easy for me to "acquire" a ten pack.

I then cycled off down to Billingborough where the lads would all be congregated in the churchyard behind a high stonewall. This was far from the prying eyes of any adults. I casually wandered up and sat down in the middle of the group of about eight or nine boys ranging from ten to fifteen. "Anyone for a fag?" I proclaimed, casually producing my ten pack of Woodbine filter tips.

Most of the kids already had one lit and only one hand came out for the offer. I popped one in my mouth and looked around for a light. Several boxes of matches flew in my direction, as the group now seemed to be taking more notice of what I was doing. I lit a match and held it under the nervously shaking fag sticking out of my mouth. Apart for a burning smell not much seemed to be happening.

Then one of the kids shouted out "You prick, Manty, you're supposed to suck the fucking thing." With that I made a large suck on the end and inhaled an enormous lung full of toxic gas. My eyes watered and I started to cough. "You're a bloody tart if you can't have a fag" retorted another kid. With that I soldiered on trying desperately to not swallow the smoke but appear to be casually drawing away like the rest.

During that afternoon I got through the remaining box by which time I was feeling very strange indeed. After making sure they all knew I had smoked the lot I made an excuse about chores on the farm, picked up my bike and started to walk down the church path to the road. Once out of sight round the corner I leaned over someone's garden wall and puked up the most awful green bile.

Now very dizzy and feeling like I was dying I started the near three-mile trek home. I could not get on the bike as I felt so dizzy and it took me over an hour to the top of the hill a quarter of a mile from the house. I then decided to climb on the bike and freewheel down the hill and into the gate as normal lest Mum should detect anything unusual. Unfortunately, in my sick state I did not get through the narrow hand gate into our front garden. I buckled my front wheel on the gatepost and slumped down by the bike totally defeated.

Hearing the commotion Mother came out of the kitchen to see me propped against the gate and looking very poorly. Her first response was to believe that I was ill so she helped me into the house and sat me in front of the fire.

As a smoker I can only assume that she could not detect the smell of smoke on my clothes but I could. I stank and I hated it, and even now the smell of cigarette smoke turns my stomach over like nothing else.

Other than the odd occasion when some idiot pushed one in my mouth during my time in the navy, I have never smoked another cigarette to this day. Even on those occasions the smell and taste prompted immediate vomiting, usually assisted by many pints of ale. Whatever gets me in the end it won't be smoke-related, unless I get hit by a Winston delivery truck.

After the smoking experiment I decided that I should turn to alcohol as that surely could not be as bad a taste. In Billingbourgh there was an old stone pub called the Fortesque Arms that at the time was run by an old widow who must have been in her eighties. By age fourteen most of us looked like we could be eighteen, at least to a partially sighted eighty-year-old.

On Saturday afternoons when the village men would be in the smoke room at the front of the pub discussing football and other critical issues, several of us underage hopefuls would congregate in a back room that remained largely unused other than by underage drinkers.

The landlady, probably sure most of us were too young for the front bar, would allow us to whisper our order through a little window in the hallway designed for off sales. That way, if the local bobby, Constable Handly, came by on his bike, she could pretend to be shooing us away and not actually selling to us.

Some of the lads would order half-pint bottles of beer but I really didn't like the taste too much after the first couple of tries so I decided to switch to cider. (Since that time my taste for beer has improved somewhat!) Unbeknown to me at the time the cider was probably five percent alcohol whereas the beer might have been three. Anyway, I preferred the taste so it was cider for me.

As long as I only had two bottles I was fine but a third would cause me to get very silly and going home silly could well have alerted Mother to some illicit substance. We would sit around swearing as much as we could to underline our adult thinking, telling exaggerated stories about how we had snogged with a particular girl or traveled at the speed of light on our racing bikes.

I could inject some sort of truth into bike feats but I was not entirely sure what snogging actually was. When one lad proclaimed he had had a bit of smelly finger I could not for the life of me figure out what the hell he was talking about. I concluded that his dad must be a fishmonger because he kept referring to the smell being like fish.

Anyway, these Saturday afternoon get-togethers in the pub were pretty happy times no doubt enhanced by the early (and continuing) comfort from alcohol. They were also a great source of education with regard to the sort of things girls would let you do if one should happen to take a fancy to you.

It was about this time that I was "seeing" Sondra but I just could not build up the courage to ask her if she would like a snog or even better let me have a smelly finger, now that I had worked out the fundamentals.

Around this time I was beginning to feel a bit more comfortable with myself and had made several good pals of my own age. Some were from Pointon where I had attended infant school and others were from Billingborough where a good deal of them went to the same school in Sleaford after age eleven.

One lad I was befriended by was Constable Handly's son Michael. He and his sister and I were mooching about in the village one day when we decided we were going to raid the local fish and chip shop. This little shop was in two parts, one side was the traditional fish and chip counter littered with bottles of vinegar and salt pots, the other side was a tiny general store and greengrocer.

The shopkeeper was Mr. Bennett. He was quite used to the kids coming in with just a few pennies to buy scraps. Scraps were the bits of batter that broke off the fish in the fryers. Mr. Bennett would strain these out of the tank and keep them on one side for the kids. Thruppence a bag was the going rate and a bag of scraps would keep you going for several hours. Our strategy to raid the shop required Daphne, Mike's sister, to enter on the fish shop side and ask for the scraps.

Mike and I then slipped into the other side out of Mr. Bennett's sight and grabbed a few items that were easiest to get at without making any noise. Before he could waddle round to our side after serving Daphne we had casually wandered out as if we had not seen anything we fancied.

The raid went off as planned and we ran off down the street and shot into the railyard where a big storage shed provided a refuge for us to examine the plunder tucked inside our shirts. A tin of peaches, two bags of hard toffees, a pan scourer, and a bottle of lemonade was the total take.

We all sat on the floor in a shaft of light to tuck into the goodies. Mike was sure Mr. Bennett would see what had gone missing and call their Dad, Constable Handly. I tried to reassure him but he continued to get more worried about being found out and refused to eat any of the toffees or drink the lemonade that Daphne and I were taking in turns gulping down.

He just sat with a gloomy look on his face as I then tried to open the tin of peaches. This proved to be quite a feat without a tin opener and eventually I had to bash the tin with a brick till it burst. The thick syrup squirted out all over the place but we managed to salvage most of the peaches.

Tinned peaches were a Sunday treat at our house for tea, and to have a whole tin between just three of us was heaven indeed, particularly if Mike was not going to have any. Sure enough he was still too worried about getting caught and expected any minute for the tall blue bobby's helmet to come into view round the shed door.

Daphne and I took it in turns to poke out the peaches till they were gone and then sat back to gloat on our triumph. After a few minutes of silence I put my hand over Daphne's as a sign of solidarity and she didn't seem to mind. She was two years younger than me so with me at fourteen, it was entirely a big brotherly thing to do as her own brother was clearly falling apart.

We got up from the floor and headed for the door, Mike slowly following on behind. I pulled the heavy sliding door just a couple of feet open to survey the yard before venturing outside.

Mike's worse fears were realized as Constable Handly and Mr. Bennett were purposefully striding in our general direction some way down the street. "Quick, hide," I whispered as loud as I dared. The approaching posse had not seen us yet still several hundred yards away, so we dived behind some old pallets and buckets at the far end of the shed. As we trembled in the semi darkness I realized we had left the sliding door open about two feet. We could hear the approaching footsteps as they came into the railyard and onto the gravel outside the shed. Mike was whimpering but I had my arm around Daphne's shoulder as if in some way it would protect her from the advancing menace. We heard muffled words outside and then the screeching as the huge door was pulled open, letting a full shaft of light into the shed. We all crouched down trying not to breath or make a sound. More crunching footsteps and then Constable Handly's voice boomed out:

"Michael, you little bugger, if you're hiding in here you had better come right out." I grabbed Mike's arm and gripped as hard as I could but to no avail. Stumbling into the light he started to cry and babble. "Where's your sister?" yelled his father.

No response from Mike and I wondered if we could remain undetected but at that point Daphne, peering at me in the gloom behind our refuge, looked into my eyes with a sign of resignation. She pulled my arm away and put her fingers to her lips to silence me and stepped out into the light.

"Right you little buggers, get yourselves back home and wait for me." I still crouched in the darkness behind the pallets praying that I would go undetected. The door screeched again as it was pulled shut and I heard footsteps start to move away and mumbled voices start to fade.

At last maybe fifteen minutes later I felt safe enough to creep out of my hiding place and approach the door. After listening for a few seconds I decided it was safe to venture outside. I grabbed the big metal handle and gave it a tug. Nothing moved so I tried a little hard. Still no movement.

Now I started to panic; I could not move the door an inch.

The realization dawned on me that on departing, the constable had flipped over the locking latch on the outside of the door that usually held a padlock. But even without the padlock it was firmly in place as to not allow the door to slide a fraction. I looked around the dim barn trying to see if there was another way out.

Sure enough at the bottom end past the pallets where we had hidden I could make the outline of light around a small door. I ran to the door and grabbed the handle that was turned into the doorframe. It too would not move, obviously locked from the outside. Now in blind panic I ran back to the big door at the front and tried again to move it to the side. Nothing. I was trapped.

I was going to die of hunger and thirst in this awful shed, alone and forgotten. It was retribution for stealing, I knew it. Somehow I was being punished for my crime and not owning up with my friends as they took the rap.

All of a sudden I felt a terrible surge of remorse. I would make amends, and I would pay for the stolen items and clean Mr. Bennett's windows for nothing every week.

As I sat on the ground contemplating ways to compensate for my crime I again heard footsteps, this time lighter, and chatter and laughing.

A loud bang and then the door started to open. The light surged in and I could see the silhouettes of two people as I stumbled into the outside world. Mike and Daphne were standing there with huge grins on their faces.

"What happened, what's goin on?" I said totally confused by the apparent turnaround in events.

"We told Dad it was some boys from down the fen who stole the stuff and they had made Daphne help them in the shop or they were going to beat me up," blurted Michael. "He's gone on his bike to try to catch them up."

The fen was a road that wound its way out of the village coming to a dead end by a deep drainage dyke some four or five miles away. Some of the kids who lived in the farm cottages were easy targets to lay blame on for crimes where there were no witnesses. This seemed to be as good a time as any to blame them as Mr. Bennett had not actually laid eyes on the perps and therefore could not be sure who was to blame. All he had seen after noting missing items was Daphne and two lads heading up the street in the direction of the railyard, hence his call to Constable Handly for assistance.

After agreeing to stick to that story if ever questioned we parted company. We gathered the evidence from the raid and made sure it was well buried and would not be found. I retrieved my bike and headed home to the farm vowing never to steal anything ever again. Apart from the odd apple or plum "scrumped' over someone's fence, since then I have stuck to that vow.

The village continued to provide a haven for me whenever I could ride my bike after finishing up any chores that were assigned to me at the farm. Brother Pete was now twenty and already preparing to go off to Nottingham University by working at the local planning office of the County Council in Sleaford.

My older sister Liz had started her training at Harlow Wood Hospital to become an orthopedic nurse. I still had no idea what I was going to do with my life nor even thought very much about the future. All I did know was that I did not want to stay in Lincolnshire and work as a farm laborer like my dad.

I would take every opportunity to leave the cottage and go to one of the villages for whatever entertainment was available. On Saturdays the village football team would often play at home so that was usually a good diversion.

Occasionally the team would run a bus for an away game and some of the supporters could ride on the bus to the neighboring village to watch the match. Listening to the older lads and the adults that were team members bragging about their exploits with the girls was another source of education for me. Even though none of these opportunities seemed to come my way I was building up a great source of information for the moment that I got my first chance to try out the theory.

On Wednesday evenings for a period of time we were treated to a traveling cinema show that visited Billingborough and set up a temporary theater in the village hall. One night I had been to see a film, the title of which I have no recollection of, and was on my way home on my bike at about 10:00 P.M.

It was late summer so it was dusk but still light enough to see where I was going without any lights. The road home passed a green lane that led to the twelfth-century Sempringham Abbey that was always a bit spooky even though the Abbey was at least a mile from this part of the road.

As I approached the end of this lane I began to make out the outline of a person standing by the side of the road. My first impression was that it was an old tramp that was often seen around the area. We called him old Joe and he had a couple of makeshift camps he would stay in. I think Joe was a war veteran who had never adjusted to a normal life and just wandered around the local area looking for handouts.

Neither of his camps were near this spot so if it was Joe he was a long way from home. As I got nearer, maybe now thirty yards away, I realized that this figure seemed to have no bottom half, furthermore it was a man with a large hat and Elizabethan ruff around his neck.

In total disbelief and shock I began to pedal like crazy as I passed this silent, motionless figure. It was gray and still but the eyes seemed to follow me as I, in turn, stared at it as I went by.

Now terrified I continued to pedal as fast as I could not

daring to look back lest this ghost should be floating along behind me. Finally, exhausted, I slowed down and glanced behind me. The lane was now a half mile behind me and there was no sign of the figure. I continued on home still not really believing what I had seen.

I never told anyone about this until many years later when the subject of ghosts came up in a conversation. Whenever I recount this experience I get very disbelieving looks from listeners. All I know is that the image of this man is still very firmly fixed in my brain and I have no doubt that what I saw was truly a ghost. As I write this account the now familiar cold chill goes down my back.

As I reached fifteen in February 1962 I was approaching the mock GCE exams at school. This was the test to determine which O levels I would pursue into the fifth year. On the run up to the tests in spring I was still having a great deal of trouble with several subjects. Algebra was a complete mystery to me as were other math-related subjects. Geography and history seemed to come fairly easy but most of the other subjects I was really not very good at. We took the tests in May and June just prior to the summer holiday that would run from early July to September.

My test results were awful and the prospect of me improving during the fifth year to the point where I would take and pass the GCEs for real was remote to say the least. My parents, bless them, really did not have the time or sophistication to help me through this dilemma.

Sometime around then the old Foreman Clarkson had retired and we had moved from the little semi cottage into the old stone farmhouse. Dad was now the sole permanent employee on this part of Proctor's enterprise and there was always plenty to do around the place for idle hands.

I remember on many occasions sugar beet singling. This entailed crawling along sugar beet rows pulling out double seeds so the ones left had space to grow much bigger. It was grueling work and we got paid a modest fee by the row.

Dad was just happy doing his stuff around the farm and Mum had found a job working at the village bakers. They were so proud of Brother Peter who was now at University and so obviously talented that I sort of blended into the background.

Dad would sometimes say he would have a word with Proctor so that I could get a permanent job on the farm. Although Mother did not subscribe to that being my only option there was little talk of anything else for me.

In 1962 the legal age where you could leave school was fifteen, an age I had now reached. Terrified of going back after the summer for more miserable education I was beginning to think about what my alternatives were.

I remember Uncle Arthur's stories about the navy and I was still fascinated by the thought of traveling around the world. So much so, that I decided to make a visit to the naval recruiting office in Lincoln. As this was a thirty-mile bus trip I had to share my thoughts with my mother.

To my surprise she seemed to be quite keen on the idea of the visit so, after a couple of phone calls to make an appointment, I was on my way to Lincoln.

At the interview I discovered that at my age the only way into the navy was to enter HMS Ganges. Ganges was a youth training facility near Ipswich where a one-year junior training program was available to youths who could pass an entrance exam. With nothing to lose I agreed to take the test.

I don't remember much about the content but to my surprise I received a letter a couple of weeks later saying I had passed the exam and was eligible to enter Ganges as a junior seaman. The next step was the medical, which was going to take some time, as they made an appointment for me for about a month later.

This was to be at a place in Derby that was even further away. By now I was starting to get used to the idea that I might just make it into the service. Mum and Dad had agreed to sign the consent papers as I was still under the age where I could do my own thing. During the rest of the summer I continued to fool around with my pals while I waited for the medical appointment to come round.

Idle time usually involved more tearing around the villages on our bikes and generally killing time until school started again for those who were going back after the summer. One or two lads had already started work on various farms; some had started apprenticeships and of course I was in waiting for my navy medical.

One afternoon several of us decided that we were going to have a contest to see who could ride their bike the fastest around a tight corner which turned up a dirt track off the main road in the village.

We marked a starting point some way up the road and each of us was to line up ready for the start. The idea was to see who could get to the turn first and navigate it without slowing down. The dirt rack ran up between several houses and just into the turn was the back of a brick outhouse.

By now my cycling skills were well developed and because I went everywhere by bike, I was very fit and in with a good chance of being first. We set off as fast as we could and sure enough I managed to ease out in front of the five or six contestants.

The turn was fast approaching and I needed to move well to the left to cut the corner as tight as I could as this would require banking over to the limit. Still marginally ahead I made my move and cut across the others to lean into

71

the turn. All was going well as I rounded the blind corner but then disaster struck.

My front wheel started to slide in the gravel and I began to drift to the outside of the track. Nowhere to go, I tried to straighten up but I was going way too fast to stop the rot. With a sickening crunch I struck a glancing blow to the back of the brick building with my right shoulder and fell to the ground dazed and bruised. The other bikes came rattling by around me, fortunately missing me as I lay on the ground with my bike on top of my legs.

"Fucking hell, Manty, are you alright?"

"Oh yeh, do I look alright, you prick?"

I tried to get up but I could not move my right arm. I had banged my head either on the wall or the ground and it was pounding like crazy.

Several hands came out to help me up and I gradually got to my feet. Someone picked my bike up and proclaimed the front wheel was a bit bent but other than that it was OK. It was me that was not OK. I quickly realized that I had either broken my shoulder or at least severely buggered it up, so much so that I could not lift my arm an inch.

This was not good; in less than seven days I was going for a medical that could determine my whole future and here I was looking like a pigeon with a broken wing. After a few minutes of comforting from my mates I decided there was nothing else to do but to go home. I hung my arm over my bike seat and started the long walk home, leaning and pushing my wobbly bike as I went.

I waited till I was well away from the village before I let the intense pain overwhelm me and the sobbing that followed was heard by no one. It took what seemed like ages to get to the farm. I eventually made it home and sank into a chair. "Dr. Henderson, oh Dr. Henderson."

A brief visit to Doc the next day and the usual "Oh, has

the wee laddy hurt himself again" from the good doctor. It was determined that I had severely bruised my shoulder and had probably dislocated it but it was now back in place. "Give him some wee aspirin and some rest and laddy will be as good as new in a couple of weeks."

My arm was strapped across my chest and Doc said I needed to keep it like that for a while to let the shoulder heal.

A week later I am sitting in another doctor's office in Derby. "What on earth do you think you are doing turning up for a fitness medical with your arm in a sling." The doctor's question seemed reasonable to me so I had little to say. I was told to come back in a month, at which time if I could pass the medical then I could still make the entrance date of October 3rd to enter HMS Ganges.

If I missed that I would have to miss a three-month period and go next year. My shoulder improved and by the time I made my next trip to Derby I was almost back to normal. Lots of prodding and poking and several strenuous exercises later I was dispatched home from the doctor's office to await the results.

By now it was late August and time was running out for me to make the entrance date. About two weeks later the letter arrived from the Ministry of Defense with instructions for me to return to the recruiting office in Lincoln to sign on the dotted line.

1962 was just two years since national service had ended. Therefore the army, air force and navy were now reliant on mugs like me who actually volunteered to get their heads blown off.

It was also the beginning of the Vietnam conflict for the Americans and cold war was in full swing, so times were a bit on the uncertain side to say the least. Nevertheless I had made my mind up that the navy was the life for me and nothing was going to stop me from going. This was regardless of the fact that I had to sign on for nine years, the time not counting until my eighteenth birthday.

In effect I was committing myself to the navy for almost twelve years.

When one contemplates the world's problems that also came along in the '60s including the Arab-Israeli six-day war, Rhodesia declaring independence, the Cuban missile crisis, Britain's withdrawal from Aden and the troubles starting up again in Ireland to name just a few, I feel sort of lucky to still be around. Any one of these crises could have dragged me into all kinds of trouble, but apart from a few punch-ups on shore leave I escaped more or less unscathed.

However, my seven years afore the mast (and sometimes up it) included a great deal of strange, sometimes dangerous and often bizarre events that I would need a series of books to tell it all. Instead I have selected a few of the more interesting events that follow in the next chapters.

One of the most compelling things about this period was the people, some of whom were damaged goods right from the word go. I had spent the first fifteen years of my life hidden away in rural Lincolnshire with virtually no exposure to the world outside and incredibly naïve about the ways of the world in big cities or other countries.

We did not have a television and I rarely listened to the news on the radio.

When the choices were the "Goon Show," the "Navy Lark," or the "Glums," who wanted to waste time listening to some crusty old BBC news reporter telling us that the Americans had initiated an invasion of some little island off Florida and got a black eye for their trouble?

Some of the significant events that happened in 1962 as I was preparing to join the navy included John Glenn going into space, Adolf Eichmann getting hanged in Israel, Marilyn Monroe departing this Earth and Nelson Mandela finding out what life was like on Robin Island in South Africa. We were also treated to the first publication of *Private Eye,* and the TV show "That Was the Week That Was."

4

You're in the Navy Now

The day came to go to Lincoln to sign on at the recruiting office. There I met several of the first of nearly two thousand boys who were to become a close part of my life for the next year. HMS Ganges was a huge youth training camp at the village of Shotley Point just South of Ipswich. Many people who are old enough may remember the famous mast at this establishment.

Built using original mast sections from two famous 19th-century navy vessels, the *Agincourt* and the *Cordelia,* it had been built with five stages. The first level had a wide area of rope netting around its full base rising up maybe 45 to 50 feet at a steep angle where it connected to a cross beam, the name for which I have completely forgotten. The next stage was much narrower and the netting hung almost vertical again rising up another 25 feet or so to another cross member.

The next step was even more narrow still, rising a further 30 feet to the last cross section. Another narrow piece rose 20 feet more where it was so narrow only two boys could stand and then 15 more feet of round wooden mast above that.

At the very top was a wooden bowl 11 ½ inches across, known as the button. All told, from ground to button, the mast stood 143 feet and ten inches high. Quite a long way down unless you took the express lift!

This mast was often featured in news bulletins when the navy had open days or they had found out some hapless recruit had fallen off and crashed through the base post office roof located nearby.

Legend has it that this did actually happen, but the truth of it was in 1949 a lad did fall but got stuck in the netting and lost most of the skin round his neck.

I seemed to be in a daze for the next few weeks waiting for the date to come round for me to board the train and head for Ipswich. When it finally came Mum drove me to Lincoln where I again encountered the two boys who had been at the recruiting office the day I signed on. This was some adventure for me because apart from a couple of previous trips riding a train was a big deal.

I think we had to change in Norwich on the way but eventually we arrived at Ipswich sometime late in the afternoon. The navy had arranged to collect me and to my surprise what seemed like hundreds of other kids on busses and take us the eight or so miles to the camp. I had arrived, Junior Seaman Manton, official service number PO70000.

I was part of a group of several hundred boys who entered this establishment in early October 1962. The first part of the program was intended to be a six-week basic training period. I say intended because the fall out rate was very high.

We had thrown our suitcases and bags into the luggage bay at the back and climbed aboard four or five blue busses parked at the end of the platform. By the time I got on, most of the seats were taken and from the conversation it became obvious that some of the boys had been waiting for a long time for the last few of us to arrive.

We set off from the station and wound our way out of Ipswich now with a hazy sun low in the sky. After about

77

twenty minutes we pulled into a large wire gate that was closed behind us.

We all climbed out onto a wide open tarmac area surrounded on all four sides by what can be best described as long wooden huts, with names above the entrance, like Benbow, Ashanti, Rodney and other famous historic names from naval history.

These huts were not too dissimilar to the chicken deep-litter, houses of my native Lincolnshire. Several boys were moving about the parade ground (as I soon discovered it was called) hurrying from one side to the other and not taking much notice of the new arrivals. These boys were all dressed exactly the same in light blue shirts, dark blue baggy trousers and wearing brilliant white sailors' hats with HMS Ganges written around the hatband.

This establishment, I was about to learn, was known as the Annex.

The nervous chattering on the busses had been replaced by an almost silent calm, as we all stood around not sure what to do.

That problem went away very quickly. "Alright you 'orrible little buggers, stop that facking babbling and fall in. My name is Chief Petty Officer 'Utchins but if I let you speak to me you can call me SIR."

Fall in, fall in what I wondered. Before I had time to solve the riddle there was an immediate shuffling about and we all miraculously seemed to end up in several almost straight lines three or four deep. I had had the misfortune of finding myself on the front row only a few feet away from the yelling and spitting CPO Hutchins.

Now I was faced with the awful reality of what I had signed up for. We stood silent, eyes fixed on CPO Hutchins' mouth waiting for the next onslaught of words.

We were all silent other than one poor lad on the back row who was starting to cry. Not daring to move it was hard to see who the lone blubberer was.

Hutchins strode forward pushing his way past me as if I was invisible, carving a path through the throng of silent faces. I dared a glance over my shoulder to see the CPO with his face only inches from the blubbering boy. "Your mother, you want your mother." He screamed, "I'M YOUR FACKING MOTHER NOW LAD."

I was dumbstruck, I couldn't believe anyone could be so nasty on our first day; after all, we had volunteered to come here and all he could do was yell at us. "If all you can do is cry, lad, you might as well get back on that facking bus and fack off home to your facking mother."

This seemed to calm the lad as he went silent. I returned my head forward and stood as still as I could hoping to not attract any attention. The CPO barged his way back to the front and with his arms again, locked dead straight at his side and as stiff as a telegraph pole he screamed "TeeeeeeennnnnshaaaaaAA."

Having seen several war films I cottoned on really quickly and clicked my heels together and stood even straighter with my arms straight down like the CPO. If nothing else I was going to do exactly as I was told.

In the seven years I was in the navy I never heard one command to come to attention that bore any relationship to the actual word attention. Even later on when I had a small band of underlings to march around myself, whenever I called them to attention I seemed to be afflicted with the same speech impediment as everyone else.

Some of the other kids had obviously seen the same film I had because enough of us hit the spot so that the rest followed suit by example. Now all standing bolt upright with our arms welded to our sides like the Chief, we waited in silence for the next verbal onslaught. Hutchins spun round away from us and with his arms swinging to the height of his shoulders like a demented chimpanzee he marched off into an open doorway at the end of one of the huts.

He was replaced by another uniform, this one with less gold braid on display which turned out to be a Petty Officer. "The CPO has gone to fetch the Annex Commander so I want you all to be still and quiet till they return," he said, this time in a more relaxed manner. I was a little relieved, as I had begun to think that everyone here just yelled at you. The peace did not last long as Hutchins came striding back toward us still imitating the chimp.

Behind him followed this rather elderly officer with two gold rings around each arm. Hutchins snapped to a stop and then shuffled sideways with a couple of grunts. The officer ambled up beside him and asked the CPO to stand us at ease. "Stand at . . . HEEEEEEZE," screamed the CPO, again giving me another liberal dose of spit in the process. The officer seemed to cringe away from the noise as Hutchins stamped his feet wide now clasping his hands behind his back.

Again I was on to it in a flash and imitated the stance followed by the others around me who were also getting with the idea.

"Good afternoon boys. I'm Lieutenant Baxter and I am the Annex commander who will be responsible for your first six weeks of basic training." Lt. Baxter looked like he wanted to be anywhere other than here but he went through the motions. He droned on about how we were entering the most noble of forces in the service of our Glorious Queen. There was no greater honor than to take up arms in defense of our great country and to proudly serve as millions had served before.

The speech went on for what seemed like hours but he eventually fizzled out and handed us back to the CPO.

After the soft tones of the Lt. Hutchins brought the level back up. "Right then, P.O. Jones will give you your mess name so listen up carefully, get to your mess, select a bed and place all your personal belongings on that bed."

Personal belongings. I had hardly thought about my little brown case that held just one pair of trousers, two shirts, two pairs of pajamas, a toothbrush, toothpaste and my underwear, still in the luggage compartment on the bus.

We had been instructed to only bring a minimal amount of clothing, as most of our time would be spent in uniform. What they really meant was that *all* of our time would be spent in uniform.

The next half an hour was a roll call of names as each boy was called forward and told his mess name. The navy called living quarters the mess, which I found confusing at first as in the movies the mess always seemed to be where the soldiers went to eat. But I wasn't a soldier I was now a sailor, although it would be some time before I could equate the stories of Uncle Arthur to the experiences to come.

"Jones, Jacobs, Johnson, Kline, Kingston, Lorrimore, Lewis, Manton," the names were coming thick and fast and I stood rigid as mine came and went. I suddenly sprang into action and ran forward to the PO to hear the mess name. I had missed my turn and afraid to interrupt I just stood like an idiot as the list continued. Eventually he got to the end, "Wilson, Watkins, and Zeal," that was it. All the boys had by now grabbed their bags and cases from the busses and disappeared into the various buildings.

I still stood in front of the PO as he continued looking down at his list. Finally he glanced up to see me standing there like a lost puppy on the side of the road. "What's your name, lad?" barked the PO.

"Mmmanton, Sir," I stammered.

The PO glanced back at his list flipping over pages with obvious annoyance. "Manton, Manton, ah, here you are, Ashanti mess." I remained standing still as he stared at me.

"Well, go to it, lad, do you want me to hold your bloody 'and." With that I turned round and headed to the bus for my suitcase. The driver had closed up the luggage bay in the back and was climbing into the cab as I ran up.

He could see me approaching and I despaired that he would drive off with my stuff, never to be seen again. After a glance in my direction he climbed back down and ambled to the back. Without a word he opened the bay, pulled my lone little suitcase from the back and dropped it at my feet. He raised his eyes up as if to say, "You idiot" then he ambled back to the driver's door and climbed in.

I grabbed my suitcase and ran to the hut with Ashanti over the door as fast as I could. Once inside I realized that the inside of the hut did not look any more attractive than the outside. Passing the toilets and shower room by the front entrance I shuffled down the middle between rows of iron beds along each side.

At the side of each bed was a metal locker. The other boys had all selected a bed and were busy emptying their belongings onto their chosen spot.

I walked to the far end and then, not having seen one unoccupied space, headed back to the other end in the vain hope that I had missed one somewhere in the middle.

Back at the entrance I discovered just one bed space empty, all alone and very near to the toilet door.

After yet another look up and down I concluded this was the only spot left so I lay my little case on the bed and sat down beside it. I was not sure what to do, as all the other boys seemed to be busy shifting things around on their beds.

"It's by the door," said the boy at the nearest bed to

mine. I found out later that this was junior seaman Read, later to be called Yetti Read due to his incredible amount of black body hair.

"What is?" I offered feebly.

"The orders, it's pinned up near the door."

I followed the line of his pointing finger to the door that I had come through. Now closed, I could see a piece of paper pinned to a board near the door.

I walked over and started to read the sheet headed, Daily Orders HMS Ganges Annex, October 3rd 1962.

1. Select a bed, unpack all personal belongings and place neatly on your bed.
2. Place suitcase / other bag under the bed at your sleep station.
3. Place any valuables such as watches, rings or other items in the locker allocated to your sleep station, lock door and remove key.
4. Muster at front of mess building for further instruction.

I didn't have any valuables and it didn't take long to tip my meager suitcase contents onto the bed. I had just pushed the case under the bed when PO Jones opened the door and yelled at the top of his voice, "Right O lads, everyone outside and fall in."

I now knew what fall in meant, but for what I had no idea. Despite being at the front of the hut I ended up in the middle of the gaggle as we all filed outside to see what the next surprise was going to be.

"Fall in. Fall in. Right, we are all going to go over to the dining hall to feed you lot, after that you come back to your mess take a shower and turn in." I hadn't thought much about food which was unusual for me as I was normally ready to eat at the drop of a hat. With so much going on I had taken little notice of the fact that it was getting dark and very cold.

We followed the PO across the tarmac (I was soon to understand the significance of this seemingly large unused parking area) to another identical hut on the far side. As we filed in I could detect the smell of food. By now I was hungry as we lined up in single file at the buffet counter.

Behind the counter were several scruffy-looking men, all dressed in the same blue outfits as the boys I had seen earlier outside but this time the clothes were faded and crumpled. These men might have been in their mid twenties but to me at fifteen they looked old. On approaching the food we picked up stainless steel trays that had several indented compartments to accommodate the various components of the meal.

As I got closer I could see huge steel containers of stew, vegetables, potatoes and something unidentifiable at the far end. This turned out to be spotty dick pudding on which the last "chef" in line slapped a thick layer of immobile custard on top.

Now, with probably four pounds of food weighing down my tray, I picked up a plastic mug of water at the end of the line and found myself a seat at one of the many wooden benches set at tables for eight.

I sat down trying not to nudge the boy next to me for fear of having to speak and began to eat the food. Surprisingly it tasted quite good and despite the rather strange consistency of the mashed potato I tucked in till my tray was empty. The custard was more like a slice of yellow jelly but it too tasted OK. In my seven years of service I rarely ever complained about the food, three hot meals a day and as much as you wanted. Only problem is that this conditioned me to always take large quantities and eat it all. OK when you're a growing teenager using four thousand calories a day rowing boats and scaling masts. However, as a sedentary adult, scaling down has always been a problem for me.

The boy next to me introduced himself as Bill Teacher from Newcastle.

Bill was shorter than me but about twice as wide. I had never met a sixteen-year-old that looked like this; he wasn't fat he was just big. It later transpired that Bill was a boxer and was also very fragile emotionally.

Another boy from the Newcastle area, Chris Thomson, told me that Bill had been in reform school and the navy was his option to stay out of going to jail if he kept up his former activities. Right then he seemed pretty nice to me but I was to find out otherwise a few days later.

We walked back to Ashanti mess in groups of three or four. I didn't say much, just answered questions if asked. Like, where I was from, how old, brothers, sisters that kind of stuff, but not offering to add anything. I felt incredibly out of it; they all seemed to know each other and were chatting away about all manner of things that were completely alien to me.

Once inside the mess I collected my toothbrush, paste and PJs and headed into the shower room. Inside the door was a pile of towels so I bent down and picked one up and continued on. To my horror there was line of naked boys all standing under showerheads laughing and shouting and seemingly oblivious to the fact that everyone could see . . . their willies. My god, I had never ever let anyone see my willy and I didn't plan to start now. I shuffled about in the doorway for a few seconds and then turned round to the row of sinks at the end of the shower room. I must have brushed my teeth for fifteen minutes, occasionally glancing into the steamy mirror to determine if everyone had finally left. Eventually only a couple of boys remained so I scurried past them to the furthest point in the room and slowly removed my clothes.

With my back to the others (not a practice that was to be recommended in some circumstances), now naked, I stepped sideways under the shower and turned it on. A flood of ice-cold water cascaded over me as I frantically tried to adjust the control. This did nothing for my shrinking assets as I fumbled with the ancient plumbing trying to find a temperature that didn't scald me or form ice on my head.

The other two boys were laughing, and I was sure they were laughing at my skinny hairless body huddled under the shower. I dared a glance in their direction but to my surprise they were not even looking at me. The joke over, they grabbed towels and walked out of the showers.

Alone, I turned off the shower and sat on the wooden bench next to my little pile of clothes draping the towel over my lower half. I sat for a few moments contemplating the day's events. I was miserable, alone and scared, and I wanted to go home to my Mum. The tears welled up inside me and I started to shudder and blubber trying not to make any sound lest I alert all those macho types who were in the mess telling jokes and stories about their exploits. I was sure I was going to fail every test the navy put me to. What on earth was I doing in this awful place?

After a few minutes I managed to get my blubbering under control. I was determined not to let the CPO hear me crying as I didn't want him to yell at me after seeing the display when we had arrived with the other boy who cried.

After drying off and donning my PJs I went for a pee and went back to my bed. I put the little pile of clothes in the steel locker and crept into bed. The main lights were out but the mess was dimly lit by red lights dotted along the walls at various intervals. That became another consequence of seven years in the navy. I have always been able to sleep despite being in a lighted room. Some of the boys were still chattering but gradually the sounds died down till all that could be heard was the odd squeak and rattle of the bed frames as they tossed and turned getting settled in for the night.

5

A New Day

"WAKEY, WAKEEEEE, 'ANDS OFF COCKS ON SOCKS." I jumped awake at the yelling at the foot of my bed. The lights were full on and blinding as I made out the shape of a man doing the yelling. For a few seconds I was totally confused, my room was different, there were beds all over the place and noise and people moving around. Then the awful truth dawned on me and the experience of the previous day came flooding back. PO Jones grabbed the end of my bed frame and jerked it hard. "Come on, lad, get yer arse out of that bed and get dressed."

I tumbled out of bed and ran to the toilet to find several boys already standing in a queue waiting to relieve themselves at the urinals. The mess held about fifty boys but the facilities were designed for far less.

After taking my turn I splashed water on my face and ran back to dress, which took about ten seconds. I then ran out of the mess after the rapidly exiting crowd to fall in to the now familiar three rows, at the front of the hut. It was cold and I had not put my coat on but it was too late for that. After making sure everyone was outside the PO led us off again to the dining hall.

Breakfast was another feast; bacon, sausages, scrambled eggs, baked beans and huge chunks of white bread. A giant rusty-looking urn at the end of the line dispensed steaming mugs full of strong dark tea.

I filled my steel tray to the brim, filled a mug with tea and sat down to tuck in yet again. Eating seemed to be the main occupation so far. This time I sat next to a tall skinny boy who introduced himself as Chris Thompson; he was the one who later told me about Bill Teacher's sordid past in Newcastle. Chris was from Morpeth and it took several attempts for me to understand his accent.

The dialect was so thick it was like listening to a foreign language but eventually I tuned in to what he was saying. His dad was a shipyard worker and he had two brothers and a sister. He had joined the navy because there was no work in the Newcastle area and no room for him at the little prefabricated house they had in Morpeth.

He couldn't stop talking and I listened as I ate my mountain of breakfast. Chris was a nice lad with a big smile and seemed incredibly happy to be here. I started to feel less isolated as he volunteered his life story, speaking at a tremendous pace.

Other boys were chattering around us and I began to detect all kinds of accents as a cacophony of sound filled the room. These sounds mingled with the clattering of metal on metal as two hundred breakfasts disappeared into two hundred boys from every walk of life imaginable.

Until now I had not thought much about who else would be entering Ganges at the same time as me. Other than the two boys who had boarded the train in Lincoln with me I had not considered where else they might have come from.

My thoughts were interrupted as PO Jones banged on a tray in the doorway. "Right O lads, as soon as you have finished eating, Ashanti and Benbow mess's muster outside. We are going to take a bus over to the main camp to get your uniform issue and get your 'air cut.

"The rest of you go back to your mess and I will come

and tell you what's next." It transpired that Petty Officer Jones, like Chief Petty Officer Hutchins, was a cockney and in cockney land the H is silent.

Haircut, I didn't need a haircut, just a day before I left, Mum had taken me to the little barber shop in Billingborough where I had lost enormous amounts of my thick brown locks to the wastebasket. I was sure once the barber in the camp saw how short it was he would move on to the next boy, many of whom had hair much longer than mine.

Eventually we were all loaded on the same blue bus we had arrived in and we set off through the wire gate. We crossed over a main road straight through iron gates that were supported by large brick pillars. At either side were massive ships figureheads just inside the entrance.

Several uniformed sailors were standing under floodlights at the gate. This time the uniforms were all dark blue—number 3's, I later discovered—heavy serge material with tight-fitting jackets over a white front and bell-bottom trousers. A piece of white string was looped round the neck and hung down the front. Again the white round hat perched on top with HMS Ganges around the hatband. I noticed that these hats were curved down at the sides and not as bright white.

As the bus pulled up by a building the light was beginning to get better as the sky brightened. By now it was probably seven o'clock but as I had no watch it was hard to tell. We climbed off the bus and formed yet another queue which disappeared into the front of the building.

The familiar barber's pole projected from a rusty angle iron over the door. As we waited outside in a gaggle Petty Officer Jones had us fall in again. As we lined up in our usual three rows I could hear the sounds of shouting across the parade ground as several groups of boys were being marched around with their arms swinging. At the side of each group was a Petty Officer barking orders. "RIGHT HAWHEEEL, LEFT HAWHEEEL. KEEP UP, LAD, KEEP UP. GET IN STEP, YOU STUPID TURD."

The sounds mingled together as each group responded to the commands of their instructor. Many recruits were out of step and obviously having trouble keeping in any kind of alignment.

I had misplaced my new pal Chris so I waited in silence as the line of boys began to disappear into the barbershop. After a few minutes they began to re-appear from the barber's shop door rubbing their heads that now had very little hair. I was still convinced I would get a pass, as my hair was shorter than I had ever had it. Finally it was my turn and by now I had seen how things were done.

The barber was a tiny little man with a limp, probably in his sixties and bald in the middle of his head. He had a cigarette hanging out of his mouth with a long column of ash. Periodically the ash would fall off onto the head of the individual in the chair. Shotley, as the barber was called, would dust the ash of the hair and carry on clipping with his mechanical clippers.

As each victim sat down the clippers would be run up the back and over the top till all that was left was a short stubble all over. "Sir, I don't think I need a haircut, sir. I had one the day before yesterday." I half addressed my plea to the PO who was reading a newspaper in the corner. Shotley laughed and then coughed and hacked as he pushed my shoulders down in the chair. I closed my eyes so I could not see myself in the dirty mirror as I felt the first tugging at the back of my head.

I opened my eyes and looked helplessly across at the PO who was muttering something about what he was reading in his paper. The headline on the front was "Nehru warns

China." I had no idea who Nehru was, or what he was pissed off with China for. Of course this reference was to the border war between China and India which was building up to armed conflict at the time in which the Indians got a bloody nose.

Within about a minute I was done. Little spots of blood had appeared on the top of my head where Shotley had dug in a little too hard and my hair was at best a quarter of an inch all over. I walked outside and stood silently with the rest until everyone was shorn. "Right O, follow me," barked PO Jones. He strode off in the direction of another building with a sign over the door identifying it as the Quartermaster Stores.

I had now managed to get in the line behind Chris and we picked up on the breakfast conversation while the queue shuffled forward. I told him I was from a farm in Lincolnshire and my Uncle Arthur had been on the Battle-ship *Ajax* in the Persian Gulf and my brother Pete was going to be an architect and my sister was a nurse at Harlow Wood Hospital. Chris listened with interest as I blurted out my life story. I told him about my mates at home and hurting my shoulder and failing the first medical until eventually we found ourselves inside the door.

" 'Ow tall, waist, weight," yelled the first of several sail-ors behind the wooden counter. As each boy gave his vital statistics the sailor behind the counter pushed a neat pile of clothing across.

We then moved to the next person until we had a huge pile of clothing. At the end of the line were the shoes. "Size," mumbled the guy behind the counter. "Er, er," I stuttered. I couldn't' remember my size. Without waiting for me to col-lect my thoughts he yelled, "Give me a shoe." I thought the idea was for him to give me the shoes so I still stood motion-less, not sure what to do.

"Give me a fucking shoe," he yelled even louder. I now got the message. I leaned down and pulled off my shoe and placed it on the counter top. He glanced inside the shoe and turned to his racks behind him. "Eight, you prick, you're going to do really well round here if you don't even know your own fucking shoe size." He slammed the shiny black shoes in front of me and yelled "Next."

I moved along balancing my pile with the shoes on top, out of another door and back to the bus. Chris was waiting for me. He just raised his eyebrows and said, "Fucking twat."

We both laughed and climbed onto the bus. That was the first time I had laughed for over two days and it felt good. "We're going to beat the bastards," he said with that big wide smile on his face. "Yeh, we're going to beat the bastards," I said in response. Inside I was not quite as sure as Chris but I said it anyway.

When we eventually arrived back at the mess and spread out the pile of clothes I discovered I had two sets of the light blue shirts and trousers, two blue woolen jumpers, four pairs of enormous underpants, a baggy pair of swimming shorts, four white vests, four pairs of socks, two pairs of pajamas and one pair of black lace up shoes and pair of white plim-soles. In addition to that, hidden in the middle, was a rolled up blue cloth-bag. I inspected this little bag trying to figure out what it was for.

It was tied with a piece of ribbon so I undid the knot and unrolled the bag. Inside were several bundles of cotton, some sewing needles, several large blue buttons, safety pins and a thimble.

As I pondered over this discovery Yetti Read, as he was already nicknamed, over at the next bed, came over and pointed out that we were expected to mend our own clothes. Before I could ponder any more CPO Hutchins appeared at the door. "Petty Officer Jones is off with the other lot so listen up." He marched further down the mess to make sure the boys at the far end could hear him.

"I want you to put all your personal belongings into your suitcases, clothes, watches everything and wrap it up in this 'ear paper." He turned and pointed at a small table at the side of the entrance upon which lay a thick pile of brown paper and several bundles of string. "Write your home address on the top and put it on the trolley outside the 'ut."

"What are we going to wear on Saturday night to go out?" said one boy moving into the middle of the room to address everyone in general.

I had not even thought about going out anywhere, but now that he had brought it up I wondered too. If we sent our clothes home we would only have these blue work uniforms to wear.

I suddenly began to realize that we were prisoners. We couldn't do anything unless someone came in and told us what to do. How would we go anywhere? Up to now I had thought once the training day was over we could hop on a bus and ride into Ipswich and go to the pictures or try to get a pint in a pub or something.

Everyone began to grumble and moan as they too began to understand the situation we found ourselves in.

The rest of the day was taken up by embroidering our names on our repair kit, packing out stuff, eating lunch and being shown around the various classrooms and other facilities that were to dominate our lives for the next six weeks, at least for many of us.

I gradually got to know some of the other boys as we mingled in different groups as the day progressed.

I was amongst the youngest at fifteen and a half with some almost a year older. There was also a huge difference in size and maturity because some of them already looked like they shaved and some had a lot of body hair. I, by contrast, had hardly any body hair and what I did have was blond and light.

I was quite tall for my age but very thin and with little muscle. That was to change over the next year as I packed on the body weight and muscle. I went from an eight stone weakling to an eleven stone strong man.

By evening I was starting to feel more relaxed and less intimidated by my surroundings. In conversation with several boys I discovered they too were apprehensive about what was going on and that made me feel less isolated. Dinnertime came round fairly quickly and it was time for more food. I was beginning to look forward to the training we were to begin the next day.

This was going to be split between classroom study where we did subjects like English, math and navigation and parade ground training where we learned to march and do drill. After the basics we were to then move onto rifle drill. At that time the navy was still using the standard Lee Enfield 303 bolt-action rifle.

This weapon weighed in at just over nine pounds and I discovered that after several hours of throwing it about on the parade ground it felt like ninety pounds. Like much of the equipment in the navy at this time, it was old school. This gun was a modified version of what the British used in the Boer War and had gone through many incarnations eventually being used right up to the '80s for training purposes. It would be some time before I experienced the awesome power of this beast in live firing.

The first few days in the classroom involved learning about the training schedule; we had to do all of the basics in the Annex in six weeks before moving over to the main camp to start the full program. All this was very mundane stuff but unless told how, we had no idea. I had arrived on a Tuesday and on Friday we were allowed to call home and tell our families that we were OK and happy.

I called my mother and told her I was fine and having a great time. I didn't tell her that I was having bad dreams, sleepwalking and waking up in the night in a cold sweat.

On the second or third night I had a very strange dream in which I was floating above my bed looking down at my sleeping body. I floated out of the door and across the parade ground looking down at all the huts.

I floated up higher and felt like I could fly away. The next thing I knew I was standing outside in my pajamas, in the freezing cold by the door of the mess. I had woken with a start and realized I was outside. I went back inside and approached my bed. The only problem was that the bed had someone in it. I was totally confused. I ran outside again not sure where I was. As I started to waken further I could see the name Ashanti on the front of a hut across the other side of the parade ground.

Now I understood. I had walked right across to the other side, some one hundred yards. I ran back to my own mess and was relieved to find my bed empty. I crawled back in, frozen to the bone.

For the next several weeks I had at least three other occasions where I found myself outside in the night. The days began to rush by filled with fervent activity, up before 6:00 A.M. and something going on all the time till about 7:00 P.M. When the pressure was finally off and we were allowed a couple of hours to ourselves in the mess till lights out. After such an intensive schedule I was ready for bed even before the lights went out. I was actually beginning to enjoy the discipline and routine till one morning about two weeks into the schedule I read the daily orders pinned by the door.

ANNEX, BOXING CHAMPIONSHIPS.

Now I was born with a fine specimen of a nose and one

thing I had discovered early in life was that getting whacked on my nose hurt like hell. All of a sudden I was staring at the prospect of going three one-minute rounds with some thug weighing twice as much as me, thumping me on my nose with a bloody great pair of boxing gloves.

The orders specified the pairing for the contest to come only five days away. I frantically scanned down the list to find my name. Sure enough there it was, Junior Seaman Manton vs. Junior Seaman Williams.

Now Williams was a year older than me and at least forty pounds heavier but in their wisdom the PTIs (Physical training instructors) had used height as the matching criteria. I was quite tall but, my god, so skinny.

Williams was also a boxer of some reputation in his hometown, wherever that was.

It was time for the Manton ingenuity that has kept me out of many a punch up over the years. Call me a coward, OK I'm a coward, but the thought of someone punching me in the face for fun has never been something I have been prepared to risk other than in the most extreme circumstances.

The boxing was to take place on a Friday and this was Monday. I had just four days to hatch a plan to keep me from getting my lights knocked out but without flunking the course. If there was any hint of cowardice I would be kicked off the course in seconds and suffer the same fate as a couple of dozen boys who, for various reasons, had already got the boot.

The prospect of returning to the farm in disgrace with my limited employment options was not an option. I had to do this with cunning.

My chance came the next day when we were engaged in a football match to select a team to play the main camp at the end of our Annex training. I wanted so badly to get onto the team but my focus was on getting out of the boxing.

We were grouped into several teams and the tournament was to be played with several thirty-minute halves to give all the boys who could half kick a ball the chance for glory. I waited around until my team was called, the yellow team, which was somewhat ironic under the circumstances.

I was pretty fast on my feet, probably enhanced by the times I had to run for cover after committing crimes in my school years. I was designated to the right wing where my job was to lob the ball over for the center forward to shoot for goals. This was soccer before the continentals had corrupted the set-up where everyone seems to be in the middle and the back.

We had played for about twenty minutes and I decided it was time to hatch my plan. Someone played the ball out to my wing and I set off at full speed in the direction of the corner, but instead of taking it wide I dummied the full back and turned toward the center; like someone possessed I evaded a couple of other players and found myself facing the goalie just a few feet off the goal line.

I could see out of the corner of my eye another lad was hurtling toward me from my left; so I lunged forward as he hit me in the side with a sliding tackle. I flipped the ball over the goalie's head into the net. At the same time, with the inertia kindly provided by the defender, I rolled to my right and gracefully slid into the goal post, banging my left knee with a resounding thud.

In true professionals style I rolled about groaning and clutching my knee as if my leg was broken in twenty places. The cheers of my teammates were still ringing in my ears as I was carried off on a stretcher to the sick bay.

Still pretending the pain was intense (which it wasn't) I was looked over by the medical officer who eventually pronounced that nothing was broken but I would need to have it strapped up for a few days to recover.

"Will I have to miss the boxing on Friday, Sir?" I asked nervously.

"Sorry, lad, you won't be doing any more sports for at least a week."

Mission accomplished.

Friday came and I watched the boxing from a front seat and by the end of the afternoon I had as much blood on me as some of the hapless youths that were being beaten to a pulp in the ring. Williams had now been paired with another lad who made a valiant attempt to defend himself for about fifteen seconds. After that it was brutal. The PTI leapt in between them to prevent a murder being committed as Williams, flailing like a mad thing, flattened the poor kid to the canvas.

I was then witness to Bill Teacher, the boy who was twice as wide as me who I talked to on the first day. He was fighting another boxer called Ghent from Ireland. These two went at it like pros. Teacher won this time but this bout started a rivalry between these boys that lasted for the whole year as they both represented the navy in various inter-service tournaments.

On several occasions during the next few weeks I witnessed Teacher's obvious fragile emotional state. It seemed to take little provocation to cause him to flare up and threaten to pummel someone for no real reason. Consequently, for the protection of my nose, I made sure I did not get on the wrong side of him. I learned several years later that Bill Teacher had tried to commit suicide.

After the boxing was out of the way my knee began an incredibly rapid recovery such that, by the next weekend, I was back playing football. Having not made it into any sort of proper team at school I desperately wanted to get into the

Ganges team and play inter-service games. Despite incredible effort and enthusiasm balanced with very little skill I did not get picked for the Annex team to play the main camp. This was just another example in a long line of rejections.

During the next few days we sensed a great deal of tension amongst the staff and we finally found out that the Americans were threatening to attack Russian ships bound for Cuba. History tells us the rest but at that time we were convinced we would be drawn into a nuclear war with the Russians.

After about two weeks we had all been taken over to the main camp to go to the swimming pool. This was a huge Olympic-size pool with the high boards and a fifteen-foot deep end.

I was not a swimmer, despite going to the local pool at home in the summers I had not overcome the fear of water and consequently I could not go out of my depth.

We were ushered into the changing rooms and much to our surprise were told to don blue boiler suits over our swimming shorts.

We were then marched out to the side of the pool and formed up in several lines. A Chief Petty Officer in immaculate white tee shirt and shorts, with his rank proudly displayed on the chest, strutted up to the front. "Right HO lads we are about to find out which of you lot can swim."

That's OK, I thought, they are going to let us get in at the shallow end and swim up and down and see who can and who can't, so that can't be too bad, can it!

Little did I anticipate the navy's method of separating the wheat from the chaff. About forty of us were now lined up around the edge of the deep end.

I was a little apprehensive in case I fell in but still had not fully understood what was about to happen.

The anticipation did not last long. Several PTIs, all immaculately dressed like the Chief, were standing behind us as we faced the pool. "ALL RIGHT LADS . . . EVERYONE IN THE POOL." I couldn't believe my ears, here I was in a bloody great oversize boiler suit being told to jump into fifteen feet of water. I was rooted to the spot, but only momentarily. I felt a sharp push in the back and I was in the water, to be precise, under the water.

The suit weighed heavy as I scrambled to get to the surface.

By now I was gasping and terrified. I could feel the water around me churning as dozens of bodies thrashed around trying to get back to the air. After what seemed like several minutes my face broke the surface and I gulped in volumes of air, only to go down again under the weight of the suit.

I must have surfaced at least three times and I was beginning to grow very weak when I felt the hard end of a pole thrust into my chest. I grabbed the pole like a rat in a sewer clinging on to a floating turd. I was only in the water maybe three minutes but thought I was going to drown.

The blurred image of a PTI appeared on the other end of the pole as he urged me to hold on while pulling me to the side. I banged against the side of the pool and then felt several strong hands grab my wet boiler suit and haul me out of the water.

I lay on my back on the side coughing up water and bile as a PTI stood over me with a big grin on his face. "Sign on for swimming lessons then, lad, come on we 'ain't got all day."

I lifted myself up and followed several other boys to the far end of the pool area where another PTI was sitting behind a desk writing down names of each dripping spectacle that approached him.

For the next six weeks I attended swimming lessons at 6:00 A.M. every morning for one hour. I suppose you would be in deep shit if you fell off a ship in your work clothes and couldn't swim. That seems perfectly reasonable now, but right then I thought they were crazy for throwing forty kids into the deep end without any idea who could actually swim. In less than six weeks I had passed the Duke of Edinburgh award at the bronze level for self-survival at sea. This required me to swim a mile, tread water for half an hour in the dreaded boiler suit and then remove it before climbing out of the pool unassisted.

The six weeks in the Annex passed very quickly and as boys dropped out on a daily basis I began to believe that I was going to make it and pass over in to the main camp for training to begin in earnest.

Although I was still having bad dreams I had now discovered that wonderful comfort of masturbation. I had tried it a couple of years before when prompted by several girls who were playing in the unused attic of a family's home who we were friendly with. I was the only boy in the crowd and the girls were very curious about sex. I was pretending to know all about it although this was before the training sessions with the older lads, so my information was somewhat flawed.

I think I had bragged that I could "do it" so the daughter of the householder who was also about thirteen provided me with a plastic dish and said the girls would wait outside the empty attic room whilst I wanked off to prove my boast. I tweaked my equipment for some considerable time in a vain attempt to produce the demanded substance but nothing seemed to be happening.

The girls were taking turns to peek through the keyhole to see how I was doing but in the end I had to admit I was not able to perform. I tried to get one of the girls to help but got no takers. Very humiliating indeed for a thirteen-year-old.

Now, with about fifty other boys periodically thumping away under their blankets in the semi-darkness, I very quickly perfected the art of self-gratification.

The time came to transfer over to the main camp and up to now we had not been allowed outside the grounds of the Annex. Once we transferred we would be issued with a dress uniform and on Saturdays would be allowed to go outside on shore leave for several hours.

Something like twenty-five percent of the original intake had been thrown off the course for various reasons. Some were ousted for stealing, some for having two left feet and not having a clue how to march in formation.

One boy was made to stand in a large dustbin in the middle of the parade ground one night shouting "I am rubbish" because the PO had despaired at his incredibly filthy bed and clothing. He was sent home just a few days before transferring. I don't remember ever seeing that boy in the shower in the previous six weeks.

We were allocated new sleeping quarters and on the first day were issued with our number 3's. This was the heavy serge bell bottom uniform so familiar to anyone in a naval town. We would only be issued our number 1's on graduation. Number 1's were the same set-up but in a much smoother lighter fabric that did not itch like the number 3's. At least now we had a way of getting off the camp and checking out the local girls in Ipswich. By now it was the middle of November and the icy wind would blow off the wide River Stour estuary that went out to sea past Felixstowe and Harwich. One of the almost daily routines was to row the heavy clinker-built lifeboats that were moored on the jetty.

These boats had an uneven oar arrangement with three rowlocks on one side and only two on the other. As I was tall I got the job of stroke oar sitting facing the coxswain near the stern of the boat. The Cox would call the stroke as we pulled out into the river-mouth to a buoy way out in the middle.

I think the course we rowed was seven-eighths of a mile and half a dozen crews would be pitted against each other. As the stroke, I was responsible for keeping a good rhythm for the other four oars to follow, so if I got out of whack everything went pear-shaped. Not wanting to incur the wrath of the PO I pulled my heart out to get it right.

Once positioned out in the river by the first buoy we would wait for someone to fire a starting pistol and off we would go. The Cox would be yelling right into my face, "HINA, HINA, HINA." In the heat of the battle it's amazing how much effort you can exert as the adrenalin mounts to the sound of all the Cox's yelling at their crews.

"Come on lads, don't let those fucking girls from Ansen mess get in front." Seven-eighths of a mile may not seem far but under that kind of pressure it was like rowing the Atlantic. By the time we got to the second marker buoy most of us were physically sick over the side from pure exhaustion.

In just one year I packed on over forty pounds of solid muscle and my shoulders grew to almost twice as wide as they were on the first day.

This was not the only form of physical exercise. Every day included some kind of activity (other than masturbation). After I had finished my swimming training I was now as keen as mustard to be in the pool at every opportunity.

On top of that we did gymnastics two or three times a week, cross-country runs and, of course, marching.

I quite enjoyed marching; there was something pure about twenty or thirty lads all dressed in their smart blue uniforms marching along completely in step. After a while, we got pretty good at the various maneuvers.

The next phase was rifle drill. Now once again this interjected an element of risk, rifle, right. Even worse, during certain types of drill, we were required to fix bayonets and then march around swinging that 9 lb, 303, bolt action antique weapon through all the maneuvers with a pig sticker bayonet on the end.

"TeeeeeeeenSHAN, ORDER, HARRRRRRRMS, STAND AT, HEEEEEEZE ... TeeeeeeeeSHARRR, SHOULDER, HARRRRRRRRMS."

Getting on the front row was always a problem as whatever the particular movement was it could be seen instantly by the petty officer yelling out the orders. I always tried to get on the back but being quite tall I usually got placed on one end or the other and almost always on the front row.

One day, quite early into the rifle drill, with bayonets fixed, we were called to shoulder arms. This required pulling the rifle upright at the right side from the at attention position, lifting to the shoulder level by using the left hand across the body, transferring the hand position and then, with a sharp upward movement, placing the rifle across the left shoulder supported by the left hand under the stock. Easy peasy!!

Not so this time. On the swing up the body to get it in position for the drop onto the shoulder I somehow managed to aim the end of the pig sticker bayonet under my left armpit. With the movement now having its own momentum I jammed the end of the sharp point up into my flesh. I let go of the rifle but it was so jammed into my armpit that it just hung as if suspended by an invisible wire.

It hurt like hell and I let out a yell of pain. The petty officer marched up to me and pushed his face about two inches from mine. "You fucking prick, Manton, you're supposed to stick the fucking HENAMY, not your fucking self."

It was very strange that the cockney accent, which dropped the H from many words, always seemed to be then implanted on words that began with an E if uttered at high volume. I still stood rigid, not quite sure what to do. I was convinced I was mortally wounded as I could feel the blood running down the inside of my uniform.

The petty officer made the next decision on my behalf as with a sharp tug he pulled down on the rifle and extracted it from my underarm. Before I had time to consider what my next move should be he rammed the rifle across my chest and bawled: "RIGHT LAD, TEN CIRCUITS WITH YOUR RIFLE OVER YOUR 'ED BEFORE YOU FIND THE SICK BAY."

I had done this before, and seen many others subjected to the same torture. The first couple of circuits were not too difficult but a nine-pound rifle held above the head gradually begins to feel like ninety pounds. This was compounded by the fact that I had a bloody great hole under my arm and I was bleeding like a split pig.

Off I went muttering obscenities under my breath as I trudged round the outside edge of the parade ground. Every time I allowed the rifle to come lower the PO would yell at me to keep it high.

It was probably close to a quarter mile round the full perimeter so ten laps was pushing more than two miles. It became a battle of wills. On one hand I knew that if I stopped I would be subjected to more verbal abuse, but allowed to give in; but if I kept going I would probably pass out or fall down. But something made me keep going way beyond the point where I would have been capable without the threat of humiliation, or ridicule. Eventually the PO decided that I had done enough and he indicated for me to head for the sickbay. I was totally exhausted and my left arm was numb but I managed to keep my head up and trot off in the direction of his pointing finger.

The bleeding had stopped, or had subsided to the point where I couldn't detect anything running down my arm, or maybe I was empty! By now the rest of my group had left the parade ground and gone on to the next activity so I made my way to the sick bay. No Dr. Henderson here, mate.

Oh no, here the bedside manner was more, let's say functional.

After explaining to the duty medical officer what I had done, he almost pushed me out of the door into a treatment room where a grizzly old-looking medical technician proceeded to jab me with a needle, clean off the wound and then strap a bulky dressing under my arm.

That done I was off to find my mates for the next fun and games at Camp Ganges.

I had got to know several other lads as time passed and one of them, called Geoff Lewis, from the east end of London, was full of all kinds of stories about life in the big city. Geoff had volunteered to become a bugler, mainly because he thought it would help him get away with things he didn't like to do.

However, one duty of a bugler is to keep your bugle shiny. Geoff was not good at the fancy stuff, in fact he was a lousy bugler all around. Not only did he fail to keep it clean, he couldn't play the damn thing properly either.

He would have to get up early on certain days to play reveille so the rest of us would know it was 6:00 A.M. and another day of fun was about to begin. Whenever Geoff was on bugle duty the sound was unmistakable. It was akin to listening to Les Dawson playing Rachmaninov's 3rd. He managed to miss umpteen free periods because his bugle usually looked like it sounded, nasty.

Christmas came quickly and I was able to go home for a two-week leave to the farm over the holiday. Winter of '62 was one of those occasions when England got its fair share of snow and I spent much of the time helping my family digging out the lane.

This led from the farm to the nearest road where the local council had managed to put a snowplough through. Without that we were going to be short of food for the Christmas feast and for that I would have a dug a hundred miles.

The holiday went by in a flash, where I got reacquainted with Mother's fabulous cooking and then resumed my training in January. We were now trusted to go off camp on Saturdays for several hours.

Some of us would catch a bus into Ipswich and go to the pictures or hang around in the town trying to talk to girls. Problem was that we were all dressed in our heavy number three uniforms because civilian clothing was not allowed. The girls would look us up and down and then make jokes about penguins coming to town.

Only occasionally did anyone get to the point of actually dating a girl because they all knew we were only allowed out for a short time and that once we finished training we were off to sea. Not the best prospect for a long-term relationship. To try to give the impression that we were not "Nozzers," a term used to describe new recruits, we would go to great lengths to bend and shape our brilliant white hats to make them look used and older, as if in some way this would afford us some kind of credibility with the girls. It's laughable now to think that such a futile effort could carry any esteem whatsoever, but at the time it seemed so important.

As the trips into Ipswich didn't seem to work I figured out another way to get hold of a girl and that was to join dance classes at the camp. One night of the week a local dance instructor would come to the base and hold a two-hour ballroom dance class. With her, she would bring about half a dozen girls from the local village to partner the boys in the class.

We started off with the waltz and progressed to the

quick step. All I was interested in was progressing to the point where I could grab one of the girls close enough to me to feel her nipples pressed into my chest. It's worth remembering here that we were all in our midteens full of developing testosterone and only the privacy of a blanket at night to relieve the pressure.

Little wonder we were close to sex maniacs and found it hard not to make it too obvious during the quickstep. Not many boys attended classes as it was considered a bit too unmasculine to ballroom dance. That was especially now that we had the option of jiving to the Four Seasons, Elvis Presley and Little Richard in the NAFFI club.

The lack of competition cleared the field for those of us who did go to get quality time with one or other of the girls. Some of them were quite pretty but now and again a really ugly girl would turn up and we would all try to latch on to someone else lest we were left holding the dog. It sounds awful now to think back how shallow we were but I guess nothing has changed since. Oh, for teenage boys I mean, not me. I am now much less shallow . . . really.

As time progressed I really began to grow, not just physically but mentally too. For most of my life up to then I was always the skinny wimp that got pushed around by everyone else but now I was gaining confidence in myself.

The training was hard and long but interesting too. There were options to choose a specialized trade part way through like engineering or signals, but for the most part the seamanship branch seemed to be where most of us were encouraged to go. Looking back now, this was mainly because the navy was short of seamen.

They are the sailors who actually ran the ship's routines. We made up the radar operators, gunners, helmsmen and general dogs bodies that performed most of the basic functions of operating the vessel we were eventually assigned to.

I, in my wisdom, decided I wanted to be a gunner as the thought of firing those massive six-inch guns I had seen in pictures was very exciting. If I had known up front what the accident rate was, and that was just in the training, I might have had a different idea. One has to remember that in 1962 most of the hardware that the British navy had was WW2 or at least based on that era of technology.

The newer county class destroyers with missile technology were still under development, the destroyer *Deyonshire* being one of the very first to emerge that very year. We had seen the last of battleships and heavy cruisers but there were precious few new ships in the fleet that could be considered modern.

Summer was nearly upon us and I was beginning to get myself noticed on the soccer field. I still had my dream of winning a place on the Ganges team where we would be entered in inter-service competitions against other youth teams from the air force and the army. These spots were highly contested because it provided a chance to travel off the camp to away games and it also afforded more concessions from the training staff.

As the spring season games came to an end I was finally picked for the team to play the air force right after summer leave at the start of the new season.

I had managed to secure the right wing position as first pick so I was bound to take the field for the first half at least. Sometime in July my section was granted a two-week leave. I planned to go to Morpeth for the first weekend with my pal Chris. After that I would head home to Lincolnshire to spend the rest of the two weeks with my family. Now I had a special reason for this much more than just spending time with my pal. He had hooked me up with a girl from his hometown and I had been writing to her for several weeks.

Jane sounded like a nice enough girl from her letters. I

had a photo and she looked pretty good too. So at the risk of upsetting my Mum I boarded the train for Newcastle with Chris and finally arrived in Morpeth on the last leg of the trip by the local bus early on a Friday evening. The serge uniform was not the best thing to wear on a long journey so it was good to get off the bus and walk the last two miles to his home.

The area was dotted with gray prefabricated homes that should have been demolished many years ago. All the time Chris was chattering away about his mum and dad and brothers and sisters and I just listened. The plan was to drop our bags at the house and then walk into the little town to the grocery shop where Jane, my new pen pal, was working. Only problem was that we had not told her I was coming.

We arrived at the house and Chris introduced me to his mother and father. Here in came my first problem. They both started chattering away at me with huge smiles on their faces and outstretched hands but I could not understand a word they said.

Try as I might I could not tune into the accent. I had thought Chris's was broad but he sounded like he came from Harrow when compared to his parents.

I muttered my thanks for their hospitality basing my responses on what I thought they might be saying. I was too embarrassed to admit I had not understood one word. Thankfully Chris was keen to get me down to the shop to meet my pen friend so we dumped our bags and headed for the town center.

On the way down we took off our crisp white hats and gave them another good bending. No Nozzers here, my friend!

We arrived at the shop just before the six o'clock closing and boldly marched right in. I looked around at all the people to spot the girl whose photo was in my hip pocket. There were three girls in uniform that obviously worked in the shop so I went up to a rather plain short girl and asked her to point out Jane. She was holding a tray of eggs with both hands as I stood in front of her waiting for an answer.

She let out a sort of strangled gurgle and dropped the eggs at my feet. With that she spun round and shot out of the back door. I was dumbfounded for a second—wondering what on earth had spooked her. Chris nudged me in the ribs and whispered, "Haway lad bein off weya," which I took to mean let's leave.

We returned to the pavement outside with me completely mystified with the events in the shop. "That's her, man," he muttered. "That's her." I took the photo out of my pocket and took a hard look. If that was her then the photo I had was certainly not. Blonde, tall, shapely, attractive, none of these adjectives could be applied to plain Jane. It now began to sink in, Plain Jane had probably never expected to meet me in the flesh and Chris had not seen the photo I had coveted in my pocket for so many weeks. I stood for a moment staring at him, not knowing whether to laugh or cry. After a few seconds I just burst out laughing and had to lean against the shop front. If the poor girl was in any position to see us at that point I'm sure she must have died of embarrassment at the two of us falling about at her expense. If you are reading this, Jane, I'm very sorry.

"Haway lad wein dune the fucking pub and let's get pissed." I needed no further encouragement.

We walked into a pub just down the street and Chris was greeted with slaps on the back and jabs in the ribs. The place was already half full even though it had only opened for the evening about half an hour before we arrived.

Many of the locals looked old and wizened, with weathered faces and hands that suggested hard work. Others were fresh-faced youths not much older than we were. "Ya wannin a peent, lads," yelled one of the teenagers by the bar.

Two large glasses of Newcastle Brown appeared in front of us and I gingerly picked mine up and took a gulp. I had not had an alcoholic drink for several months and had never had a whole pint in one glass.

My drinking experience had been limited to maybe two or three half-pint bottles of cider in the Fortesque Arms in Billingborough. I was allowed to have the odd beer at home but this was a whole new ball game. I was sixteen years and five months old when I drank that first full pint of beer in a pub.

Newcastle Brown became a particular favorite of mine and still is today. This brew featured quite a lot over the next several years as my drinking skills escalated to heights that dwarfed most others.

After several pints and a gradual descent into a semi-stupefied condition that bordered between a string puppet and Marcel Marceau, we staggered on down the street in search of food. Sure enough a fish "n" chip shop came into view and we wolfed down cod and chips laced with salt and vinegar with a hearty helping of mushy peas.

Oh, I miss that taste, as no one outside the UK anywhere in the world has been able to faithfully recreate that bastion of true British culinary art which must be up there somewhere close to Yorkshire pudding.

Full of beer and food and feeling pretty tired after the journey, we headed home to Chris's house. His parents did not bat an eyelid at our obvious state of inebriation as we flopped on the floor in the tiny living room.

The weekend had just begun as I was due to catch a train on the Monday morning to head home to Lincolnshire and this was still Friday night. I tried my best to understand the conversation as Christ gabbled on about Ganges and all the characters we shared our training with. Every now and again he would shoot a question at me to seek clarification of some event.

By now Chris had reverted to his natural tongue and I was having a hard time catching what he was saying, too. His parents might as well have been Chinese for all I understood. Thankfully his siblings were not at home so I escaped having to tackle that hurdle too. Eventually we retired to bed. I was shown to a bedroom that was at most, six feet by eight with just enough room to stand at the end of the little single bed to undress. After a trip to the equally tiny bathroom I sank into the middle of the bed which twanged and creaked with every move.

I had trouble sleeping because I kept thinking about how I could get through the weekend without understanding anything that was being said.

By the morning I had built up such phobia about the language problem that I blurted out an excuse that I had forgotten my sister's birthday and I really needed to go home early. Chris's mum seemed to understand my discomfort and made it easy for me to bow out. After a walk down to the phone box to check on train times, I packed my hold-all and with Chris in tow headed back to the bus depot to catch a ride into Newcastle. Chris looked like a puppy being left by the side of the road as I waved from the back seat of the bus. I felt awful for his parents as they were great people but my embarrassment was such that I felt I had no choice but to leave.

Once, on the train heading for Grantham, I managed to find a compartment where only one other person was inside. He had a battered old navy hold-all on the luggage rack and was laid flat out across one side of the compartment fast asleep. I had been up and down the corridor several times but this was the only place where I could get a seat.

The compartment stank of stale beer and it was obvious why my naval friend was the only person on the train with a place of his own.

Not to be intimidated, I sat down and stared out of the window thinking about the events of the night before. Would I write to Jane when I got back? I didn't think so. Should I write to Chris's parents and apologize for being rude? My thoughts were interrupted when the sailor woke up and stood in the window.

He was about six foot six with fire red hair.

He muttered something in a broad Scottish accent and then, as he stretched his arms up, let go to the loudest, longest fart I have ever heard (from another person). I couldn't believe it, dirty bastard. The smell was unbelievable, so I grabbed my bag and ran out into the corridor. I spent the rest of the journey sitting in the corridor by the toilet door. That is one hell of a way to get a compartment to yourself. I eventually arrived home in the late evening after Mum had picked me up at Grantham station.

By now my Dad was the only remaining permanent employee on the farm, but that did mean we now had the farmhouse to live in which was much roomier than the little cottage over the road. Quite a change from just ten years ago when at least seven or eight men were regularly seen working around the place, every day.

The farm was now fully arable and equipped with modern machinery, which included combine harvesters and diesel tractors. It was also equipped with a dog left behind by the old foreman and his family.

The dog's name was Paddy and he was a sort of lab mix. Paddy's specialty was crouching under the hedge beside the road and waiting for one of the half dozen vehicles that might pass the place on any given day. When the car or van was almost level with him he would scoot out at incredible speed and try to bite the tires running as fast as he could at the side of the vehicle. This practice was eventually to be the cause of his premature journey to that great kennel in the sky.

My parents now had a little Ford Thames van with just two seats in the front. The back was empty other than a loose old seat that slid about with every small amount of G force. The driving age was seventeen so I was still too young to go on the road . . . legally. I was desperate to drive and couldn't wait to have a go.

My dad let me take the van and drive down some of the farm roads to get used to handling the vehicle. He didn't even get in with me, he just said you will figure it out and walked off. It had a three-speed floor change gear stick and very few refinements. That didn't matter to me. I was driving and that's what counted.

I had figured out the basics so I knew how to slip the clutch to get going; the rest was easy. After bouncing along the tracks for a couple of hours I felt ready for the real thing. However, that would have to wait till I could get my license in about six months. During the next ten days I renewed my acquaintance with of my old school buddies. I was now full of stories about life outside Lincolnshire and couldn't wait to impress my friends with my worldly experiences.

Of course there was a little storyteller's license in the telling, but mostly it was based on actual events! They were all amazed how much I had grown since Christmas and I seemed to be the center of attention whenever I turned up at the village.

Lobby Harris had called on some girls that he had got to know in another village about ten miles away and had impressed them with my impending arrival.

So, one afternoon near the end of my leave, I was to meet Lobby in Pointon and we were then going to cycle over to see these young ladies. Lobby was a really good-looking lad with blond hair and was always lucky with the girls. I, on the other hand, was a bit less photogenic so tagging along with Lobby always helped to get the girls' attention. However, it often proved a problem once first contact had been made, as I was the "dog."

I left the farm on my trusty racing bike and headed along the country road to the village. Part of the way was a slight downhill run of about half a mile where I could get my head down and reach maximum speed. At full tilt, I rounded a slight bend and hit a bloody great pothole in the road.

The pothole was not there the last time I had ridden this way six months before. My front wheel hit the hole and buckled, and I went over the handlebar and head first into the road. After an unknown period of time I came to lying on my back on the grass verge several yards from my bike. I don't know how long I was out cold but I tried to stand and promptly fell down again.

Blood was all over my face and hands and my shoulder was hurting like crazy and my head was throbbing. It gradually dawned on me that I was hurt quite badly. I managed to get up the second time but was very groggy on my feet. I looked around for help and saw a man I knew from a nearby farm working a tractor in a hay field.

I staggered over to the fence and began to shout to him for help. Finally he saw me waving and drove over to where I stood. "Arrgh boy you buggered yer sen up there lad." He told me to sit on the grass while he fetched his car.

He drove me to Billingborough to Dr. Henderson's office which was the nearest medical help. To get an ambulance would have taken at least thirty minutes from the nearest hospital in Bourne town about ten miles away so he decided the local doctor was probably the best option. I bled all over his car seats, which fortunately were so dirty with farm grime a couple pints of my life's blood was not going to be an issue. "Och, it's that laddy again with blood all over his wee face."

The good Doc had probably thought he had seen the last of me but not so. He patched me up again and I called my Mum where she worked at the bakery to take me home. After a couple of uncomfortable days resting I climbed aboard the train to get back to Ganges. I had discarded the sling from my arm but still had a bandage round my head and two bandaged hands.

When I reported for training on the Monday morning I was told to report sick to the medical officer. He gave me a once over before telling me I could attend classes but not take part in any physical activities for one week.

Friday was to be the football match against the air force team. Despite my pleading with the PTI in charge of the squad I was not even allowed to travel with the team. That was the end of my football career, as I never made it into another side.

Our time in Ganges was coming to an end and we had all received our various assignments for our step into the navy for real. Mine was to be HMS Cambridge, a gunnery training school at Wembury Point just south of Plymouth. However, before we were to leave, some of us were invited to take a trip over to Holland on a fishing boat, captained by one of the Petty Officers.

About twenty were selected to go on the trip and one Friday afternoon we set sail from the pier at Ganges on an old wooden fishing trawler. The sea was a slight swell rising and falling about six or eight feet but it made this boat pitch and roll and yaw and dive like nothing else. Once clear of the river estuary the PO had put one of the boys on the wheel up top and was busy cooking up bacon, eggs and tinned tomatoes for the feast before we reached our destination. We planned to put into Den Helder, about 120 miles from the base high up the Dutch coast on the Zuider Zee.

Like ninety percent of the rest on board, I was seasick. This was the one and only time I have ever been seasick and it was horrible. The stench of fuel oil mingled with the smell of vomit topped with frying bacon pushed me over the edge.

Once we docked at Den Helder I was fine. It was way too late to go ashore so we all turned in for the night lying around on any flat surface we could find (after a clean up to remove the vomit). Next day we surged ashore in our uniforms having been read the riot act by the PO not to go in any bars or start any fights. Right! Fights I could do without but bars? This was my first venture outside of England and as it turned out only the beginning of a long journey that continues today.

We had all day Saturday to explore and managed to stay out of trouble and on Sunday left just after noon to head back to Ganges. I had discovered a new delicacy available on every street corner which was little cone-shaped bags of thin potato chips (or French fries to the non-English speakers) with a big dollop of mayonnaise on top.

Funny that my recollection of new places is either a drink or food. The trip back was quite rough but by now I was a seasoned seafarer. I took a turn on the wheel and got my first lesson in following a gyrocompass. Now I knew I was really going to enjoy the navy if we could get paid having this much fun.

Back at Ganges we were told to prepare for our departure in the coming weeks. I was to join several other boys for another short stint on an RFA (Royal Fleet Auxiliary) HMS *Berryhead*. This was to fill in a few weeks before the gunnery-training program started at HMS Cambridge. Before we could leave to our new assignments we had to go through the final passing out parade.

The passing out ceremony included all of us who were leaving to dress in our brand new number one uniforms and do various drills on the parade ground. This was followed by the ancient tradition of manning the mast. On the big day many of the parents had traveled down to see their sons going through the ceremony.

I don't think I had even told my parent about the event knowing full well that they would be unable to make the hundred and twenty mile trip to Ipswich. We managed to get the parade ground drill done without any hitches and then it was time to go up the mast. I am not too good at heights so I was pleased to be in the section that only went up to the first level.

To the beat of a large drum we all clawed our way up the netting to pre-determined positions and then stuck one leg and one arm out like demented grasshoppers. One volunteer then shinned up the last ten feet of the pole at the top and had to climb over the rim of the button and stand up. Absolute, bloody nut case in my humble opinion.

Once the button boy, as he was known, had trapped the lightning conductor between his knees and saluted, the drum resumed beating and we all worked our way back down to terra firma.

6

The Real World

I boarded a train the next day and traveled to Chatham in Kent to join the *Berryhead*. We spent a couple of days in port fueling up storage tanks for the exercise. We were due to head out to the English channel and go through some ship to ship refueling exercises with a destroyer. The night before we left I went ashore with a few other new recruits to sample the local beers.

After more than enough beer and a good dollop of Vindaloo (a new experience for me) at one of Chatham's finest ethnic locals, one clown spotted a tattoo parlor. Before common sense and reason kicked in I was sitting in the chair with my right sleeve rolled up watching a grubby old bloke with bad body odor drilling my arm with colored ink. I awoke the next morning with a bandage round my arm and blood all over my sheets. The evening's events flooded back and I ripped the bandage off to reveal a puffy arm with a very bright colored picture.

In the bathroom I washed off the blood to take a look at my new artwork. I didn't have much time to worry about it as another problem was making its mark being the Vindaloo in this inexperienced system.

Once that was dealt with I had a chance to pay attention to my arm. I was now the proud owner of a green and red heart interwoven with a black anchor with Mum & Dad written across it at an angle. This was probably the most common tattoo ever drilled into any sailor's arm.

That damn tattoo and several others that came later haunted me for most of my post-navy life. If anyone reading this is thinking of getting one, think very carefully indeed. I have spent over $10,000 trying to rid myself of these hideous blemishes and they are still partially visible today.

We prepared to depart Chatham that morning and I was assigned to help slip the ship at the forecastle. (Pointy end for the non-nautical.) The *Berryhead* was quite a big ship, some four hundred and forty feet so the wire hawsers were pretty heavy and thick. It was also quite old having been built in Canada during the Second World War.

My job was to wait by one of the winches and at the given signal run the winch out a few feet. This was to create some slack so the dockyard worker on the jetty could slip the eye of the hawser off the bollard.

My line was to be the last to go as the Captain was "springing" the ship forward to swing the stern away from the berth and run astern to enter the shipping lane to leave harbor. All was well till the PO in charge of the forecastle yelled at me to slip. Instead of pushing the lever, I pulled. The steam winch cranked into life and started to reel in the line instead of letting it slacken off.

I could hear hysterical shouting from the open bridge up in the superstructure, as the ship was being pulled toward the jetty. The PO leapt past me, almost knocking me through the guardrail and reversed the winch.

By now the ship's engine was in reverse and the PO had to slip yards of hawser to give enough slack to the guy on the jetty. He has started to walk backwards as the 20,000-ton ship was coming straight at him but he did get the eye over the bollard in time. The Captain managed to prevent the ship from actually hitting the jetty but it was close. The PO clouted me across the back of my head with his hand as I stood feeling very stupid. "You fucking idiot, you damn near had us demolish the fucking jetty." He was interrupted by more screaming from the bridge calling for him to report to the officer of the watch after he had secured the lines on the forecastle. Not a good start to my seagoing career, but memorable.

During one related incident several years later I was on a towing crew moving the retired Aircraft Carrier HMS *Centaur* from Portsmouth to Plymouth. We were being towed by several ocean tugs and I was one of several on the *Centaur's* forecastle manning the towlines. The sea had a gentle swell that caused the lines to slacken and snap taut from time to time.

During one of the more heavy movements one of the eight-inch steel hawsers snapped several feet over the ship's side. The severed end still secured to our bollards came inboard with a mighty hiss as the tension was released. It snapped back through the guardrails braking off several metal rails and smashed against the roof of the deck area as the forecastle crew all dived for cover.

We all looked around to see if anyone was hurt but thankfully no one had been hit. However, when we saw what the hawser had done to the guardrail, we nearly fainted. It would have cut a man in half.

Life on the *Berryhead* was very busy as we went through several weeks of replenishment at sea trials. Rigging lines from one ship to another as they both steam at twelve knots is a precarious business and on several occasions sailors got injured from heavy equipment banging around or wires snapping at legs and arms.

We were taught very quickly never to stand in the bight. This meant always keeping an eye on the wires to determine which way they would pull if tension came on very suddenly.

In the bight meant being in extreme danger. I learned very fast, and that might have been why I escaped with my life in the later *Centaur* incident.

To get the initial line over from the supply ship to the destroyer a marksman, armed with modified 303 rifle, would fire a steel rod across the open forecastle of the receiving ship. The steel rod was attached to a light but strong line. This, in turn, was joined to a heavier line that was then hauled over to make the first connection.

Then the heavier rigging cables would follow to be fixed on both sides ready to transfer the stores. At the same time a separate operation was rigged to carry the huge fuel lines that transferred the oil.

While all this was going on the two ships had to maintain exactly the same speed and heading. If the sea was too rough this could be very dangerous because, despite their incredible strength, steel cables being pulled apart by some fifty thousand tons could snap in an instant.

Firing the steel rod was known to be dangerous, too. I was told of one incident several years before where someone on the receiving end stuck his head up too soon and was hit between the eyes, very dead. After the trials were over we returned to Chatham and I packed my kit bag and headed for Plymouth on the train.

I was picked up along with several other boys and taken by bus to Wembury Point. This was on a peninsula about ten miles from Plymouth. HMS Cambridge was a shore base perched high on the cliff overlooking the sea and in sight of the Eddistone lighthouse. The base had several types of naval guns mounted on pivots and pointing out to sea. The new arrivals were allocated billets in the stark wooden huts that were to be home to us for several months to come, through the winter of 1963.

The other big difference for us here was, at last, we

could go on shore leave, in our time off, wearing civilian clothes.

By now it was early November and the wind cut over the top of the cliff with a vengeance. The huts were poorly insulated and the only source of heat was a potbelly stove in the middle. The group of lads now included some older people who had joined the navy at seventeen and up to their mid twenties. Being too old to go to the junior training at Ganges they had done a six-week basic entrance course at HMS Raleigh over the border at Torpoint in Cornwall.

I was approaching my seventeenth birthday coming up in February. Twelve stones (168 lbs) of solid muscle and a very light hand on the rudder.

I suppose I was a bit like a mini car with a V8 engine, lots of power but very little control on which direction I might take if I applied all the power at once. After the repressive environment at Ganges I now had lots of freedom to explore life outside the confines of the navy base.

Thinking back to my school days in Lincolnshire, which quickly transcended into a full year in Ganges, I had not had much time to learn the way of the world as an adult. The brief spell in Chatham had taught me that having freedom also brought some measure of responsibility; the tattoo incident was proof of that. Let go of the reins for a second and you could hit the wall hard. Temptation was everywhere, either in the pub or lurking outside on the street. There were also lots of people around who were much more advanced than I was to lead me astray.

Wembury Point was a tiny village with no prospect of any nighttime fun so, on the weekend, the only way to find entertainment was to board the local bus and ride into Plymouth. I was now an ordinary seaman and thus my curfew had moved from 10:00 P.M. to 1:00 A.M. Once you made it to able seaman or any rank above, then night leave expired the next morning before eight.

Nothing much happened for the first couple of days as we spent our time being shown around the camp and learning the routines.

One routine was that we were now required to stand watches for security purposes. This meant working to the naval 24-hour watch system made up of seven periods. The morning watch ran from 4:00 A.M. to 8:00 A.M., the forenoon from 8:00 A.M. to noon, the afternoon from noon to 4:00 P.M., the first dog watch from 4:00 P.M. to 6:00 P.M., the second dog from 6:00 P.M. to 8:00 P.M., the first watch from 8:00 P.M. to midnight and finally the dreaded middle watch from midnight to 4:00 A.M.

We were put on a four-day cycle meaning that we would do a 24-hour watch period every fourth day. That was in turn four hours on four hours off, depending on who got the dogwatches. These were split to enable meals to be taken in the evening.

On our designated watch we were given a flashlight and a set of metal tokens. At various points around the base there were metal boxes located where, depending on which cycle we were on, we either placed the token in the box or took one out. The whole idea was to make sure the patrolling sailor actually visited all the points on the camp during his watch. Of course, during the night watches, knowing that the Master at Arms would be unlikely to do a random check, we fixed the game. In conspiracy with the guy who was to follow my rounds I would not leave the tokens.

I would hand them over to him as I came off watch and he would have them ready for the next guy. That way neither of us actually went anywhere near the full circuit. In winter this place was bleak to say the least. The pathway down to the beach was steep and dark and very eerie. The full circuit, done properly, would take about two hours so being able to cower in the watch hut by the stove was infinitely favorable to being out in the cold.

Gunnery training started in the classroom where we were taught the basics of how guns work, their range and how to aim and fire them in theory.

It was all a bit futile because the training guns at the camp were wartime relics and the new navy was beginning to get more modern weapons that had remote operating controls. These four-inch guns at the base were all hand-operated.

One man would sit in a seat at the side with little hand-operated wheels that controlled the lay (the layer), another would be in the firing seat where he would control the elevation and firing mechanism. The third and fourth crewmembers were loaders, taking it in turn to ram shells into the breach. Ramming the shell into the breach with the fist was the most dangerous part. After ramming the shell the breach block would slam shut knocking the fist upwards. As long as your hand was still on the end of your arm it then required jumping sideways in a hurry as the gun was fired hoping like hell to be out of the way when the casing ejected from the breach. It came out hot and fast and rattled around the base of the gun.

The first time was terrifying. The layer and triggerman had headphones on and were given instructions through the intercom. The loaders responded to the chief acting as gun Captain who was yelling orders from a safe distance behind the turret.

The gun we were firing was able to swing through an arc of about 60°. The rail it was mounted on had solid metal stops screwed in place to prevent the gun from firing outside a pre-determined "safe" area.

Local fishermen and general sea traffic would observe

the flag hoisted over the base so they would know when the guns would be active. It was also rigged to drop the non-explosive shells far enough away from the Eddistone lighthouse. The lighthouse was outside the maximum distance for the gun's range but it was still a bit worrying for the keeper to think of about 40 lbs of solid lead coming in his general direction at several hundred miles an hour.

Probably to make the lighthouse keeper feel safe the navy had rigged the stops on the mounting so they could not fire in his general direction. However, that was before some of us figured out that moving the stop about six inches allowed just enough extra travel to bring the gun to bear right on the lighthouse. The night before we were scheduled to do another live firing, one of the lads took an adjustable spanner and some freeing oil on his security rounds.

Quite a few of us were in on the scheme as we prepared to run the live firing drill at about 8:00 A.M. the next day. The Chief ordered everyone in position and began calling orders. We ran through several dry runs, going through the motions without actually loading the gun.

When he was ready the Chief called for a live round. I was first up as the gun was positioned to fire. I rammed my shell and jumped out of the way. "FIRE!" The sound was tremendous as the gun fired and spat out the hot shell casing that clattered onto the metal gun deck. I stared out to sea trying to see where the shell landed.

It was impossible from any angle to see where it came down several miles off shore. "10 degrees right," yelled the instructor. The gun swung to the right and the next loader stepped up to ram his shell. I stood back cradling my next shell in my arms waiting my turn.

From my position I could see that the gun had run right to its limit and lined up with the lighthouse. For a brief moment I panicked and thought of confessing to the Chief, but too late—the order came to fire. Everyone in on the secret stared at the lighthouse trying to see if the shell would make it all the way.

Of course this was logistically impossible but we had no real idea how far out of range it was. It would have been impossible to actually see the shell even if it had gone right through the wall but we kept looking. Nothing happened and the drill continued for another five or six rounds.

The chief was a lot better at figuring out where the shells were going than we were and he gradually figured out why. He marched up to the gun and started whacking his stick on the side wall. "Right you lot, fall in back here." He began to bawl us out demanding that the culprits confess or else. It apparently was a common scam for the trainees to rig the gun. Of course, no one confessed so the whole gun crew was docked two day's leave and two day's pay. Worth it though. I would have loved to see the lighthouse keeper's face as the shells came whistling toward his rocks.

The next session was firing the Bofors anti-aircraft guns. These had a large clip of shells mounted on top of the breach that automatically fed a stream of rounds as the gun fired in rapid succession. Once I had handled these shells I was convinced they were the same as the ones I had casually kicked around on Folkingham airfield whilst trying to see the BRM racing cars.

These practice shells were filled with lead shot very much like a giant shot gun cartridge and designed to be fired at a drogue. The drogue (a long tube made of fabric) was towed on a wire behind a plane, usually provided by the air force. The intention was to aim at the drogue several hundred feet behind the plane.

As expected, we were tempted to aim at the plane and on several occasions an irate pilot would radio in that he was hearing shot pellets hitting his wind screen. He then was threatening to abort the runs unless those little bastard improved their aim.

Training over one day, we had our meal and retired to the mess for the evening; it was Friday, November 22nd 1963. On the TV ten o'clock news we saw the footage of John F. Kennedy's assassination.

The camp was soon buzzing with rumors that the USA was going to war with Russia, believing that it was the Russians taking revenge for the Cuban missile standoff the previous year. As the American ally we expected to get dragged into a conflict and needless to say, we were very excited about the prospect of going to war now that we were expert gunners! How stupid that thought seems now.

The next day, myself and two other lads, based on the previous weekend's reconnaissance of the little village outside the camp, were to meet some girls. Our plan was to ride into Plymouth on the bus and go to the pictures. We met the girls at the bus stop as planned and boarded the bus. The girl sitting with me, Alice, was very quiet and looked miserable. I on the other hand was looking forward to at least a good grope and maybe even a snog. I didn't think it was appropriate to go for the smelly finger on the first date but one can be ever hopeful.

She remained quiet as we rode along. The others were chatting and laughing and I tried to get her to smile with some of my very poor jokes. I might as well have not bothered as she sat silent and motionless for the whole thirty minutes into town. We walked to the cinema from the bus station and bought our tickets for the 2:00 P.M. show. The plan was to see the film and hopefully make some progress in the dark, then get some food after the show and finally go dancing.

Once inside and the lights dim I decided I needed to make my first move. I carefully put my arm around her shoulder and squeezed her arm. To my delight she seemed to relax and leaned toward me. Better still she turned her face to my shoulder and buried it into my jacket. Yes, Yes, Yes, we have lift off, I thought.

I tried to look down at her face but she was digging in harder and gripping my hand. I suddenly realized she was sobbing quietly into my jacket. Now I as totally confused. I wasn't the most experienced guy around but how I had made her cry at this stage was beyond me. We spent the next two hours clutching each other in the dark until the film was over. She had stopped crying but had not let me kiss her or anything other than cradle her in my arms.

We walked out into the light behind the other two couples. Both couples were holding hands and laughing like they had known each other for years. Alice held my hand but still did not say anything. My technique needed improvement or I was not going to get anywhere here.

Someone suggested we walk down to Union Street where we could get a Cornish pasty from a street vendor. That was a luxury on an ordinary seaman's wages of five pounds per week. We got the pasties and sat on a wall nearby. Alice was still quiet but did say thank you as we sat next to each other, a few feet from the others. We sat in silence till the feast was over and then without warning she started to cry again.

By now I was beginning to realize that something was very wrong and it had nothing to do with my skills as a date. One of the other girls came over and put her arms around Alice and looked back at me obviously understanding my confusion and said, "Her dad died last week, and this is the first time she has been out of the house since he died."

Oh great, how had I ended up with a sixteen-year-old girl who was mourning her father? That sort of ended any aspirations of romance for the evening and I sat silent, not having a clue what to say to the poor girl. She pulled herself together and the girls made it clear that they wanted to head back home to Wembury Point. I was incredibly relieved but my mates were not quite so happy.

The girls left and I never saw Alice again. Sorry Alice!

In the early part of 1964 our next venture was to spend a two-week period on an old frigate to do real live gun practice. This assignment was to be on HMS *Venus*. HMS *Venus* was a battered old Frigate and the old lags reading this (plus anyone who has been in the same pub as me after a few pints) will be familiar with certain verses that included references to the good ship *Venus*.

'Twas on the good ship *Venus*,
By god! You should have seen us,
The figure-head was a whore in bed,
And the mast a rampant penis.

They called the Captain Slugger,
He was a dirty bugger,
He wasn't fit to shovel shit,
On any bugger's lugger

Got the drift, eh. There are thirty or forty verses to this musical narrative but over time they have been added to and modified as have many military standards. My whole navy career is full of all kinds of songs that have been sung in many drinking establishments around the world. Not just during my service time either.

On one occasion (as usual assisted by bottled bravado) I did a naval adaptation of a famous opera at a very high-class conference venue at the Green Briar Hotel in White Sulfur Springs, Virginia.

Not only that, it was in front of two company presidents,

their wives and assorted other company dignitaries, but that was many years after I left the service and at a time when I thought my civilian career could suffer little more damage.

Our second introduction to life at sea was quite traumatic. The *Venus* was old, I mean really old. It was dirty, rusty, smelly and very crowded. The living quarters were cramped and airless. Sleep stations were hammocks that had to be hoisted every night and stowed away in the mornings.

They hung in rows tied to metal rings, either side of the mess and rigged across the width of the ship. To walk about when they were rigged required stooping low and creeping underneath. Each one touched the next so there was no room to stand up other than in the area by the hatchway into the mess.

They were rigged this way to accommodate the roll of the ship; as it rolled the hammocks would swing to stay level. The principle was centuries old and did work quite well once everyone was in place. We looked like giant moth chrysalides hanging in some bizarre sci-fi movie.

As we were only on board for two weeks and still in training we did not have to do night watch duties so we did get to sleep at night. Most of the rest of the time we were put through normal seagoing activities.

This included the usual rope and hawser work, preparing lifeboats ready for putting them over the side in an emergency, and, of course tying up again as we came alongside in a port. This was in addition to the real purpose of the trip, to actually be able to fire the guns. After leaving Plymouth we made our way through the channel and up the East Coast.

As a special treat we put into Oostende for one night to give the novices a quick lesson in shore leave. I set off with several other lads to explore this strange little Belgian town.

Of course, the first thing we decided to do was go for a few drinks, what else was expected? We were sailors, right, and sailors go for a drink. Belgium was pretty liberal about drinking laws so the fact that we looked twelve did not seem to matter much. As long as you could pay, you could have anything you wanted, literally.

Several of us tried a brew called Scotch Ale. It was dark like Guinness but I'm sure was spiked with whisky. It seemed quite tame so I drank several in quick succession. I decided I needed to take a leak so I went in search of the facilities.

I saw a door that looked like it might be the gents and walked right in. I now got another lesson how different the world can be. As I entered there was a row of urinals to my left and several open door toilets facing me.

To my horror a lady was sitting on one of the toilets with the door wide open and her knickers round her ankles. I spun round believing I must be in the wrong place, nearly knocking over a big bloke who was on his way in. He muttered something under his breath in an unknown language that I assumed was aimed at me.

He walked up to the urinal and unzipped his fly. I was now totally confused. By now the woman was at the hand basin washing her hands and messing about with her hair. In a complete state of shock I headed back outside to the bar, still needing to pee. I decided to watch the door for a while and when I was sure no women were inside I shot back in and furiously peed as fast as I could before another one appeared. I went back to the bar to resume drinking my new favorite brew. What strange people would put blokes and ladies in the same toilet?

Last I remember was trying to call my mum from a phone kiosk that was fixed to a wall on the harbor. I had no idea how to dial the right numbers and finally fell backwards still holding the phone. The whole phone assembly came away in my hand and lay on top of me as I lay looking up at the stars.

I was conscious of being hauled up onto my feet and being pushed into the back of a vehicle. I spent some time in a dark room at the police station before being taken by the MPs back to the ship in the early hours of the morning.

I received a good bollocking the next morning from the officer of the watch but was relieved to know I would not be reported back at HMS Cambridge. Not bad for my first real shore leave, but I knew I could do better . . . much better.

Back at sea we were now allowed to practice on the ancient four-inch guns that made up the bulk of the *Venus's* weaponry. Ramming those shells in a fast fire drill is extremely dangerous. First, you have to make sure that you keep your fist closed as not to let the fingers follow the shell into the breach.

Then you have to jump out of the way very quickly to avoid the hot shell casing as it flies back out of the breach and crashes into the back of the turret. The yelling of the gun captain and the monstrous bang of the gun all contributed to some kind of manic order. This was practice in peacetime, god knows what it must have been like with the ship under attack during a war. I managed to survive without losing anything vital and looked forward to the next session on the anti-aircraft guns.

We were entertained by some of the old lags helping us to rattle off a few hundred rounds of anti-aircraft shells from the Bofors guns. I got to sit in the hot seat for a few minutes as I loosely aimed at a target towed by an air force plane somewhere off the coast of Norfolk. I don't recall if this pilot got the same treatment as the ones at the training school, but it was great fun. Mind you it was fun this way, I doubt it was fun when the plane could fire back.

We put into Plymouth at the end of our two weeks and I

returned to HMS Cambridge. The threat of nuclear war had abated and I went home to Lincolnshire for leave over the Christmas holiday.

I had mastered the little van on the farm roads so it was quite easy to drive on the road with no other traffic around. Fortunately we lived far enough out in the sticks to not have to worry about other vehicles. If one came by I would pull onto the grass till it had passed and then carry on with my training.

During that holiday I got to know another lad from Billingborough called Rodney; he and I became great mates over time. Rodney had started an apprenticeship at Blackstone's in Stamford working on building huge diesel engines. As, far as I know, forty plus years later, he is still there.

7

Little Guns Can Be Fun Too

Back at HMS Cambridge we were told we were to go over to HMS Raleigh for a small arms training course. Raleigh was in Torpoint, over the Tamar River, in Cornwall. There they had a thousand yard shooting range with a huge earth bank behind the targets. The course was to include a .38 caliber pistol, a Lee-Enfield 303 rifle used on targets at three hundred yards and machine guns. The navy also had the Bren gun, which was a tri-pod mounted light machine gun version of the 303. Finally, there was a little handheld machine gun called the Lanchester.

The Lanchester was a naval adaptation of the German wartime MP 28 machine gun. This had been modified to carry a short magazine across the body. It was designed for use in close quarters to allow you to run through narrow corridors on the ships during boarding parties without knocking the magazine off. Unfortunately this weapon like other small rapid firing weapons had a vicious pull during use.

We started with the six shot .38 pistol, as each of us was called up to face a man-shaped cardboard target set at about ten yards distance. The instructor demonstrated the action to each student in turn and then handed over the weapon for the first shot.

One of the lads in the group was called Ordinary Seaman Jones—Jonah, as he became known very quickly.

He was just at the minimum height limit to get in the navy—in fact he must have had thick shoe soles when he signed up. He was also totally incompetent. I mentioned in an earlier chapter that I had learned that if a gun is going to fire be behind it! Well, this was the time to remember that lesson. About a dozen of us were standing several yards behind the area where the action was taking place, considered the safe zone when this lesson was to become paramount.

How could anyone hit you facing a target in the opposite direction? The Chief ran through the drill for Jonah and handed him the weapon. It was loaded with six bullets. Jonah raised his arm straight pointing the gun at the target. He cocked the hammer and pulled the trigger. His hand shot up in the air with the recoil and then the idiot turned round still with the gun in the air at shoulder height.

The Chief was bellowing at him inches from his ear but Jonah, now waving the gun around like a flag, seemed oblivious to the Chief's instructions. He had a stare of surprise on his face as if he had not expected anything to happen. The Chief grabbed his arm and pushed it up, forcing the gun to point to the sky. Somehow Jonah managed to pull the trigger again and another shot rang out.

By now we were all flying in different directions and hitting the ground. Jonah finally let go of the gun and the Chief hung it in his belt holster and strapped it in place. He yelled at Jonah some more and told him to get out of his sight. There were no holes in the target. Training continued until we had all shot off six rounds. I managed to get all six on the target but if it had been a real man he might have lost an arm or leg but could have survived. That .38 was heavy and very hard to hold level. Jonah was rated not competent to operate a pistol.

Next session was rifle training that required operating the 303 from a prone position. I am left-handed and could not get comfortable firing the rifle from my right shoulder so the chief told me to use my left shoulder. Only problem is the rifle was made with a bolt action to operate with the right hand. Not easy if you had it to your left shoulder as your right hand is supporting the barrel. I had to operate the bolt by using my left hand over the top of the weapon.

The 303 had a clip that held ten rounds. Each round had to be rammed by the bolt and then released and then the next one rammed. So, operating the bolt with the left hand made it hard to be as smooth as a right-handed operator.

We were positioned three hundred yards from the first set of targets that were two-foot square steel plates. The plates were set to pop up at irregular intervals and we were supposed to fire when they popped up and hopefully hit them. You knew it was a hit by the loud clang, if you were on target. The dirt bank behind the butts extended about twenty feet out to each side but the designer had not anticipated Jonah.

The land was rented out to a local dairy farmer for grazing. At each side of the range was an electric fence that kept his cows off the range during firing practice.

We were laying six at a time and were supposed to fire in sequence. Right position first, five rounds as the plates popped up, then number two and so on.

We had already been shown how to operate the rifle and given tips on how to look down the sight. That was just a pin with a tiny knob on the end of the barrel protected by a raised metal tag either side, to be lined up with a little flip-up sight in front of the bolt. I watched the first group get in position which included Jonah. It all started OK with the odd clang being heard when someone actually hit a plate until it was Jonah's turn. The Chief was paying very close attention to Jonah after the pistol incident. He straddled Jonah as he lay on the ground wrestling with the bolt. At least two plates popped up and went down again but Jonah still did not get a round off. The Chief started yelling at him to take the next one or else.

Up came the plate and BANG, Jonah let go a round. No sound from the plate so we knew he had missed the target. What we didn't realize until one of the lads started shouting and pointing, is that a cow had toppled over in the distance just over the electric fence beyond the bank.

He must have been 25 degrees off the target to hit that cow. It was dead, shot clean through the neck. A Lee Enfield Mark IV 303 firing at 2440 feet per second was capable of passing through a fairly thick tree so a cow was no contest. I'm sure the navy had a bit of explaining to do.

During the course of the rifle training, those of us who could hit the plates were given an additional opportunity to try for a marksman qualification. I hit every plate so I was invited to go on to paper targets where actual scores were kept. To attain the marksman badge we had to score over 85 percent. I got 87 percent and received my badge.

The badge was two crossed rifles and was sown onto the number one uniform's left arm just above the wrist.

During our small arms training our group was invited to play a game of rugby against the HMS Raleigh team which consisted of several quite large and knurled Chiefs who looked like they could bite the heads off chickens without a thought.

I reluctantly agreed to take part and lined up with the HMS Cambridge Light Weights to face the front row that probably could have taken on the England team and given them a run for their money. It started badly and got much worse. Fifteen minutes into the game we had lost two players and were down about 20 points to 0.

I was suddenly confronted by one of their forwards hurtling toward me with the ball barely visible tucked under his enormous arm. I closed my eyes and waited for the impact, which took me clean off my feet and set me on my backside ten feet back. It was a bit like a bicycle trying to stop a 20-ton truck at a traffic light!

Winded and bruised I managed to get back to my feet and resume. By the end of the game I had been kicked in the balls and had a tooth loosened and had decided without doubt that I was not interested in a career in Rugby.

Many years after my encounter with handheld weapons I was at a hunting ranch in Texas with some American colleagues where the company would entertain customers to deer hunting. I was not a deer hunter but had to be there for the sales meeting being used as a lame excuse to go hunting on company time.

A colleague of mine, Bradley, was a hunting fanatic, like most of the others that grew up in the US. He had his own arsenal of weapons including a seven-millimeter rifle he used for deer hunting. Although I would not shoot deer, I was happy to shoot birds, or skeet (clay pigeons) or just targets.

Before going out to the hides at dusk, where they would wait for the deer to wander by in search of food, Bradley decided that being a Brit I needed some coaching so he invited me to go to the target range to watch him "sight" his rifle.

He sat down to a low table facing a wooden board mounted on poles about a hundred yards away. A ringed paper target about eighteen inches across was pinned to the board. Bradley shuffled about for a few seconds peering down the telescopic sight making various little adjustments and then fired one round. His head jerked up as he strained to see the hole in the target.

He picked up his binoculars and brought them into focus. "God damn," he muttered. He lined up another shot and fired. Again he peered through the binoculars. "God-damn, this god damn sight is not worth a shit." He started to fiddle about with the sight still muttering under his breath. I picked up the binoculars and looked at the target. One hole was on the far right of the target the other was eight or ten inches off center, low on the left.

"Can I have a go?" I said. Bradley was not too sure about this Brit that had just invaded his cozy management team but he handed me the gun and proceeded to explain how to use the bolt action and load a single round. I must have forgotten to tell him about my marksman training so many years before.

I knelt down at the table and loaded a round. I had never looked through a telescopic sight but it seemed pretty obvious how it should work. I set the cross hairs on the bull's eye and squeezed the trigger. Bradley grabbed the binocu-lars and looked at the target. "God damn lucky shot." I took the binoculars and looked at the target.

My shot was almost dead center. "Let's see you do that again, clever ass," he shouted. I lined up another shot and fired a second round. "Ha, miles away, it's not even on the damn target," he yelled with obvious glee.

I was sure I was close so I said we should walk down to the target to take a closer look. On close scrutiny it was clear my second shot had widened the hole that the first one had made. He didn't ask me to use his rifle anymore after that.

The last part of the course was the Lanchester, that little machine gun that could blast off many rounds a minute from its fifty-shot magazine. We were now all highly sensitized to the potential risks when Jonah had a weapon in his hand. So was the Chief, so we were all made to stand a long way back behind the firing range.

We used the same targets for this that we had used for

the pistol. We were instructed to fire short bursts of five or six rounds and then survey the target to correct our aim. He gun was made to fire from the hip and be moved from side to side to cut down a target. It was quite easy to chop the cardboard targets in half if we were allowed to keep blasting away. Everyone overdid the burst as we all enjoyed the experience.

The gun did pull hard to the left and required plenty of concentration to not let it turn you around. You guessed, Jonah completely lost it and gradually began to turn to the left, spraying bullets into the ground.

The rest of us were well out of range rolling about and laughing like crazy. The Chief grabbed the gun and yelled at Jonah: "Get off my fucking range, you idiot." Jonah was deemed unfit for small arms duty under any circumstances.

I on the other hand was now a marksman, and for that I think I got another two shillings and sixpence per week extra.

Soon after returning to HMS Cambridge I received a letter from the navy telling me to report to HMS Drake in Devonport, the huge naval dockyard adjoining Plymouth. I was to join the aircraft carrier *Ark Royal* for a two-year commission that included a year in the Far East, based at Singapore.

The *Ark Royal* was undergoing its first major refit since it was commissioned in 1950 and was in dry dock in Devonport. The crew assigned to the ship were billeted in Drake Barracks, as she was not ready for occupation. The crew numbered a little over 2,000 and would grow to 2,800 when the naval air arm joined, when it was ready to receive the aircraft at sea.

The barracks were old and very much like the wooden huts I was now very familiar with. Heat again was provided by the stove in the middle of the room and did nothing to heat the room sixty feet away where my bed was.

Once we had settled into the mess we were told to gather at the dockside to receive our work orders. With the ship in dry dock none of the regular duties were required. We were all assigned to various jobs that included the tedious security patrols mainly looking for fires or floods. With hundreds of dockyard laborers welding on the ship during the days, fire was a real hazard.

I was amazed at the size of the vessel. In dry dock it looked even bigger than when it was in the water. She was 803 feet long and weighing in around 51,000 tons when fully loaded with all the aircraft and equipment onboard. Standing on the flight deck and peering over the side to the bottom of the dry dock was quite something.

One good thing about the situation was that there were so many of us available to cover watches that the duty intervals were infrequent. That meant we got lots of time to discover the delights of this naval city.

Devonport and Plymouth are joined at the hip and it took very little time to travel from the dockyard into Plymouth City Center.

One street in particular, Union Street, was known for lots of pubs and night life. At that time I think there were at least fifteen pubs actually on Union Street alone, apart from the many others in the side streets.

I turned seventeen on February the 1st at which point I applied for my provisional driver's license. Driving was one of my major priorities because it could provide a level of independence that I had not yet enjoyed.

Weekend leave was now possible and, due to the minimum duties, I could get three out of four weekends off. That meant from about 4:00 P.M. Friday to 1:00 A.M. Monday morning. At a push it meant I could travel home to

Lincolnshire on a regular basis. Only problem was train fares.

The navy issued three free travel passes per year, anymore than that and you were on your own. However, this was a time when hitchhiking was very easy. I would wear my uniform to hitchhike and rarely stood for more than five minutes at a prime pickup spot before getting a ride.

Mind you it could be quite hazardous riding in all kinds of vehicles. Lorrys were the most likely to pick up but they were also slow so I always tried to snag a car if possible.

One guy picked me up outside Plymouth and told me he was going as far as London. Not the most direct way but in one shot was worth the dogleg.

The car was something like a Vauxhall and we set off at breakneck speed along the A38 toward Exeter.

We exchanged the usual banter about where I was from what he did for a living and so on. Then he started to talk about some strange stuff like how the new E Type Jaguar was usually driven by men who had a penis fixation. Being very naïve about the ways of the world I listened with amusement.

He went on about certain kinds of art where the human form was represented in different ways. How a painting of two men entwined naked on the ground could be beautiful. I still didn't get it!

I got it when we stopped at a roadside service area and he asked me to come into the same toilet with him and close the door. I got my thumb out very quickly and took the next lorry that slowed to forty miles an hour!

Hazards aside, it was a cheap way to travel and often quite interesting. I would often not get home till the early hours on Saturday morning and had to leave in the afternoon on Sunday. That did give me all day Saturday and of course Saturday night for fun. My first priority was getting in Dad's van and driving.

145

I had applied for my driving test right away foolishly believing I could pass without a hitch. After a couple more hours with my mum I decided I was fine on my own—illegal of course—but who was to know?

Now Saturday night took a whole new dimension whenever I could get home. Very few of my mates had cars if any; so now that I had the wheels I called the shots. We could get six or seven of us in this little Ford van if we threw out the rear seat altogether. We would go from pub to pub for a while and then try to find a village dance hall. The roads in the area had some gentle sloping hills and if I could get a long enough run down one I could get the speedometer needle to hit eighty miles an hour with the engine screaming and blue smoke pouring out the back. (Sorry about the van, Dad.)

It was exhilarating and the freedom was overwhelming. I thought the world was a wonderful place.

In 1964 the breathalyzer was still five years away. If you could stand up and walk a straight line you could probably convince the police you were still competent. I cringe to think how stupid we all were, as if there were no limits on our excesses.

My driving test date came through for a Saturday morning to be taken in Boston, about fifteen miles from the farm.

I had gone home on the Friday night to be ready for the big day. No one could go with me as my co-driver—which was a legal requirement for a provisional driver—so I decided I would go on my own and hope the driving examiner didn't ask how I got there.

I found the test center and found the guy who was to be my examiner and we walked to the van. He looked around a bit surprised, presumably looking for my co-driver, so I said my Dad had gone off to do some shopping.

The van did not have seatbelts as they were not required at the time. Everything went well for the first few minutes as

I followed his instructions. "Turn left at the next light, take a right turn by the post office." "What was the last road sign we passed?" I was doing great and thinking I had it in the bag.

We drove along a quiet road away from the town center and he told me we were going to do an emergency stop. On his signal, which would be his hand banging the dashboard, I was to stop as quickly as I could. No problem.

After a few more seconds, as we were doing about forty miles an hour, he suddenly hit the dashboard with a thump.

I hit the brakes. The jack shot out from under the passenger seat and hit his ankles. The loose seat in the back flew forward and hit him in the back. His head hit the dash. His clipboard hit the floor and the van swerved left and hit the curb.

Not pretty, but we stopped! We sat silent for a few seconds as he rubbed his ankles and tried to gather his stuff off the floor. He adjusted his glasses and turned toward me with a very stern look on his face. Still silent I thought I had better say something.

"How was that?"

"That, young man, has resulted in three reasons to fail the test, loose objects in the vehicle, defective brakes and exceeding the speed limit."

Bugger, that didn't go well did it? I had not even noticed the 30 mph speed limit.

We drove in silence back to the test center as he scribbled his notes on my test sheet. I pulled up outside the door and he got out. He came round to my window and thrust the sheet in to my hand. He turned away and started hobbling up the steps of the test center. I drove off and my last sight of him he was standing on the steps looking at me and scratching his head as I drove off on my own.

I reapplied for my driving test but this time in Spalding, to make sure I didn't get the same bloke. It came through for a month's time so I took the precaution of booking a driving lesson for one hour before the test. This would also allow me to use the school car for the test.

Back in Plymouth I was getting bored with the routine of trudging round the ship looking for fires. We also had to do some maintenance work to keep us out of mischief. This sometimes involved hanging over the side in a flimsy bosun's chair and chipping rust off the side, around some of the fittings.

The days went slowly but the evenings went fast.

By now I had teamed up with four other lads all about the same age. This was the first real assignment for us all and we hit it off well. Saddy was from Banbury, Taf was from Milford Haven in South Wales, Stevo was also from Banbury and Taffy was from Borth on the West Coast of Wales. With two Welshmen we had to differentiate by adding the Y to one of them. We made up a motley crew indeed.

We used to all go ashore together and indulge in as much drinking as we could. It was a regular event to start at one end of Union Street and see how many pubs we could have one pint in before one of us fell over. Considering that none of us was over eighteen we were getting in plenty of practice for when we could go out to start drinking for real. I had not developed much of a taste for some of the southern beers so I would often resort to the local Scrumpy cider. This also had the advantage of being cheaper than beer. However, it was sometimes so sour that I would top it with blackcurrant juice to improve the taste with a little sweetness. Only problem with this mixture was that any vomit was very purple and stained like hell.

One night we had got about halfway down Union Street and had made it through the United Services, one of the oldest pubs around, and I had probably drunk eight or nine pints of my mix when my legs gave out in a shop doorway and I threw up. I was on my knees facing the door allegedly using the letterbox as a receptacle when I was hauled to my feet by two constables. My mates were all standing about laughing as the constables threw me into the back of their land rover.

I spent the night in the cells back at the barracks and appeared before the duty officer the next morning. Two day's pay and two day's leave docked were the standard for this common misdemeanor!

About sixteen years later I was on a trip to Cornwall to visit the sales manager of a company who had their office in Plymouth. At the time I was the Western Regional Manager for Union Carbides Agricultural Business in the UK.

Thomas's of Plymouth had expressed an interest in becoming a distributor for Union Carbide and I was on my way to meet their sales manager and consummate the deal. I met Mr. Piper in his office and we talked over the distributorship and then went for lunch. He kept looking at me a bit strange and then he said, "Have you ever been to Plymouth before?" I said I had been in the navy and was stationed here in the mid sixties and why did he ask. "Oh, I used to be a special constable and I recon I seen e afore and arrested e."

Despite my drunken state on that night sixteen years before I did have a faint recollection of the arresting officer. It was indeed Special Constable Keith Piper. We laughed like drains and became good friends after that.

8

Love Is a Many Splendor'd Thing

Despite the nightly drinking sessions I was always on the lookout for some female company. Up to now I had not had a serious girlfriend, in fact I hadn't really had a girlfriend at all. That is unless you count Sonia at school. So I was quite curious about the prospect of a liaison with the opposite sex.

It's hard to plan such an event when you go out with a bunch of yelling degenerates, so I just put my trust in providence and carried on as normal. Then one night it hit me. I was hooked, I was enthralled, I was captivated, I was in love.

I met Shelly in the Haddington Arms in Devonport. She was almost sixteen years old and I was just seventeen. She was at the pub with a Petty Officer and his wife, who were friends with her parents, although they were not there on this occasion. She had been allowed to go out with her father's permission for the first time, this Friday night.

At first I just kept smiling at her across the smoky room.

It was noisy and crowded and my mates and I had all had several pints so they were acting up as usual. However, I was in good shape and something told me to be a bit more restrained than usual. She returned my smiles and so I started to work my way across the room trying not to make my approach look too obvious.

At last I was by her table and gave her another big smile and leaned down and said something stupid like, "Do you like Manfred Mann then?" Manfred was oo wa diddying like crazy from the juke box much to the dislike of the older Petty Officer. He wanted to know what the hell "oo wa diddy diddy dum diddy do" was supposed to mean.

I did my best to convince him this was the new music and it was great. It's ironic that I have since spent many hours trying to convince my daughter as a teenager that Frankie Goes to Hollywood were not proper musicians and that she should listen to something that had meaning.

Anyway, now I was next to the young lady but I still didn't know her name. So I thought that would be a great opening line. She responded in a smooth Devon accent and told me her name was Shelly Eldridge. I now sat straddling a chair facing her and she followed on by saying she lived out at West Park and soon had to go home as her curfew was fast approaching.

It was probably about 9:30 by then so I guessed her Dad had told her to be home by ten. I told her my name and where I was from but not much more. It was obvious I was in the navy although none of us were in uniform. Civilian clothing was usually drainpipe trousers with a shirt that had a tiny narrow collar.

The outfit was usually finished off by winkle picker shoes or chisel toe slip on boots. I had the winkle pickers and they were horribly uncomfortable but fashion is fashion right? I also had on my new collarless Beetle jacket. (I know, I know, but this was 1964.)

For the first time in my life I now had a little money to spend on myself so why not. Although our wages were low it was all spending money because our living costs were covered by the navy.

I asked her if she would like another drink before she had to go. She flashed a smile and flipped her long wavy hair in a nervous response. "Can I have an orange juice?" she

151

said, still with a smile on her face. My legs were like jelly as I fought my way to the bar. As I waited my turn at the bar I kept looking back at her with stupid grin on my face. I finally got the drinks and made my way back to her table.

I couldn't believe it—another lad in the bar had stolen my chair, sat down next to her and was doing his best to chat her up. I coughed as I stood behind him making it obvious that I was with the lady. Shelly held up her hand for the drink and he got up and walked away. OK, now we were in business. I knew I had very little time to make an impression so I started to spill out everything I knew in the world.

Before I knew it the landlord was calling time. The ten o'clock curfew had gone by over an hour ago and now we had to leave the pub. My mates had since departed to another pub after coming over making all sorts of embarrassing comments about my prospects.

I started to feel panic as we walked toward the door. Shelly was following the Petty Officer and his wife and I thought that she would have to go with them. However, once outside, the PO said, "Is this lad going to make sure you get home safely?" I could have kissed him.

She gave me a coy look and said, "I don't know, he hasn't asked me yet."

I almost fell forward trying to get my words out.

"Er, er would you like me to see you home?"

"OK, that would be nice."

Of course I had no idea where West Park was and I did not have any means of transport.

"Come on, we can get the bus at the end of the road," she said, holding out her hand. Now I nearly began to believe in God; she wanted me to hold her hand and take her home.

I held her warm little hand as if it was a delicate flower petal as we walked along the street toward the bus stop. I don't think my feet were actually in touch with the ground at all.

"I thought you had to be home by ten."

"I only said that in case you were boring."

"I suppose I am not boring then."

"No, I quite like you."

"Wow, I like you too."

We reached the stop and waited for the next bus to appear.

She told me the busses ran on the half hour from this stop and it was nearly half eleven. I turned to face her and took her other hand in mine. I just stood looking straight into her eyes not quite sure what my next move ought to be. If I tried to kiss her would she think that was too forward? If I didn't would she think I was too slow or not interested? All kinds of thoughts raced through my mind trying to figure out what I was expected to do. At that very moment in time I now know what it was like to love another person. At the time I really had no idea what was happening to me but I knew I liked the feeling. Before I had time to fully understand what was happening the bus arrived.

We got on the bus and sat near the back.

It was almost empty so we were able to sit well away from anyone else. I still held on to her hand like it was the most precious thing in the world. I couldn't believe this feeling of incredible happiness. It was intoxicating. We chatted about all sorts of things as the bus chugged along its route. It took about twenty-five minutes to reach her stop.

We got off and started to walk along the street for a few hundred yards. We turned a couple of corners and finally came to the door of her house, which was a gray pebbledash semi-detached council house. There was a low wall that ran along the side of the yard outside the back door. We sat on the wall, still holding hands.

"Would you like to sit on my knee?" I asked, half expecting a definite no.

"OK," she said, sitting on my right knee, half facing me in the dark. I put my arms around her and pulled her gently toward me. We kissed very softly for a long, long time. We eventually came up for air and I just muttered something incoherent. Just feeling her warm body pressed to me with her little warm hands around my neck was incredible.

The rush of passion was overwhelming. If she had asked me to fly round the moon I would have found a way to do it. There it was, in less than two hours, I was in love; I mean really in love.

We sat and talked and kissed and talked and kissed and talked for what seemed like no time. (Quote, "If a man sits on a hot stove for one minute it seems like one hour. If a man talks to a beautiful woman for one hour it seems like a minute." Albert Einstein.)

Our world was interrupted when her Dad opened the back door in his dressing gown. "Shelly, it's one-thirty, time to come in now." His voice was soft and friendly and had an Irish lilt. He smiled at me but did not say anything directly for my attention. I stuttered something but he closed the door and was gone.

We kissed again and she stood up and straightened her clothes, not that I had been responsible for any deliberate attempt to rearrange them. I had felt her small breasts through her clothing and she had not tried to stop me but that was the most forward action I had taken.

"I have to go in."

"I know, when can I see you again?"

"How about tomorrow?"

"Yeh, that would be great."

"OK, can you come and pick me up because Dad will want to meet you."

"Er, yes I suppose so."

I was bit perturbed by the thought of meeting Dad but I would have walked through fire to see this girl again.

"What time can you come?"

"Oh, how does five o'clock sound?"

"That's too early, can you come at six?"

"Yes. Yes of course I can."

We kissed one more time and she turned and was gone.

I stood looking at the door for several seconds before walking back down the garden path to the road. I had no idea where I was. I had not taken any notice of the turns we had taken, so finding my way to the bus route was going to be difficult.

It didn't seem to matter as I took various different turns working my way back to the main road. I was so happy I didn't care.

Suddenly I remembered my leave expired at 1:00 A.M. Damn, I was going to be AWOL. That meant losing shore leave privilege. I wouldn't be able to see Shelly the next night. I didn't know the telephone number so I had no way of calling her. I started to panic as I now ran as fast as I could to the bus stop.

I frantically looked at the bus timetable stuck on the shelter window to see when the next bus was due. To my horror it said the last pick up at this stop was 11:45 P.M. I was screwed. I was about eight miles from the barracks and I had about two shillings in my pocket. Not enough for a taxi even if I could find one out in the sticks at this time of night. If I could get back before the morning watch started at 4:00 A.M. I might be able to persuade the guard to give me a 1:00 A.M. stamp, that way I could get away with the late hour. If the morning watch had started they would have to sign me in late regardless.

155

Could I run eight miles in less than two hours? I wasn't sure.

I did.

I arrived at the gate about ten minutes before the watch changed. I crept up to the guard who was an old able seaman with three good conduct stripes on his arm. (Old was probably twenty-eight.) I showed my ID card and he looked at me with a contemptuous grin. "You're AWOL, lad."

"I know, but I met this great girl and forgot the time and—" He interrupted me before I could finish.

"You've been out getting your end away and I've stood here all bloody night freezing my balls off and you expect me to let you off." He took out the night log and started to write.

"Please mate, give me a break, before the others turn up."

By now the morning watch keeper would be on his way; if he came before I could get in I was done for. I had to think quickly.

"200 blue liners," I blurted out.

"All right, you better get them to me tomorrow or else."

"Thanks mate." I was in.

At that time the navy kindly provided each enlisted man over sixteen with 200 unfiltered cigarettes (called blue liners due to the stripe down the side that designated them as duty free) per week for the princely sum of about two shillings and six pence.

I did not smoke so the "fags" were great bargaining chips as almost everyone else did smoke.

The next night and many others were a blur of ecstasy. I couldn't wait to be with Shelly. By now I had met her family, Mum, Dad, brother Frank, her sister, her other brother and I was getting my feet under the table.

It was all I could do to go home a couple of weekends later to take my driving test again, this time in Spalding. After an hour lesson with the instructor and the test in the school car I now sailed through with flying colors.

Now armed with my driving license I had a plan in mind to utilize this new attribute to my advantage. Shelly's brother Frank owned a car, a little Ford Prefect, which was the saloon version of the van my parents owned.

However, neither he nor his dad had a driving license. But I did.

Furthermore the family owned a little weekend cottage out at a local beauty spot called Shaw Bridge. It was a small wooden hut that had a little living room and kitchen and bedrooms with bunk beds. This was where the family liked to go at the weekends and now I provided the means to get there without undue complications.

Shelly's other brother could drive but he lived further out of town with his wife and children and was relieved to not have the responsibility to transport the rest of them. Frank was a bit miffed that this spotty teenager was driving his car but he sat quietly in the back and said nothing as we headed out to Shaw Bridge for the first of several visits. I think we had six of us in that little car.

We spent the day out at the cottage, and Shelly and I managed to get loose from the rest and walk in the woods by the rocky stream. Just walking along together holding hands was enough to make me believe that the world was a wonderful place and I did not want the day to end. We met up with the family at a little local pub for lunch and we just sat glued to each other almost totally oblivious to everyone around us.

It was early summertime and Shaw Bridge was just beginning to show signs of life. After a long day we drove back to their house and unloaded by the front gate.

The car had to stay put once Frank got out. After a cup of tea I kissed Shelly good night and promised to be back next day (Sunday) to see her again.

157

The summer and autumn passed in a blur of ecstasy (long before the chemical version that replaced real feelings) and by now the *Ark* was afloat and in preparation for us to take it to sea for start up trials.

This had to be done before embarking on our one-year tour of the Far East. The tour of duty was due to begin in June of 1965. The trials were to be conducted in the North Sea and up around Norway. Only the navy could think it was a good idea to do sea trials in the Arctic and then send us off to the tropics.

Time was running out for me to spend with Shelly and I was already mapping out our life together once I returned. Crazy idea at seventeen but I was so enamored with her that I honestly believed I would spend the rest of my life with this girl. As yet our relationship had involved some fairly passionate petting but we had not progressed to the Full Monty stage.

That was to change one evening just before we were due to leave port en route to Norway. By now I was a regular weekend visitor at her home and I was allowed to stay in the spare bedroom.

In the morning on Sunday I would slip into bed with her in her room (wearing pajamas of course) and her Dad, delivering morning tea with a big grin on his face, would make all kinds of comments about keeping my hands in sight. On one occasion, Shelly touched my erection by accident and recoiled in horror.

I tried to pass it off as no big deal but she was very embarrassed. (Getting an erection as soon as I got into bed with her was a given.) I don't think she had any idea at the time of what went on in a boy's mind (or pajamas).

One Saturday, just days away from my departure, Frank had agreed to lend us his Ford Prefect for an evening out. I had so much enjoyed the time out at Shaw Bridge that I suggested we go out there to the same pub. I had not really thought about going to the cottage, but subconsciously it might have crossed my mind.

After a couple of drinks in the pub we decided to go to the cottage. By now it was probably after nine in the evening. Shelly knew where the key was hidden and we let ourselves in. My mind was in a whirl as we sat on the little sofa in the dark. We didn't put the light on and by now it was quite dark outside.

We kissed very passionately and I put my hand inside her blouse and felt her small firm breasts through her bra. I was so inexperienced that I had no idea how to proceed. All I knew was that I wanted to make love to this girl so badly that it was hurting.

After a few minutes she got up from the sofa and held her hand out to me. We went into the bedroom and lay down on the bottom bunk, side by side.

The next few minutes were a blur and I still have trouble fully recounting what happened. Her skirt was up around her middle and her panties had gone missing. My trousers had miraculously found their way to my ankles. My erection would have been competition for the hardest Sheffield steel in any contest. (Oh, if that were still possible.) I suppose that instinct took over because I had never done this before and just how to get where I was going was unknown territory.

I think I climaxed in less than one nano second and the mess was extensive. I lay on top of her gasping and panting as if I had run up two flights of stairs. Shelly lay passive and quiet beneath me. Like me she had little clue as to what we had just experienced. I was in a state of shock and could not find words that seemed useful at this juncture. Finally I whispered, "I love you." I thought that's what I should say and by God I meant it with all my heart.

She smiled and looked into my eyes but still didn't

speak. At last, after what seemed like ages she spoke in an almost inaudible whisper. "Will I'll get pregnant." Oh God, I had not even thought of such a possibility. I put my hand down between us and felt the warm sticky mess on our bare bellies.

Now embarrassment set in. In the gloom as our eyes had adjusted to dim light I could see her breasts displayed below her little silk bra that was hitched up under her arms. As I eased off her to one side I caught a glimpse of her belly and pubic hair. This was the first time I had seen a girl naked. I quickly looked the other way as if I were some kind of pervert for looking at her exposed body.

My erection had not subsided to any extent and I made a stupid effort to cover myself with my hand.

She put her hand down to me and gently closed her fingers around it, pushing my hand away. I lay back by her side and cupped my hand over one naked breast. It was so warm and firm and her nipple was hard. We lay like this for a while gently kissing and holding each other.

My erection would not go away despite my acute embarrassment but I was afraid to attempt to do any more with her after the pregnancy comment.

We lay still for a little while longer and finally I was able to re-stow my tackle. We got up from the bunk and standing with our backs to each other sorted out the rest of our clothing.

After a quiet ride back to her house we chatted about mundane things, neither of us having the desire to address what we had actually done. I had thought that the experience was going to be incredible but now it felt like I had stolen money from the church offering plate. Is that how it is for everyone?

When we parted her embrace took on a new intensity, and I felt so close to her it was hard to let go.

The day to leave came quickly. I was not sure how long we would be gone but I did know we were due back in Plymouth after the sea trials for some leave over Christmas and again, once more before departing for Singapore.

9

Go North, Young Man

On November 24th, 1964 we sailed out of the Tamar estuary, past Drakes Island and out into the English Channel. This followed the pomp and circumstance of the re-commissioning ceremony just a few days before.

I was among hundreds of others in my dress uniform standing to attention on the flight deck as we passed by the Naval Base and then Plymouth Hoe, flags flying and pipes piping.

I felt so proud with my chest sticking out and my head high. Here I was, the skinny kid from Beacon Hill going out to sea on one of the world's most powerful fighting machines. For anyone who has not had that experience it is hard to put into words.

I was in love with a beautiful girl who appeared to feel the same way about me, and I was embarking on a voyage that would eventually take me to the other side of the world. The conflict was incredible. I so wanted to see Norway, experience life at sea in the Arctic Circle and finally sail through the Indian Ocean. But leaving Shelly behind was heartbreaking.

Once clear of Drakes Island we were dismissed to change into work uniforms to begin the various sea duties. Everything was a blur as we scurried around tidying up deck areas. All my previous ventures onto the water had been done on vessels a fraction the size of the *Ark Royal*. This 800 ft. monster was a true behemoth and I thought we could take on anyone or anything.

Top speed was over 28 knots powered by four huge steam turbines that in turn were supplied with super heated steam from four boiler rooms. The ship's hull had originally been laid down in 1945 at Cammell Laird in Birkenhead, but the end of the war put a temporary stop to construction.

It was restarted during the lead up to the Korean War and finally launched in 1950 by Queen Elizabeth (who became the Queen Mother). By then she was equipped with the latest technology (the ship, not the Queen Mother). In 1964, when we put to sea for trials it had undergone its first major refit where it was updated again. However, apart from air-launched missiles the ship borne weapons were still 4 1/2 inch heavy artillery and Bofor's anti-aircraft guns. My kind of weapons!

The rest of us all had our various duties and mine sometimes included time on the wheel. The wheelhouse was on six-deck some two decks below the water line. The wheel was huge, five or six feet across. On each side were the four engines telegraphs that sent messages to the engine room. Next to the wheel were several voice pipes and down them without warning would come messages from the bridge from the officer in command of the ship.

Mounted above the wheel was the gyrocompass, which the helmsman would use once given a course to follow.

"Starb'd 10, mid-ships, port 5, mid-ships, Helmsman, steer 220."

As each command came down I would repeat the order and follow the instructions. It was critical to move quickly as the officer in command would be anticipating the sluggish moves of this huge vessel.

Imagine 51,000 tons of steel moving forward at 25

163

knots and you need to change direction. The response time was in minutes not seconds so every maneuver needed thinking out several minutes ahead of each command to the wheelhouse. It's easy for me to see how the *Titanic* hit the iceberg, bearing in mind its response time was much worse than the *Ark Royal*. (Mind you their sleeping accommodation was better, even in 3rd class!)

I was not allowed on the wheel during aircraft movement because this was the most critical of all. Any foul up in the wheelhouse could put a plane and pilot into the sea with the inevitable consequences. It required a person with many hours of experience to be trusted with duty on those occasions.

Other than the wheelhouse, other duties included lookout watches that required the duty hand to be positioned on the GDP (Gun Direction Platform). This was an open deck above the enclosed bridge. We were equipped with some massive binoculars that were mounted on a swivel podium that could turn 360 degrees.

They could also be removed from the stand so we could move around to follow objects that might disappear behind the superstructure at the rear of the deck. These became extremely useful appliances on occasions when we were near enough to peer at women on shore.

The purpose was to continually scan the horizon for ships, aircraft or anything else the skipper ought to know about, including icebergs, for one.

Before heading north, we went into Portsmouth for a few days and then back to Devonport for Christmas leave. I had a few days to see Shelly and then we left Devonport again, on January 14th.

This time we embarked the squadrons for the first serious flying trials, which were to be done in the Moray Firth. We were equipped with Sea Vixen and Scimitar jet fighters,

Wessex and Whirlwind helicopters and Gannet long-range radar planes.

The squadrons would only join the ship from Yeovelton Naval Air station once we were a good distance out to sea.

Watching the jets land one by one was an incredible sight. As the pilots approached the flight deck at incredible speed they would twitch and wobble trying to line up to catch the arrestor wire that snagged a hook hanging under the belly of the jet.

Once hooked the jet would go from about 150 mph to 0 in about 150 feet with the scream of the engine dying down.

This was followed by frantic action to move the jet out of the landing zone as the next one was already approaching. If they missed the hook on the first approach they would open up full throttle and roar off the front of the ship in a cloud fumes and fuel, sometimes dipping down below the front of the flight deck.

My heart would be in my mouth till the jet came creeping back into view and soaring up into the sky for the next attempt. It's amazing to me now that some of these pilots were no more than twenty-two or twenty-three years old throwing multimillion pound aircraft around like I used to ride my truck down the hill at Beacon.

It was only then that I realized how I had missed my chance to aspire to such an incredible career. Up to then I had not really thought much about what I could do.

Now I was racked with jealousy that I could never have the opportunity to do such a thing. Some of these pilots were landing on a ship at sea for the first time and it's hard to imagine what was going through their minds as they made that first live approach.

After going north to Moray we then went south to Brest (nice name that) in France for a bit of flag flying, and a good run ashore. Only problem was that Sir Winston Churchill popped his clogs a few days before we arrived so it put the dampers on our first real run ashore in a foreign port.

Not that I had much idea quite what old Winny had done for the nation but it was obvious that all the officers thought it was inappropriate to appear to be having too much fun. In fact it was rumored that we might even be sent back to base as it was such a big occasion, but in the end they decided to go ahead with the visit.

Now, me and my mates, the two Taffys, Saddy and Steve, were not going to let some crusty old statesman dying put a damper on our fun so we decided to go and look for fun anyway. After being cooped up on the ship for a couple of weeks we were ready to rock and roll.

What we did not realize was that the French did not like the British Navy too much as during the war we had blasted the port of Brest to get at the German submarines that were operating out of there. We had also sunk several of their ships in an Algerian port during Operation Catapult in 1940 to prevent the Nazis getting their hands on them.

Further, one of the French vessels that we damaged, the battleship *Richelieu,* was now a permanent fixture in Brest. When we finally got ashore many of the shops were boarded up and the bars closed. However, despite the Froggies' attempt to make us unwelcome the five of us found enough places to go to feel like we had done it justice.

Back at sea we went back to Scotland, this time Rosyth, still working up the ship's systems ready for our coming stint in the Far East.

After a few days painting the newly exposed rusty bits we headed out to sea again for the C in C's Inspection to make sure we were war ready. All we needed was a nice war, and the Americans were working on that for us in Vietnam.

We also had our own little conflagration going on in

Burma where we were to provide a helping hand in due course.

With the Admiral on board we now headed for Bergen in Norway. On the way we were involved in some kind of joint exercise but because the navy didn't actually tell we grunts what the hell was going on we just did our jobs and looked forward to the next opportunity get off the ship and raise hell.

Now almost fully operational we were all getting familiar with the various duties; one I had mentioned earlier was lookout up on the GDP.

This was great fun during the day especially when we were launching aircraft because we got the best view of the action, but at night it was desperate.

It got pretty boring up there in the middle watch (midnight to 4:00 A.M.) and on one occasion (now famous in the annals of Manton history) when we were way north I found myself actually frozen to the guard rail at the front of the GDP. This position was also serviced by voice pipes, which allowed the officer in command to issue instructions. For instance, if an object came up on the radar screen on the bridge the officer would give a bearing and ask the lookout to make a visual sighting as soon as possible.

I was conscious of a voice in the distance calling "Lookout, Lookout, can you see a light bearing port one-five?" It was like I was in a trance.

I had been on the GDP for over two hours and as the ship was due to go to the tropics in a few months we had not been equipped with Arctic clothing. Consequently I was only wearing regular clothing with a thin coat over the top. I did have pair of woolen gloves on but by now they were very cold and wet. That's what froze me to the rail. I could still hear the voice but it was as if it was in the distance. The voice started to get louder and louder but I was incapable of moving.

The next thing I was surrounded by people all shouting at me and asking me to talk. Someone pulled my hands from the rail breaking the ice away from my woolen gloves. I was helped down the steep ladder to the bridge and placed in a chair at the back. I was beginning to understand that something was wrong but I was still very confused. Someone tipped my head back and poured a liquid into my gaping mouth.

I realized later that I had been administered the navy's medicinal answer to all illness. A shot of neat 120% proof rum.

The rum brought me back to reality very quickly. I heard a voice say, "Take him to the sick bay," and with that I was escorted down below.

The duty medical officer did not seem too pleased to be woken up at about three in the morning so his bedside manner left something to be desired. However, after being administered enough alcohol to render any seventeen-year-old shit-faced, I just grinned.

"Stupid fucking idiot, you damn near froze to death."

"Sorry Sir, I don't know what happened."

"What happened is that you were going into hypothermia, you fool."

Oh great, how the heck was I supposed to know what hypothermia was?

I slept well.

In Bergen I had one of my early first experiences (no, not that kind of experience) of eating something other than the standard British fare of meat and two veg.

My mates and I walked into a restaurant and sat down. Our Norwegian was nonexistent and the locals did not seem to understand English (why on earth not?).

Ordering became a system of arm-waving, pointing, making noises like a chicken and shrugging shoulders.

After a short while the waitress wrote something on her pad and walked off. We had managed to make five beers understood and they arrived quickly. After several more beers the food finally turned up.

Several different dishes were placed on the table and I got one that was a pile of white mush in a large bowl. After a few pokes with my fork and a couple of sniffs I determined that it was fish, but fish done like this was new to me.

As I was starving (not an unusual feeling for me) I took a fork full and swallowed.

The taste was exquisite, I had no idea that fish could taste this good. Now I know that it must have been something like cod done in a white cream sauce but then it could just as easily have been moon dust.

Another first for me was to be invited to join a group of Norwegian sailors at a ski resort just outside the town. We were given our equipment and about twenty of us were taken to the top of the mountain riding on the ski lift. This was followed by a couple of hours instruction by our very helpful hosts.

This involved some gentle gliding down shallow slops by the buildings at the top of the mountain. One clown fell on his back and his skis, slowly gathering momentum on their own, disappeared over the edge of a ridge into the treetops below.

After a very nice lunch (fish again) in the clubhouse we were asked to muster by the top of the ski run.

Now I had no idea that the Norwegians had such a sense of humor but we soon found out. In broken English the main guide explained we were now ready to ski back to the base station and turned and pointed down the slope. As we stood stupefied looking down this near vertical ice wall several skiers flashed by and disappeared at breakneck speed into the distance.

My immediate response was to walk backwards away from the edge in case some loony pushed me off and I could not stop. I still could not believe they expected us to go down this suicide slope. Of course they did not, but it got plenty of laughs from their side before they explained that the family slopes were at the other side of the clubhouse.

This was a series of short, less steep slopes that wound its way back to the base over about three miles. The Norwegians were all expert skiers so they were going to do the suicide run leaving us to work our way down the "safe" part.

After two hours of tuition (and several beers) I was feeling pretty confident I could do this with no problem.

How wrong I was!

I watched several of my group set off till I decided I would tackle the first run. It was not too steep and stretched for about 500 yards with small pine trees and saplings scattered along the edges and the gap maybe fifteen yards wide. No problem!

Having no idea how to turn, with my sticks waving in he breeze, I entered the woods at about twenty miles per hour. I straddled several small saplings as I went until hitting a small tree, which uprooted under my arm, and threw me to the ground with legs and skis akimbo.

Of course, the snow in the woods was deep and soft, so I spent the next five minutes trying to stand up and get my skis on again.

My shoulder was hurt (the same one that nearly screwed up my medical) and I was now somewhat intimidated by the rest of the course. Five-hundred yards done, three miles to go. At this rate I might just tear off a few limbs before getting to the bottom.

I managed to get going again but fell at every turn. By

the time I got to the bottom where our hosts were probably on their tenth beer I was wet, bruised, injured and exhausted.

To my surprise I was one of the first to get in so I must have passed a dozen of my shipmates on the way down. God knows where they went to, off the track.

Lots of laughing and rib jabbing and several (medicinal) beers later we returned to the ship, broken and bruised but triumphant.

I was not to don another set of skis until 1985 and only then for one afternoon.

10

Now East, Young Man

Over the next couple of months we went back into Portsmouth, did trials with a new experimental navy jet, the Buccaneer, had more leave in Devonport and finally arrived back at Devonport again for more leave.

This was to be our last shore leave before departing for a year in the Far East.

I made the most of the last few days with Shelly and on the last night I saw her I told her that when I came back we should get married. Well, it seemed like a good idea at the time!

On June 17th, 1965 we once again set sail past Plymouth Hoe and Drakes Island into the English Channel. Next stop Gibraltar.

We spent three nights in Gibraltar and I had another new experience when some of us crossed over into the Spanish town of La Linea.

The nightclubs were something to behold for an innocent like me. To see totally naked women dancing on stage was one thing but to watch one pick up coins, thrown by the yelling crowd, with her . . . well, use your imagination, was something else indeed.

I heard stories told of how some old lags would heat the coins with their lighters before tossing them onto the stage. That I don't want to think about!

A bucket of nasty "Malaga" wine was about three pennies so drinking was cheap and as we were expecting to be shipbound for several weeks we made the most of the opportunity. Getting back over the border was even more interesting as a large crowd of us pushed and shoved at the checkpoint when I thought the armed border guards would actually shoot us.

General Franco was not too happy with the Brits for hanging on to Gibraltar in the first place.

The next night several of us walked to the top of the rock and one of the Barbary Apes ran off with my hat. So if you see an ape wearing a sailor's hat, next time you are in Gibraltar ask for it back. 6 7/8" with an *Ark Royal* hat band.

The next port of call was Aden, but to get there we first had to pass through the Suez Canal. We were required to lay off Port Said for several hours, waiting for a convoy of ships to assemble ready for the passage through the canal.

By now we were beginning to realize how hot it could get and at the end of June it was hot. For a lad used to good summer days in the mid 70s, 95 degrees was about all I could handle. Little did I know it would get worse.

The officer of the watch decided (in his officer type wisdom) to let the hands bathe. This was the naval order to allow the ship's company who were not on a specific watch duty to jump over the side for a swim. Now consider the *Ark* at about 800 feet long and the open decks around the side being some thirty feet above the water line. Add to that we were anchored in a moving sea channel that turned out to be running several knots.

As the order "hands to bathe" blasted out around the speaker system several hundred hot sailors jumped over the side, yours truly among them.

By now I was a pretty strong swimmer but after leaping over thirty feet down from four-deck just aft of the forecastle, by the time I came to the surface I was almost by the stern. This was not seen as immediate problem until I tried to swim back toward the ship. All around, the water was filled with sailors thrashing as hard as they could to head back toward the scramble nets that had been placed all around the ship's side to allow us to climb back on board after our refreshing swim.

The officer of the watch had probably realized by now that he was about to be court-martialed for drowning half the ship's company.

As I continued to swim as hard as I could I heard the ship's siren sound the man overboard signal. Several boats and helicopters were scrambled to pick up those of us who ran out of steam before we could grab a ladder and climb back on board.

I did manage to make it to the net but after twenty minutes in the water had to be rescued by the lifeboat and hauled up by several laughing shipmates who had the good fortune to have been on duty. Some of the poor sods that jumped from nearer the stern had surfaced way past the ship and it took quite a time to get them all safely accounted for. We did not lose one soul but must have come pretty close.

While we were anchored waiting for the correct timing to enter the canal the obligatory "bum" boats came alongside full of locals trying to sell all kinds of knock-off Rolex watches and leather gear. Some asked for food in return for their offerings.

A woman with a couple of children came alongside in a boat that looked way too tiny to be this far from the shore. I was on 4 deck with several others as she called up asking for potatoes, in broken English. One of the vegetable lockers was right behind us so myself and another seaman decided we would rob the veg locker and oblige this poor unfortunate.

By the time we got back to the side with a 50 lb bag of spuds another boat with a couple of pushy blokes in it were waving the woman away and maneuvering under our deck to grab the bag of spuds. We obliged by dropping it about thirty feet straight into the bottom of their boat. It nearly went right through the bottom. The last we saw was them paddling and bailing like crazy trying to get back to dry land before sinking.

About midnight we passed through Port Said harbor, by the statue of Ferdinand de Lesseps (canal architect) and entered the Suez Canal.

It was quite uncanny as we moved almost silent and slowly. As dawn broke it was easy to see the poverty and simple homes that the locals lived in if you leaned over the side and looked down. If you stood in the middle of the flight deck all you could see was desert for miles on both sides.

We arrived in Aden on July 1st to the news that the Yemen Freedom Fighters (terrorists) were lobbing homemade bombs into cinemas and at groups of occupying Brits, so going ashore was somewhat risky. However, the call of the cheap watches and bars was too much to deter our intrepid band.

We were anchored out in the harbor and going ashore required liberty boats. We were only allowed ashore in civilian clothes (fine by me) and in groups of six to help provide some kind of safety. The Royal Air Force had a base just outside the town and had an area of the seafront where shark nets were rigged to offer a bit of comfort for those who felt like a swim.

If the terrorists didn't get you the sharks might! Several of us ended up drinking in a hotel bar on the first night. The next night we discovered it had been bombed, presumably for catering to the devil British who were occupying their homeland. No longer thirsty we ran most of the way back to

175

the boat and played drafts on board ship for the rest of the evening.

We left Aden on the 4th and after some more mucking about at sea (which involved a 3 ship RAS) we arrived in Singapore on the 19th. This was to be our base in the Far East for the next ten months and proved to be a place full of surprises. Some of which were mind-boggling for a "skin" like me.

We couldn't wait to get off the ship and explore this new playground. We youngsters on our first trip had been primed by the old lags who were on their second or third visit to the base.

We knew that Boogis Street was the place to head for once you had consumed several pints of Tiger beer and a Nasi Goreng in the streets of Sembawang village just outside the naval base gates.

(3 ship **R**eplenishment **A**t **S**ea is a maneuver that involves a supply ship attached either side transferring stores and fuel while traveling at about 12 knots. A skin was the name for youngsters who had hardly started to shave.)

11

Girlies with Tackle!

My first visit to Singapore City was with my pals, the two Taffs, Saddy and Steve, plus another older able seaman Neil "Pusser" Holms. Pusser was from my home county of Lincolnshire and had sort of adopted me to show me the ropes.

After plenty of Tigers to loosen up we arrived in Boogis Street late in the evening.

The whole area was a collection of makeshift bars and street cafes that had outside seating down the middle of the street. More interesting were some rather dubious-looking establishments that had scantily clad girls hanging around the doors trying to separate sailors from their money.

We sat at one of the tables and were immediately pounced upon by several of the girls who offered to fetch drinks and sit on our knees. OK so far, I thought.

Pusser seemed to be enjoying himself and pretended he knew several of the girls from earlier visits. As the night progressed we were all enjoying the attention and there was no mention of parting with any money.

By now my inhibitions were in serous freefall so I ventured my hand along the very exposed thigh that was bouncing around on my knee. No resistance so far so I crept past the giggle zone to the central attraction.

Herein I discovered the basis of Pusser's hysterical

laughter. The "girl" was sporting a set of wedding tackle that I would have been proud to have myself.

I let out a yelp and virtually threw the "girl" off my knee into the street. Pusser was by now almost flat on his back roaring with laughter.

"You bastard . . . you knew all along they are all blokes . . . right, they are all blokes."

He just kept laughing and the others, who by now had either made the same discovery for themselves or had seen my reaction, were exhibiting the same kind of horror that I was experiencing.

Once we had all calmed down and started to see the funny side of the joke we carried on drinking and watching the goings-on around us. However, the initial attraction to the "girls" had subsided a little and put me off the whole idea even if I had been wavering. Sometime later the group had diminished and I was left sitting with just Dave when a real woman, I think, came over and asked us if we wanted to see a "fucky fucky show." What the hell, we thought, when in Rome eh!

We parted with a couple of dollars (probably about twenty pence in today's currency), and were led along a dark passageway inside one of the dubious wooden buildings. The woman whispered for us to be silent with her finger on her lips. She gestured to several small holes and peered through. I could make out the white backside of someone riding up on down on top of a girl whose legs were in the air. Then I caught a glimpse of the guy's face.

It was Taff.

I nearly fell backwards in surprise and saw Dave do the same thing. We looked at each other trying not to make any noise but it was too much to hold in. We both cracked out laughing so loud we heard Taff yell out from behind the wall that he was going to kill us. He probably would have if he could catch us but we were off before he could get his clothes back on. Those Asians are ingenious folks, always knowing how to make a buck or two.

With these new experiences under my belt I began to realize that the world was indeed a funny place. In my wildest imagination, back in Lincolnshire, could I have thought this kind of stuff went on around the world?

Taff was not best pleased when we saw him the next day back on board ship but he got over it quickly.

During the rest of the year we were involved in all kinds of military exercises, which included sending our jets to hit targets in Borneo. At the time, I had no idea why. After doing exercises with the US navy we went into Subic Bay in the Philippines for a couple of days.

Fortunately for me I was on duty on the first night so remained on board. I was on gangway duty from 8 to midnight and saw several of my shipmates brought back with minor knife wounds. These were inflicted by another crop of she males who were evident in Olongopo. Their party trick was to lure an unsuspecting (and drunk) sailor down a dark alley with him in anticipation of a swift kneetrembler and then stick him with a small knife. While the guy was thinking he was dying his wallet and watch went AWOL with his date. Hopefully they were spared the surprise of getting a handful of testicles before the knife went in.

I declined to go ashore the next night as by now I had decided that this whole sex thing was way too risky, and we sailed the morning after that. That was the only port of call in my seven-year navy career where I was afraid to go off the ship.

Another brief spell in Singapore and we were en route to Hong King.

We suddenly ran into a tropical storm (Agnes, very Chinese sounding name that!) the worst of the weather was during the middle watch when I was on lifeboat duty on the port side. It was standard practice to have the motor lifeboat turned out on the davits while steaming so it could be lowered and slipped in a hurry if someone went overboard. A scramble net was attached to the deck of the ship and fastened to the boat side with quick release clamps. Once in the boat the crew would release the net and the boat, one would then be lowered by the winch operator.

As the storm intensified we began to worry that the waves were coming so close to the boat it might damage it. Of course, unless given an order from the bridge, we were not allowed to bring the boat inboard.

The Leading Hand of the watch had called the bridge to report the condition but had been told to hold off for a while. By now the ship was rolling pretty heavily and the waves were smashing in on the open decks.

Finally the order came down to secure the lifeboat.

Myself, and two other seamen, ran out to unrig the scramble net to enable the boat to be turned in. Just as we grabbed the net to release the clamps a wave hit the boat and ripped it off its mountings taking it out to sea. I was pulled down to the edge of the open deck and trapped against the steel guardrails with my hands still tangled in the net. By some stroke of fortune I managed to let go the net as it tore away from the ship's fitting and I was pulled back inboard by my shipmates.

I dread to think what my chances would have been in the sea, in the dark in a tropical storm wearing rubber foul weather clothing.

We entered Hong Kong harbor on September 27th one day behind schedule. As we were so big we were anchored way out in the harbor and were serviced by the local ferry company, providing liberty boats to get off the ship.

Another new port to explore, this time with a little

180

better understanding of what delights might be on offer. Mind you, after witnessing the antics of some of my shipmates I was very cognizant of the dangers of loose women and too much booze. Several runs ashore helped us become familiar with the best places to go and we soon felt like we were old hands.

One of the traditional temptations was to get tattooed. I had succumbed to the dreaded inky needle in Chatham before leaving the UK and had decided that I was sufficiently decorated for the time being.

However, my mates thought differently. After a heavy night on the falling down water, most of which for me was a complete blank, they dragged me into a tattoo parlor and instructed the "artist" to add some memorable artwork to my arms.

They knew my girlfriend was called Shelly and my brother was Pete, who had a wife called Audrey. They also knew the flower of Lincolnshire was the daffodil. What they failed to know was that the daffodil did not come in a nice red.

I woke the next morning in my hammock to both arms covered in blood and wrapped in dirty-looking bandages.

To go with Mum and Dad over the anchor I now had a red daffodil with Lincolnshire written in a wavy line underneath on my left upper arm, a rose with Pete 'N' Aud on my right upper arm and for the piece of resistance, a flower of nondescript origin with Shelly across it on my left forearm.

I knew that Saddy was the main protagonist in this assault so I bided my time for revenge. He already had about a dozen tattoos on his chest, arms and legs so one more wouldn't hurt, would it?

After making sure he was past the caring point late one night we helped him into the operating chair at the same parlor (as confirmed by my accomplices). This time I was in

181

charge. Saddy now has a dotted line around his penis with the words "cut here" neatly underneath. It was quite an exercise watching this delicate operation, fortunately assisted by Saddy who managed a modest erection for the artist. He probably thought he was in a brothel at the time.

I managed to escape further additions for the rest of my time in the service. Since then I have spent over $10,000 having laser treatment, trying to remove them.

One other fun thing to do in Hong Kong was to ride in the rickshaws. It amazed me how these little skinny Chinese guys could run so fast with a 16 stone matelote in his chair. Of course we would offer the runner extra money if he could keep ahead of the others in competing vehicles. I'm sure the locals had seen this spectacle many times as we would remove our trouser belts and feign whipping the driver to go faster while we yelled giddy-up!

I heard tell, but never tried it myself, of another wheeze with the rickshaw. Along the harbor front at Kowloon were some old tramlines that ran a few feet from the edge of the dock. Legend has it that sailors would persuade the driver to ride in the back while the sailor ran in the shafts so they could race their buddies down the street.

At a precise moment, while running full tilt toward the dock, the sailor would ram the curved handles of the rickshaw into the tramline. The momentum of the cart would cause it to tip forward, pivot on the shafts and pitch the hapless Chinaman into the harbor, while the culprit crouched down on the ground as it all went overhead.

I bet Chris Patton didn't know about this. Not much wonder why we had to give up Hong Kong.

Back in Singapore at the end of October we had a major fire in one of the boiler rooms. By the time it was under control it had committed us to over five weeks of repairs, stuck in Singapore. This enabled us to spend plenty of time ashore but also opened up lots of opportunity for trouble.

One lot of trouble we didn't anticipate was Rhodesia declaring independence on November 11th. This was to impact our future plans more than we knew.

Car rental was pretty cheap so we decided to rent a car and do some exploring. We crossed over the Jahore Causeway into Malaysia to the town of Jahore Bahrue where we found a place that would rent us a little Datsun car.

As I was the only one who had a license, I got to drive. With five up we tore off to Singapore to see what we could find. After driving about for a bit the sky started to darken, even though it was only about two in the afternoon. All of a sudden the heavens opened and we were in the middle of a monsoon deluge.

I tried to keep going at about five mph weaving about to miss objects that came in and out of our vision but it became impossible to see anything. In the end I just stopped and we sat and waited for the rain to subside.

When it did stop we discovered we were in the middle of a huge car park area that had lamp poles every hundred feet or so. How we had got into the car park in the first place and then how we had missed all those lamp posts, I have no idea, but we had.

We set off again and saw a hotel that looked like it might have a bar. We all marched in and sat down at a table. The place was packed with mostly Asian people all dressed up to the nines. Very nice, we thought, so we decided to stay and have a couple of drinks. As it was a bit posh we all thought we would try a John Collins or a G&T.

After a few minutes a waitress came over and we all ordered our drinks. Every now and again someone would get up on the other side of the room and seemed to be talking to the crowd, followed by clapping and shouting. We didn't really take much notice of the goings on and no one seemed interested in us.

After a couple of hours and lots of John Collins, a chap in a suit approached us. At first he spoke in the local tongue but seeing our puzzled look he changed to broken English and said "Are you with Blide Fammary or Gloom?" We all realized at the same instant what was going on and started trying to emulate his accent. "Oh, me with blide, no, no, gloom."

The guy shrugged his shoulders and walked off. We got up and made a hasty exit as several larger-looking men started to head in our direction.

Because we were stuck for an extended period having B boiler room refitted the navy in their wisdom allowed a number of us some leave to travel up the Malaysian peninsula to a New Zealand army rest camp in the jungle, known as Terandak.

The ride on the Pusser's bus on jungle dirt roads was awful and long. I can't remember how far it was but it seemed to take forever.

The camp, which was surrounded by a very tight wire mesh fence, was miles from anywhere. We later found out that the wire was to try to keep poisonous snakes to a minimum. In the center of the camp was a huge swimming pool with full-size Olympic diving boards.

We soon found out that the only thing to do at this camp, apart from chasing chit-chats (little lizards) out of your locker, was to drink and swim, preferably not in that order.

Me being me, decided to do it the wrong way round. After sinking copious quantities of the beer provided free by our hosts I decided it was time to demonstrate my diving skills. Not content with the weenie boards I went right to the top.

After a little strutting and pouting, to the cheers of a dozen or so onlookers, I ran off the top board in a spectacular dive.

I woke up on my back on the side of the pool (having been pulled unconscious from the water by my mates) with a stinging back and throbbing head. Apparently my feet had overtaken my head and I landed flat on my back on the water, completely winding me.

Didn't do that again!

Several years later I saw the film *Virgin Soldiers*, which tells the story of young army recruits trying to survive in the jungle whilst fighting the Malaysian rebels, set in the late forties. It had a true sense of reality having experienced the hostile environment of that jungle. That was without someone trying to shoot you at the same time.

We went back to the ship and after a couple of departures from Singapore to test the new boiler room we headed for Freemantle, Australia, where we would spend Christmas. One night en route Pusser Holms disappeared overboard.

He was last seen about midnight sitting on the roller fairings on the forecastle drinking a beer. He was not missed until eight the next morning and despite turning back and doing a full-scale search we had to abandon him to the deep. I believe his body was brought up in a fishing net several weeks later, half-eaten by sharks.

Pusser was only 28 and was due to leave the navy when we returned to the UK.

On the 18th of December we crossed into the Southern Hemisphere. As was tradition the ship held a "crossing the line" ceremony for all those young sailors whose first time it was. Lots of giant shaving brushes and gallons of pretend shaving cream later we continued on to Australia.

We arrived in Freemantle on December 23rd ready for a five-day stay over Christmas. Apparently our gunnery officer had been flown ahead to organize a dance in Perth for the ship's company and several other Royal Navy ships, including the destroyer *Devonshire,* that were in at the same time. Further, this was the Australian Navy's base too, so there were several thousand sailors all in the same place at the same time. A recipe for some trouble one might think?

One other visitor was a Russian ship and during the five-day stay one of the jokers from the *Devonshire* decided to shin up the bow rope and try to pinch the hammer and sickle flag. He got caught in the act and the C in C Far East Fleet spent most of his Christmas day trying to avert an international incident with the Russians who, of course, at that time, were highly suspicious of any Western nation's activities.

Once secured alongside we were allowed to go ashore. Having no idea what was out there the intrepid five wandered onto the jetty and stood around debating what to do.

The dance was supposed to be the next day, so we had a day to amuse ourselves. The problem was solved when a flat bed lorry pulled up beside us and a bloke jumped out. In a broad Scots accent the bloke said, "Come on lads, we have beer and food I can take about ten of you."

Needing no further encouragement we piled on the back of the lorry and held on. As we drove off several other cars and trucks were arriving and it looked like similar invitations were being offered by the locals, to anyone who wanted to go.

We arrived at Jock's house, which was a single-story bungalow with a big back garden. He introduced us to his family with kids ranging from toddlers to early teens. His wife seemed happy to see us so we made ourselves at home.

"Beers in the bath," yelled Jock. OK, I thought, must be in a bath of ice. Not so, the beer truly was in the bath, brewed in the bath I believe. We were offered large mugs and invited to participate of the home brew. It tasted awful and warm but once you got a buzz it was fine.

God knows where these people had a shower while the beer was brewing?

They made us feel so much at home as we were all missing our families at Christmas and this was my first Christmas away from home. I'm sure we helped them with their homesickness too as they had only been in Australia for five years.

They had emigrated from Glasgow and Jock (I never found out his real name) had bought a small lorry and earned a living making local deliveries. The next few days were a bit of a blur, as the home brew, supplemented with some fine Scotch whisky that came out later, took its toll.

The dance was held in a huge entertainment center in Perth but due to the uncertainty of our actual arrival date our brilliant gunnery officer had advertised the wrong day to the local girls. Consequently the matelote to "Shelia" ratio was about 100 to 1 (in the wrong favor).

Most of us were three sheets to the wind before we got there and with so few girls to go round, drinking more beer seemed to be the best alternate option.

Now Taff was only a little guy but when he had imbibed a while he got very punchy. Taffy, on the other hand, and Dave and Saddy were much more like me. Cowards! As expected, the tension started to build as the Aus sailors took great exception to the bloody Pom's chatting up their girls.

Despite the unfavorable hen to cock ratio (must have been my good looks) I had managed to have a nice chat to several girls who had invited me and another lad (interestingly a Scot called Hamish) who was standing about at the time, to see them tomorrow. However, before I could fix the coordinates for the meeting, Taff was suddenly engaged in fisticuffs with an Australian sailor.

We were all in our number one uniforms so fighting was

a bit risky because they were expensive to replace if they got torn. The girls decided to exit the area and I turned to watch the fight. Next thing I know I got a tap on my shoulder.

"How about you and me, mate?"

I turned to see this huge grinning Aus sailor who seemed to think punching each other was some form of international bonding. My response was to emulate Roger Bannister who would have been proud of the speed if not the motive.

My nose was not going to be used to bring the UK and Australia to a new diplomatic understanding.

After enough time to allow Big Bruce to find another dance partner I ventured back to the area where Taff was last seen rolling around on the floor with his adversary. I found him propped against a wall with a bleeding nose and his white front ripped to the waist. "You rotten wanker, you left me to get thumped" was all I got from Taff. That didn't hurt anywhere near as much as Bruce was going to hurt my nose.

I helped Taff back to the ship and I think we stayed on board for the rest of that night. Next day, to my absolute surprise and delight, the girls I had talked to at the dance were waiting on the jetty. The one who seemed interested in me was called Diane and she had a huge Holden Estate car. I went to find our new friend, Hamish, who had already done some of the talking to get them interested in the first place. I knew his mess number and he was there in a flash.

We drove off to the beach and the girls had provided a sort of cold Christmas dinner in a hamper. Hamish and one of the girls were getting on really well, but myself and the others discovered they were just being friendly and that was as far as it was going.

I had a terrible guilt complex as I kept thinking of Shelly.

I had been writing letters at least once a week and I'm

sure she was so busy that the six or seven replies over the past five months was all she could manage. Anyway, we had a great afternoon and a few pecks on the cheek but it would require a visit to Mrs. Palm and her five daughters for any further relief.

Diane's father was a business owner and her friend, who was by now fully entwined with Hamish, had a millionaire for a Dad. They took us back to the ship for the night and promised to pick us up for our last day as we were due to sail on the 29th.

The next day only Diane and her friend Sally (I think) returned, so I left my pals and Hamish and I went off for the day with the girls. (They would have left me in a flash in similar circumstances.)

We had another great day but I was concerned about Hamish and Sally because they couldn't keep their hands off each other. I on the other hand was having a very platonic time with Diane. The basis of my concern was that Hamish happened to have a new wife in Glasgow. I doubt the ink was dry on the marriage certificate when we left Devonport. Oh well, I'm not his mother.

After promising to write every day we trudged back on board at the midnight curfew (we were due to sail at the crack of dawn). Back at sea I was having a chat to my new buddy Hamish when he confided to me that in the heat of passion he had asked Sally to marry him.

"You fucking pillock" was my informed response.

"Don't worry, she will soon get the message if you ignore her letters." We went back to Singapore and then, after more mucking about at sea, headed for Mombassa in Kenya.

Before we left, he got a letter from Sally telling him that her father was making an application to the navy to have him discharged so he could return to Australia to marry Sally. He must have had a screw loose to trust a three-day romance to the point where he would try a stunt like that. (Futile as it was.)

However, Hamish was worried that his wife might find out what he had been up to and asked me to write to Sally and let her down gently.

No problem! I wrote a letter to Sally telling her the tragic news that Hamish had been killed in a terrible flight deck accident and that he had been buried at sea.

That should fix the problem.

The letter would have gone a few days before we docked as the mail was often flown off the ship when we were near enough to land, for the helicopters to operate.

A few days into our stay in Mombassa he came to me and told me his mother had contacted the captain in a rage because her son had been killed and the navy had not informed the family.

It transpired that Hamish (in another stupid moment of incompetence) had allowed Sally to look in his wallet. She had found something with his home address and kept it, the home where his new wife was staying with his mother. In her grief Sally had written to his mother offering her condolences for her loss.

That one probably took a little fixing and I lived in fear of being hauled up in front of the captain for my part in the plot. However, I escaped any further involvement.

It was time to explore Mombassa.

If we had thought that Sembawang and Hong Kong had some run down areas Mombassa took the biscuit. I had never imagined people could live in such squalor. Kenya in the '60s was still a pretty poor country and the evidence was everywhere.

My most memorable recollection of Mombassa was watching two local skinny youths completely consume a metal waste bin full of cold baked beans thrown out for the rubbish barges that came alongside every day.

I was on gangway duty at the time and had to stay put. The youths, on board to load the waste barge, sat crossed-legged on either side of the bin and, using flat lats broken from vegetable crates, spooned the beans into their mouths till the bin was empty. I estimated they must have beaten at least 10 lbs of beans each. Their stomachs were sticking out like pregnant women but they seemed very happy. I'm glad I was not to be around later on if beans affected them like they do me!

Despite the Silver Sands Holiday resort, a couple of miles up the beach, most of Mombassa town was a giant slum.

Two highlights (depending on your point of view) were the Tusker Brewery, which produced a heavyweight, brown ale and the other attraction, the Casablanca club, which was basically a strip joint with a block of flats on top. This turned out to be a multi-story brothel. The brown ale tasted like I would imagine elephant piss would taste but again, after several pints, it sort of grew on you.

A group of us were invited to visit the brewery and when asked to comment on the quality of the beer, were polite in our response. We were less polite when we had the chance to pollute the crude toilet facilities afterwards. Well it was free.

The Casablanca club was open day and night and provided a 24-hour STD walk-through facility. Entertainment in the basement was a succession of "past their sell by date" scrubbers who performed all manner of extreme acts with various objects, in a zombie-like manner.

For those in the audience who were stirred from their drunken slumber a quick trip to the lift, hit any floor number, hand over ten Kenya shillings (about twenty-four pence by today's standards) and relief was a prescription away.

To break the boredom some of us were invited by ex-pat families to travel to Nairobi and spend a little time with the families there. I was not able to go on this one but Taff did. When he returned a few days later he was hauled up in front of the captain for some offense that he was reluctant to talk to us about.

Finally it transpired that he had been staying with a British family and had managed to hit it lucky with their daughter. Unfortunately for him she was only fifteen years old and her father had found out about the dirty deed.

Sounds bad but Taff was only eighteen not like he was an older man or something, and anyway in Kenya they could get married at twelve.

On another occasion our band of merry men went off to Silver Sands beach resort to try our luck with the rich folks. All we got was very burned faces and the rich folks didn't want to play so it was back to the Casablanca club for those who still had energy to burn off.

I mentioned earlier that Rhodesia had declared independence in November of '65. We were now to suffer the consequences as the *Ark* was charged with relieving HMS *Eagle* patrolling the Beira Straights. The purpose was to head off oil tankers that were attempting to break sanctions imposed by the very annoyed British government.

This involved steaming up and down the Mozambique Channel for two weeks constantly flying aircraft to make the searches. Being on a full operational basis twenty-four hours a day for almost two weeks was very tiring so we were glad when *Eagle* turned up again to relieve us.

Towards the end of those weeks the sickbay became inundated with sailors who had developed a number of social diseases no doubt courtesy of the Casablanca club. I thanked my lucky stars that the frightening experience in Singapore and Olongoo had deterred me from participating in the free for all and I felt very pious about it all. We returned for another visit to Singapore and more shore leave.

For our last trip ashore we decided to rent another car and try to see a bit more of the city. We found someone crazy enough to let us take a Singer Gazelle. Now in 1966 this was quite a fast vehicle, but unfortunately very unstable. After our usual four or five pints of Tiger in Sembawang we headed off to Singers, for our last hurrah.

One of the dangers of driving there were the pickup taxis. These taxis would have a fare but people standing by the road would flag them down and offer to share the fare with the occupant.

A great system, were it not for the following traffic. We were hammering along a rare bit of dual carriageway with yours truly at the helm and the Speedo flickering at maximum velocity (maybe 85 mph). There didn't seem to be much lane discipline so it was pass on either side depending on space.

I was undertaking several old trucks when a pickup taxi a few hundred feet ahead spotted a roadside fare and jammed on his brakes. At this speed with this machinery I knew we could not stop. No space to the right because the trucks were spread out past the taxi's smoking deceleration.

The only choice I had was to drift off the road and onto the grass verge behind the startled would-be taxi passenger. We roared behind him and bounced over some bumps and miraculously back onto the road.

No one spoke in the car as we rocked from one set of wheels to the other. To this day I have no idea how we stayed upright.

We may have cracked a couple of springs as the ride seemed a little lower after that but we continued on regardless. After a few minutes, conversation started again and no one mentioned the near death experience. (For the would-be taxi passenger.)

We decided as this was our last chance we would try out Raffles.

For those who do not know about Raffles it was the epitome of British colonial rule.

However, in '66 this once great hotel was a bit run down. Nevertheless, the staff dressed in their whites, pretending it was 1925, bowing and scraping to the "superior" occupying colonialists.

We sat in a line at the bar and ordered John Collins like the true upper crust.

It might have been the incident in the car that caught up with me but after several Tigers and two or three John Collins I suddenly threw up all over the bar.

Of course, this was a great source of entertainment to my pals who continued to sit and drink on either side of the pool of vomit that was spreading all over the top of the bar. I was escorted to the door by two very polite under managers who seemed more embarrassed than I was.

I sat in the car for a while till the crew turned up and then we set off again for more drinks. Not many people can say they have been thrown out of Raffles for vomiting on the bar! Fortunately for me (and them) the expulsion of stomach contents had sobered me up enough to get us back to Sembawang safely.

We indulged in our last Nasi-Goring in Nee-Soon, dished out of an upturned oil drum, come barbecue in the street, and then stepped off Singapore soil for the last time. We had to endure another two-week stint chasing oil tankers off the African coast before heading north to Aden where we anchored off shore to await our return passage through the Suez Canal and back to Blighty.

Ten years later I was watching a news report on TV

where it was alleged that the British Government was secretly allowing oil to be transported overland to Rhodesia while giving the public perception they were trying to stop it going in by sea.

After spending about eight weeks of my life cruising up and down the Beira Straights for no good reason I felt a bit miffed. I have no real idea what the truth was, nor may never know. This may have been the occasion when I first began to feel a sense of cynicism toward politicians and government departments in general.

The terrorist activity in Aden had reached such a pitch that we were not allowed to leave the ship. We spent several days refueling and painting the rusty bits before leaving. We passed through the Suez Canal on June 4th. This was just one year before the canal became the subject of international attention when the Arab Israeli six-day war broke out. We finally made it back to Guzz (Devonport) on June 13th just four days short of one full year since our departure. Now it was a time to cruise back into the port with all the pomp and circumstance that we had on our way out a year before, all straining our eyes to see if we could recognize anyone waving on Plymouth Hoe.

12

Heartbreak and Nymphomaniacs

We were now allowed extended leave after our duty in the Far East so my first port of call was Shelly's door. The letters had all but dried up in the last few months and the passionate language that filled the first dozen or so had been replaced by very general stuff that might have been written by my aunt.

This should have been a sign!

I arrived at the door to be met by Shelly's dad. He seemed quite embarrassed to see me and I could tell he was having trouble spitting out the truth.

"Look lad, she's been seeing this other chap and she is out with him now." The words were going in but did not register. Her mother chipped in a few comments in her defense but I was not hearing anything I wanted to hear.

"You can stay here tonight and see her if you like but I don't think it will change anything." Her dad offered this to try to give me some sort of easy letdown.

I made a stuttering excuse that I needed to go off for a while but wanted to come back later to see her.

As soon as I could get there I started to search the pubs along Union Street. If she was out with a boyfriend the odds were they would be in a pub on Union Street. Sure enough in the United Services I found her sitting holding hands with a guy who looked old enough to be her dad.

It turned out he was a marine and was ten years older than she was.

I bought a pint at the bar and then walked over and introduced myself to him. Shelly sat silent and motionless. The guy (big guy) sneered at me as I stood with a pint of beer in one hand and my other held out for him to shake.

"Fuck off" was my homecoming welcome.

Not wishing to injure his knuckles with my face, I turned back toward the bar and sat down at a table. I could hear a heated argument being whispered between them and finally Shelly came over and sat beside me at the table. She was so pretty and vulnerable I just stared at her like a lost dog.

Her explanation washed over my head as I kept glancing at the giant marine who continued to sneer at me from across the room. In the end I made an excuse and told her I was going back to the house to see her parents.

All the way on the bus my stomach hurt like I had been kicked. I was empty. It was all I could do not to cry out loud. I arrived at the back door and her dad let me in. We sat and talked for a while and it was clear he did not agree with the new situation but what could he do. Finally, about midnight, Shelly came home.

Mum and Dad had gone to bed and I sat on the sofa like an injured animal. She sat beside me and picked up on the explanation of why and when, etc. I put my hand over hers and she did not try to pull away. At that point I could not control myself. I fell forward sobbing like a baby begging her to love me like she did before.

She tried to console me but it was useless. I was a blubbering mess.

Eventually I calmed down and we talked about things in a more mature way but I was devastated. I loved this girl so much it hurt.

I left the next morning and have never seen or talked to her since, but for many months, maybe years, I thought of her every day. The pain has gone now but the memory of that innocent love lasted for a long time.

I went back to the ship and prepared to disembark with the rest of the crew who were all moving into the barracks or heading off to other assignments. As there was no reason to stay in the Plymouth area I decided I would go home to Lincolnshire for some leave. I spent a couple of weeks getting reacquainted with my old pals and family, but the pain of Shelly's memory seemed to be with me all the time.

To make things a bit better I decided I needed a car. To have a car was to have freedom in this rural backwater. During the time on the *Ark* I had managed to save a bit of money, especially in the last few months, as there had been few ports of call to spend it. Plus, despite what you might have thought in the previous chapter, very little of it was left at the Casablanca club!

It didn't take long to find a car that suited my purpose. One of my mates worked at a garage in Billingborough and he had told me he could fix a couple of problems on a car I had found, if I bought it. This was a 1957 Wolsley 690 and it was up for grabs for fifty pounds. The car was owned by a farmer, and it had been used for transporting his field gangs around.

This had resulted in it having mud all over, and on the carpets inside. The driver's door lock was broken and the door was tied with string, but other than that it was fabulous. This was a luxury vehicle, 2.6 liter straight six-cylinder engine, twin SU carb's, four-speed column change, thick carpets, leather seats, radio and room for six. (And sex, not that I had actually got any immediate prospects for that yet and after a year of celibacy, other than Mrs. Palm and her five daughters, I was ready.) But better still a car that was capable of over 100 miles an hour.

I bought the car and took it straight down to Blondie at the garage. He fixed the door lock in about ten minutes for five bob. I took it home and started to clean it up. After several hours of hard work it looked like new.

It had only done about 30,000 miles despite it being nine years old, and it ran perfectly. Road tax and insurance could wait for a few weeks until I built up my cash reserves again. After all if I bought road tax and insurance I would have nothing left for beer. Credit cards were some way away and in those days, if you didn't have cash you didn't drink.

I soon found out why it went so cheap. It drank petrol like I drank beer, a lot and often. However, this did not deter me as I had lots of mates and we could go six up; that reduced the cost of fuel if we all chipped in. In 1966 you could still buy petrol for five shillings a gallon so, a quid (one pound) was enough for sixty miles. That's providing I kept it below a hundred on the open road!

Once I had wheels I was the most popular kid around. As anticipated we could get six of us in the car and often did. Now distance was no problem. One of the options was to visit the NAAFI club at Whittering Royal Air force base near Stamford.

Because I was in the navy I could gain access to the base and sign in my pals as guests. (This was in the days before Bin Laden and other similar nuts, were hell bent on blowing up military bases.)

The location of the club, right off the A1 just two miles out of Stamford, ensured a good attendance of local girls. It was only ten miles from Peterborough also, so the place was jumping on a Saturday night.

In the '60s there were hundreds of aspiring rock bands all doing the dance hall circuits. Barry and the High-Volts,

The Jets, King Kong and the Jungle Bunnies to name just a few of the more innovative names that came and went.

The pop phenomena was in full swing and everyone was doing Beatles, Stones and Troggs numbers (most very badly) but we didn't care.

Get enough Newcastle Brown in our system and a cat howling can sound positively melodic. One night after we had some luck dancing with a couple of girls from Peterborough I had agreed to drive them home. With about seven of us in the car we set off down the A1 to their place.

As usual I was driving as fast as the car would go, about 100 mph. I noticed that we had a bit of a sway but put it down to the fact that we were well loaded. (The car *and* the driver.) However, the sway seemed to get more pronounced and with the calls to stop for bladder comfort, I finally decided to pull into a lay-by.

All the lads jumped out and lined up to pee, while I walked around the car to try to identify where the problem might be coming from. I discovered that the left rear wheel had only three of the five nuts remaining and they were so loose they could have come off at any time.

One occasion where drinking did actually prevent an accident!

I was spending a bit of time with pal Rodney who had just started his apprenticeship at Blackstones in Stamford, where they built huge diesel engines and were one of the larger employers in the area.

Rodney was prone to overconsuming beer to the point of oblivion so it was usually up to me to remain reasonably sober to get us all home safely.

Too soon my leave was over and I had to return to my ship. Because I had not purchased any insurance or road tax for the car I thought it best to leave it on the farm and travel by train.

I got back to Plymouth to discover I was to join a new mine layer still under construction in Southampton, sometime later that year

For now I was billeted in Drake barracks, the same miserable huts that we lived in before moving aboard the *Ark* prior to departing the first time. One of the delights we were subjected to was spreading DDT powder on the mattresses to kill the bed bugs before we could make up the beds.

There followed a few weeks were I was once again a free agent along with my friends who had endured the year in the Far East with me. We settled back into the old routine of hitting Union Street and "doing" the pubs. For entertainment one night we pulled the old vomit-eating stunt. This stunt was well known amongst ruby players and military men alike, and involved several props. A hot water bottle, a can of vegetable soup and several "eaters."

One designated vomitor would fill the water bottle with the soup and place it inside his shirt with the opening just below the shirt neck, out of sight. Half a dozen of us would walk into a nice bar (not our regular haunts) and after about half an hour of making it clear we were going to be trouble, but just prior to the call to the cops it was action stations. The designated vomitor suddenly clutching his chest, would declare he feels sick. Sure enough, with a good squeeze of his shirt out shot a warm (by now) can of vegetable soup all over the bar. (Vomit, to the non-informed onlooker.) The rest of us started grabbing at the "vomit" and licking our hands, proclaiming "Oh great, food at last." It's not hard to understand why several people in the bar did actually run to the toilet vomiting.

Despite fun nights like this I was still hurting inside and most of my sober hours I was miserable. I remember sitting by the potbelly stove in the middle of the mess one evening throwing in all the letters Shelly had written to me while we were away.

One of the wags in the mess said I needed to go ashore and get drunk, as that was good therapy for a broken heart. Well it was good therapy for anything in the navy. The last item to enter the open door of the stove was a rumpled photograph that had been tucked in my wallet for over a year. I watched it blacken and curl and finally burst into flames. As I watched it disappear I decided I was going to take my messmate's advice and get drunk, I mean really drunk. Bitch!

I left the barracks on my own and hit Union Street with a determination not felt for several weeks. I patronized most of the pubs one after another, sitting alone in a corner in each one as I worked my way toward the city center. I felt like I was the only person on earth who could feel this bad. I was miserable and I wanted everyone to see I was miserable. Despite more than ten pints I was still thinking about Shelly, expecting to see her in every place I looked. Finally it was closing time but I was not done yet. Now, as an Able Seaman my leave expired the next morning so I was good for the night.

Plymouth had a number of late night venues that had after hours bars so I decided to try the dance hall over the Burton men's tailors shop.

I had a couple more beers and I was about to cry in the last one when I noticed a girl across the room staring right at me. I offered a lame smile and peered back into my beer. Next thing she is right in front of me.

"Would you like to dance?"

"Err, I'm not very good and I'm a bit pissed but . . . er . . . ok."

I got to my feet now realizing that the gallon and a half of ale had begun to take its toll. We made a feeble attempt to jive and eventually gyrated together for several numbers. Although I was pretty drunk I couldn't fail to notice the very sexual way she rubbed her body against me. It was impossible to hear anything due to the volume of Bert and the Bricklayers at maximum volume so I had no idea what her name was.

Finally, using hand gestures and body squeezes, I realized she was ready to leave. We held hands down the stairs and emerged into the street outside Burtons.

"What's your name?"

"Keith, what's yours?"

"Glenda."

"Nice to meet you, Glenda, can I walk you home?"

"No, we have to get a bus, I live in Devonport."

That's handy, I thought, right outside the barracks.

With that she put her hands behind my head and pulled me forward and kissed me hard on the lips. The tongue was in my mouth in an instant and I was concerned that I might be sick after all the beer. I managed to return the tongue favor for a few seconds and not throw up.

It transpired that her dad was a Petty Officer in the navy and they lived on a street about 400 yards from the barrack gate.

We got on a bus and sat on the back seat. The girl wanted to kiss. I hadn't really taken much notice of what she looked like but coming up for air a couple of times I saw that, despite rather sharp features, she had a very nice figure and firm-looking breasts. I guessed she was a bit older than me but not by much. I never did find out how old she was.

I was quite relieved when the bus stopped and she indicated this was her stop. By now, despite my drunken demeanor, I was getting pretty excited. We walked along a dark street and turned into another street that was very steep. At regular intervals she would stop, and turn to me and kiss me hard on the lips in a very passionate way. Finally, with me nearly out of breath, she turned into a small gate and fumbled in her bag for a key. It must have been well after midnight and the place was in darkness.

She put her finger to her lips to indicate silence and opened the front door. About three feet inside was another door. She pulled me into the little porch way and closed the outer door very slowly as not to make a sound.

Once inside facing each other in the gloom we started to kiss again. Only problem now, I was desperate for a pee. As all beer drinkers know, a gallon of beer can generate four times the volume of urine. Now it was downright painful. To compound the problem Glenda was not waiting for the traditional male initiative to start the customary body search. She had her hand inside my trousers and was clutching at my somewhat depleted resources in a vain attempt to discover life.

In the end I put my mouth to her ear and whispered I just had to go.

"Oh, please don't go, you will be OK in a minute."

"No, you don't understand I have to GO."

"Oh, a piss you mean."

"Yes, a piss."

"You can't go in the house, my dad will kill you."

"Oh shit, I have to go."

"Do it in the front garden, and be quiet."

"OK, OK."

I opened the front door and stepped into the tiny front yard that had several flower tubs in it. I tried to pull the door shut so she couldn't see me taking a pee but she came out behind me.

I stumbled about in the tubs frantically trying to locate my best friend. It was too late for modesty. I think I might have reached number 36 and her house was number 22. The pressure would have been enough to start one of the *Ark Royal's* steam turbines.

Once done the release was heavenly. We squeezed back inside the door and resumed the mauling.

Now I could take part. Glenda had opened her blouse and pulled her bra up over her breasts. I helped her get her skirt round her waist and in a series of very difficult contortions managed to do some justice to all the goodies on offer. Unfortunately the beer had done its damage; not helped by the "knee trembler" stance, I was unable to complete the mission.

Once she realized I was beyond providing anything more than another face full of beer fumes she calmed down. I made a pathetic attempt to give her some pleasure with my hand but to no avail.

Embarrassed, and now painfully sober, I helped her relocate her clothing to more or less its original condition. My friend had already retreated to a stowed and secure position and a flip of the zip did the rest.

We stood facing each other in the dark with our arms around each other's necks.

"Can you come and see me tomorrow?"

"Er yes, yes I can."

By now it was tomorrow but I knew what she meant.

"OK, I will meet you at the corner of the street at the bottom of the hill."

"OK, I will see you then. Oh, what time?"

"Six OK?"

"Yeh, six is fine."

She let me out of the door and leaned out for one more mouth full of beer fumes.

I walked off down the hill and looked back to see her waving farewell as if I was going for more than seventeen hours.

Seventeen hours later I was walking out of the barrack gates heading for the meeting point. Right on time she was waiting exactly where she said. As I walked up (now completely sober) I was not sure it was the same girl. It must have been because as soon as she saw me, she ran forward and greeted me as if we had been lovers forever and I was returning from a long trip.

Not bad looking, I thought, and a great body; perhaps I will go easy on the beer tonight.

We visited a few pubs and she told me her life story. Her dad was divorced and her mother lived somewhere else.

She was an only child and worked in an office in Plymouth. I'm not sure how much I told her about myself but it didn't seem to matter.

It is obvious to me now that she was desperately lonely and wanted someone to love her. At the time I was not worldly wise enough to know. I just thought she wanted to screw. And screw we did, standing up, lying down, in the doorway, in the park, in an abandoned car and on the sea front. I think I got a whole marriage worth in, over a few months period.

Throughout the remainder of 1966 I was still living in Drake Barracks waiting for my transfer to HMS *Abdiel,* the ship that was being constructed in Southampton by Vosper Thorneycroft. To get a bit of relief I took some more leave back in Lincolnshire to try out my new car and spend some time with my old mates.

One night, Rodney and I headed off to a village dance not far from Billingborough. This was to be a very fateful evening as we both made contact with the two girls we were later to marry. Rodney knew both girls, one was his next-door neighbor and the other lived just a quarter mile away in the same village.

As usual Newcastle brown ale was to feature promi-

206

nently in the evening's proceedings. After the required amount to remove all common sense but leave enough brain function to drink, dance, and pee, we finally decided to try our hand with the girls. Rodney already had designs on Ann and I naturally adopted the other one, Sue. The village hall had a small grass paddock behind it and during a "fresh air" breather outside with the girls Rodney spotted a horse standing in the dark minding its own business.

The horse was probably thinking that Barry and the High-Volts were not going to make the top ten when Rodney, to impress the girls, decided to make a rearward assault on the horse. No, not that kind of assault; he tried to run and mount the horse like the Lone Ranger.

Now this horse may not have been a pop fan but it knew better than to let some drunken teenager hitch a free ride. As soon as Rodney touched the horse it jumped sideways, leaving Rodney flying through the air with only the ground to break his fall. To top that, the horse leaned down and bit him on his hand.

All jolly funny, and the deed no doubt clinched the deal because within two years we were both married. (To the girls, not the horse.)

When the dance ended it was customary to offer the girls a ride home but in this case Sue's father was collecting them. He, no doubt, was aware of types like Rodney and I, who just might take advantage of his daughter and steal a kiss or . . . three.

We were able to establish a second date so the next day, Sunday, we picked the girls up and went off for a picnic. I guess Sue thought I was quite a catch—big car, plenty of cash, world traveler and my family living on a farm. Little did she know I was one step from broke, the car cost fifty pounds and my father was the farm laborer, not the land-owner. Even when she found out the truth it didn't seem to deter her and by now I had discovered that she was not yet sixteen, let alone eighteen as she had told me on the first night. Now Rodney knew how old she was because she lived next door but he decided it didn't matter. I discovered how old she was when I turned up on her doorstep and she appeared from the house in a school uniform.

I was required to return to Plymouth for several more months before transferring to Southampton. Back in Plymouth I was trying to figure out a way to let Glenda down gently as I was tiring of our relationship being 75 percent sex, 20 percent drinking, and 5 percent evading her father who by now was on my case.

He apparently did not approve of any boyfriend who was in the navy. I don't blame him because all his instincts were right.

I began to limit the visits, making up stories about extra duties and training programs. On one of several weekend passes I was back home seeing Sue, by which time our relationship was beginning to take on some meaning. I had decided I needed to change my car to something I could afford to put petrol in *and* own insurance.

Rodney and I took it to Spalding and found a garage that would swap it without cash for a Ford Consul, circa 1954. The garage got the better deal but I gained ten miles to the gallon. On the way we traveled down one of the fen roads, which had a four mile straight. As a last hurrah I drove the Wolsley at over 100 mph till looming bends forced us to slow down. The Ford was a bit rusty and nowhere near as fast or as comfortable as the Wolsley but it did do more miles on a gallon.

I bought insurance and decided to drive the car to Plymouth so I would have wheels at the barracks. By now I had decided that Sue was the girl for me and Glenda had to go. I called her (Glenda) and arranged to pick her up to go out for a ride.

Like an idiot I took her out to Shaw Bridge, the place where I had such good memories of Shelly. Instead of telling her the truth and giving her the brush off, we ended up in the back seat making love for probably the fiftieth, but last time.

When we got back to her street I still had not had the guts to tell her it was over. I left like a skunk in the night, never to return another call. Character, nil points. Sorry Glenda!

As noted the car was bit rusty so I thought a coat of paint might smarten it up a bit. One day on damage control watch on the ship I persuaded the quartermaster to give me a gallon of paint and a couple of brushes out of his store.

The next night an accomplice and I brush painted the car. It was a bit streaky but a beautiful rich green, and not a patch of rust in sight. Holes were covered with a bit of masking tape several layers thick and painted over.

Last for years like that, I thought. A couple of weekends later I was driving out of the barrack gate and was stopped by the security detail.

"Nice color, lad, that wouldn't be Pusser's Brunswick Green by any chance?"

"Oh no, sir, it's, er Christmas green, I got it from Woolworths."

"Mmmmm, I bet it is. Go on, bugger off before I ask you to scrape it off and put it back in the tin."

After my sacrifices so far the navy could well afford to let me have a tin of paint.

Back in Lincolnshire the weekends took on new meaning as Rodney and Ann and me and Sue became a foursome, going out whenever I could get home.

Another favorite drinking and dancing place was the

Marco's workingmen's club in Grantham. Good thing about working men's clubs is that the beer is subsidized and you don't look out of place if you are full of it. Rodney was always a good laugh and would always end up passing out or vomiting or both.

The road home from Grantham took us up Spitlegate hill past another RAF base. We were half way up the hill one Saturday night with the engine bursting at the seams when Ann shouted from the back seat that Rodney was about to erupt. I jammed on the brakes, pulling up on the grass verge.

I ran round to the back door to drag him out before he could throw up inside. In my rush to get him out I pushed him toward the hedgerow by the side of the road. Rodney fell face forward on top of the hedge, which turned out to be Hawthorne. He was so drunk he hardly noticed the many punctures in his face and arms as we dragged him back in the car. On another occasion we were parked down a fen road late at night (for medical reasons) when he decided he needed to get out and pee. I had not realized how close we were to the ditch at the side of the lane and as he opened the back door and stepped out, he disappeared in the dark.

I opened my door and from the interior light could see the wheels were only inches from the edge of the ditch. Rodney was in the bottom, up to his knees in water and shouting at the top of his voice. It transpired that he was straddling a strip of barbed wire fencing, long past its sheep containing duties, and the more he tried to get out the deeper he was sinking in the muddy water. It took a little careful manipulation to extract him from that one.

Time flashed by and I finally transferred to Southampton in the autumn of 1966. The *Abdiel,* navy identification number N21, was in the final stages of construction but not yet ready for the crew to move on board.

The advance party, about ten of us, were required to be billeted in the little town of Shirley, just up the road from the shipyard.

Myself, a Leading Seaman and another AB, Jan, found ourselves billeted with an old lady who had three rooms to let. Jan and I were driven to the digs by the First Lieutenant, Lt. Shirley Lietchman. I had never heard of a man called Shirley so that in itself was a bit disturbing.

I do believe he came from a family with pots of money because he had an AC Cobra, yes a real AC Cobra, before they were legends in the auto world. Getting two big lads and their kit bags in an AC was quite a feat but somehow we made it the half-mile to 80 Bishops Road.

Ma was a great cook of the meat and veg brigade and her pork chops and applesauce still make my mouth water when I remember Tuesdays. We called her Ma and she called us Son, so it was a very nice place to be living especially after the wooden huts in Drake Barracks.

For some reason I had traveled to Southampton on the train and my car was back in Lincolnshire. I fixed that on my first weekend off by hitching home and coming back in the car. The incentive to go home was now high as Sue and I were getting on very well. Life was good.

There was precious little to do on the ship as the shipyard constructors were still finishing off the final fittings. Consequently we spent most of our time playing cards or walking about the shipyard looking at the expensive yachts that were under construction. I think one of them was for the Aga Kahn.

Another consequence of the ship not being ready was no weekend duty, or very little. This meant that providing I had enough money for petrol I could go home to

Lincolnshire as often as I wanted. The Leading Hand and another lad had homes en route to my place so we did a deal on petrol and I would drop them off on the way, one in North London the other in Luton.

On one trip we were driving out of Southampton when the clutch went on the Ford. This car had a low revving, 1,500 cc four-block engine with a three-speed column gear change. Consequently the torque was low in the rev range and allowed it to pull from very low speeds.

The clutch was completely fried so the only way to move was for the other two to jump out wherever we were forced to stop and push. I started the engine on the key with the car in top gear. With enough push it would start and they would jump in and off we went. This system worked fine until I was due to drop my second passenger in Luton. To anticipate the problem I decided if I stopped on a down facing hill I could get going again without too much trouble. Sure enough, with my last passenger waving in my mirror, I rolled downhill till the engine spluttered into life. All I had to do now was not stop-dead for another 100 miles.

Somehow I made it home without getting stuck. The next day, I borrowed the family car and headed for the nearest scrap yard. I found a donor Ford Consul and proceeded to lie underneath swearing until I had a replacement clutch in my hands.

Back home I spent several more hours, and all my expletives, till I had the "new" clutch installed. This was the first time I had ever separated an engine from a gearbox (or any other mechanical feat that was not part of a bicycle or a shotgun) and I was ecstatic that it worked. Little did I know that the 180-mile run without a clutch had taken its toll on the gearbox itself.

Weekends became my introduction to basic mechanics.

I could not afford to take the car to a garage so the only way to keep it going was to fix it myself.

Dismantling a Ford gearbox without an instruction manual required some trial and error. The gear wheels seemed to go in in any order, and the gear connecting rods had a mind of their own. Nevertheless I got it all back together and it seemed to work fine.

The next problem was a disturbing rumbling noise coming from the bowels of the car. I wasn't sure if it was the gearbox or the back axle.

A hand full of warmed cart grease with a similar quantity of sawdust mixed and forced, some in the gear box and some in the differential, seemed to deaden the noise and I ran it like this for several weeks. Finally I realized that something terminal was going to happen and I needed to get a more reliable car.

My dad had some modest funds in the bank and he agreed to let me borrow 200 pounds to buy a decent car. That way they wouldn't worry about me traveling home almost every weekend.

Sue's other next-door neighbor was a Scotsman who had lots of kids. He was asking me about the car one day on the road outside his house. I saw a chance to offload the car and help fund the new one.

"Fifty quid and it's yours, Jock."

"Fifty quid, that's about right, I'll take it."

The deal was struck. I hoped I would be well out of the way before he discovered the sawdust in the gearbox and the rust lurking below the Brunswick green, waiting to burst through the sticky tape.

We agreed that he would get the money the next day and I would go off and find another car to replace it using my Dad's loan. Rodney and I headed off to Spalding as we had seen several potential candidates in the local papers that might fit the bill. The emphasis was on reliability and economical on fuel.

We looked at several cars and finally came upon a garage that had two vehicles each on offer for about two hundred pounds. One was a little Triumph Herald, sporting a 995 cc engine and four-speed floor change.

The other was a strange-looking sloping big black thing that was older and had a little oval back window. It also had a two-liter engine and would no doubt drink fuel much faster than the Triumph.

With cash in hand and a quick test drive I decided it was to be the Triumph. The other car was a Bristol 403, circa early '50s, and probably now worth upwards of many thousands of pounds. Sailor V as they say.

Sure enough this little Triumph did about forty to the gallon and would just about top seventy with a following wind. However, it was so low to the ground and so stable after the top-heavy Ford it felt like I was flying.

13

Rum and Scotland the Brave

I had turned twenty in February and at twenty it was a momentous occasion for someone in the navy. At twenty, once on a ship borne commission, we were given RUM. Every day at 11:45 A.M. precisely, the call "Up Spirits" would sound.

We had now moved onboard *Abdiel* and were undergoing the first sea trials having got rid of the constructors a few weeks earlier. Most of the crew had joined, probably only about seventy officers and men in total.

The *Abdiel* was what was known as an "Exercise Minelayer." Loosely speaking this meant we would steam around dropping dummy mines and a flotilla of minesweepers would steam around picking them up.

Good deal eh. All this activity was to take place in and around the Firth of Fourth. Our base was to be HMS Lockinvar, which was essentially a jetty under the Fourth Road Bridge just north of Edinburgh. However, before we could take up station and start dropping dummy mines in the North Sea, we had to make sure the toilets worked and the ship went in the direction we pointed it.

All this activity was to be fueled by rum. Many old soaks were addicted to this nectar as the Royal Navy had been using it to coerce sailors for more than 300 years.

The rum was a 120% proof brew originally from Jamaica, although by the time I got it I believe it came from

Australia. For those below the rank of Petty Officer it was diluted in two parts water when handed over to the trembling seaman.

The mix just about filled a half-pint glass so it's not hard to see that, for a lad just starting out, instant inebriation was inevitable. We always thought if the Russians were going to invade Britain they should come about noon. We would have all been so drunk we would have asked them in for a party. Mind you the Ruskies would have been toasted on vodka so it still might have been a fair fight!

The other good thing (apart from instant inebriation) was that rum was a form of currency. If I was due to go home for a weekend I could swap just one tot, as it was known, for a seven-pound fillet of beef. Fortunately the ship's butcher had access to the officers' food stocks and he loved his rum. The grunts in the mess only got stewing beef but the officers got fillet!

There were only four or five officers on this ship so it was a complete opposite to the *Ark Royal*. Although I was still an Able Seaman I was assigned the duties of a leading hand because we didn't have many available.

We left the dock with half a dozen Vospers engineer on board and did a number of runs up and down the English Channel to test the ship's systems.

There didn't seem to be too many problems and finally the Vospers people released the ship into the capable hands of the Royal Navy (and me, who was blind drunk for two hours every day). As soon as we had finished sea trials we had to depart for Scotland. As this was to be a year-long commission I had taken the Triumph home and sold it to repay my dad his loan. That was after spending a whole weekend fitting two new drive shafts and a head gasket. So much for reliability!

If I had been kicked out of the navy I could have made a living fixing cars!

By now I was best pals with Jan from Exmore in Devon. He had an old Norton Dominator motorbike that had low gearing to pull a sidecar, but the sidecar was long gone. This meant it would scream up to eighty but was then flat out and very loud. The captain, a Scot with fire-red hair, had a little mini estate car. A couple of days before we were due to sail to Scotland he had us lift the car on board and stow it in the mine magazine at the stern of the ship.

Inspired by this flagrant departure from naval rules Jan and I, under cover of darkness, wheeled the Norton on board and hid it under some canvas in another part of the magazine. If the skipper could have his vehicle, we were going to have ours.

The ship had been officially transferred to the Royal Navy on Jan 22nd 1967 and, after completing the sea trials, we left the comfort of Vosper Thorneycroft in Southampton and cruised out into the English Channel.

Our course was to take us east through the narrow Dover Straits and into the North Sea. This boat was so small by navy standards that it only required the officer of the watch on the bridge with one lookout, a helmsman in the wheelhouse, a couple of engineers below and the leading hand of the watch to circulate the ship during non-working hours.

The wheelhouse was unique on the *Abdiel* because it was just below the bridge and had a porthole in the front looking out over the forecastle. Once we were under way and out of the Isle of White navigation channel the skipper left Sub Lt. Bride in charge on the bridge and went below to get his dinner and turn in for the night. I was Leading-Hand of the watch and proceeded to take up my first ever seagoing trip actually in charge of something.

I put a lad called Pete on the wheel and sat back in the

wheelhouse to read a magazine before I took the mandatory walkabout to see everything was OK around the ship. Pete was a boxer from Derbyshire and although a nice enough chap was not the sharpest knife in the drawer. It might have been the constant blows to the head that made him that way but he did require some extra attention.

Sub Lt. Bride was enjoying himself on the bridge being his first shot at being in charge too.

"Leading Hand, can you see that ship dead ahead?"

I jumped up to the voice pipe and answered as I peered out of the little round porthole. "Yes Sir, I see it."

"Well, follow that ship."

I had never been told to follow a ship before but it seemed reasonable to me. I gestured Pete to sit down and took over the little wheel. We followed the lights for about half an hour till "Dickey" called down a course to follow as I guess the other ship had gone in a direction we didn't want to.

I put Pete back on the wheel and picked up my magazine again. "Steer 085 helmsman," came the order. "Aye Aye Sir."

The ship was equipped with the same type of gyrocompass that the *Ark* had. It was quite simple to follow unless you suffer with a tendency to "follow the lubbers line." This referred to the mistake of turning the wheel in the complete opposite direction to what was needed.

The problem was that the display on the compass was a narrow oblong window in which the numbers moved across behind a static line in the center, as the ship's head turned. If you wanted to alter course to starboard (right to you land lubbers) you turned the wheel to the . . . right, got it. Simple enough, but of course the compass numbers would click away to the left creating an optical illusion that you were doing it backwards. When given an order "Starboard 5" it was easy enough to put 5 degrees of turn on the wheel and wait for the order "Midships" at which point you returned the wheel to the center. Once the officer on the bridge saw he had adjusted his course to where he wanted it he would then say, "Steer 085" or whatever course suited his purpose. At that point it was up to the helmsman to keep that course until told otherwise.

To control the heading required small adjustments on the wheel to keep the designated course right on the line in the compass display.

I was deeply into trying to separate the center page of a crumpled two-year-old *Playboy* when I felt the ship beginning to list to one side. I looked up to see Pete frantically spinning the wheel with a look of extreme panic on his face.

I knew instantly that he was following the line. The more he spun the wheel the harder the ship turned the wrong way. By now we were heeled over at about a 15° list and things were beginning to fall off shelves and out of lockers that were not closed properly. I could hear Dickey screaming down the voice pipe but Pete was in a trance. I pushed him out of the way and grabbed the wheel just as the skipper, red hair flowing and with only a towel round his waist, come barging into the wheelhouse. At the same time I was conscious of a distant ship's siren sounding. As the skipper came in the door he managed to put his flip flopped foot right into a metal waste bin that had rolled across the deck.

We now had the skipper clanking about with one foot stuck in the waste bin, his towel starting to fall off, Dickey yelling down the voice pipe like a demented mental patient. Pete standing rigid at the side of the wheelhouse, unable to speak and me desperately trying to unravel the ship from its 360° spin.

To compound the problem we were doing this about half a mile ahead of a huge oil tanker (sounding its sirens)

219

because in the narrow English Channel shipping lanes he had nowhere to go other than right over us.

Despite the seriousness of the situation my sense of humor got the better of me and I started to laugh out loud. Bad plan. The skipper was bright red in the face as well as on the hair and he was still trying to get the bin off his foot and yell at me from about two inches away.

Fortunately for me I remembered the course we were supposed to be on and decided it was quicker to go the full circle and straighten up than try to reverse the turn.

Dickey had gone quiet on the bridge and I looked out of the porthole to see the lights of the tanker passing quickly by looking extremely close to our bow.

Still no orders from the bridge so I spun the wheel hard opposite to stop the turn and the ship heeled upright as I managed to get her back on course without too many more erratic turns of the wheel.

We had made a full 360° circle less than a quarter mile ahead of an 80,000-ton taker in a very narrow shipping lane.

I'm glad I was not responsible for the explanation to the Admiralty when the skipper of the tanker called that one in. It was an event fully worthy of HMS *Troughtbridge* of the "Navy Lark" fame, the comedy show I loved when I was a kid on the farm on those Sundays I enjoyed so much. The skipper marched off back to his cabin, after finally extracting his foot from the waste bin and only just stopping his towel from coming right off. No doubt I was to hear about this in the morning. Finally Dickey's shaky voice comes back down the voice pipe. "Well done, Manton, you have probably just completely fucked my career." Pete had regained some semblance of reason and started to stutter an explanation for his screw up. "Forget it, Pete, if I ever write a book it will make a great story."

I did hear about it in the morning and the skipper decided that Able Seaman Peter Boise was not to be assigned helmsman duties again, anywhere within 500 miles of another vessel. (Basically, anywhere in the sea.)

Dickey had been given a good talking to but the skipper seemed to understand that everyone and everything was new so he gave us a little slack.

We steamed up the East Coast into the North Sea. Next stop was Hartlepool in County Durham as the *Abdiel* was the adopted ship of this town. We got in on the Friday and were due to leave on Monday morning.

This was particularly good for me as my Uncle Ray and Aunty Eve lived in Hartlepool and they were known to throw the odd party.

Sure enough they were planning some R&R for me when we arrived, me having called them ahead of time. Once we had docked Uncle Ray picked me up and took me to their house. That Friday night we went to a nightclub near Billingham where Roy Orbison was performing.

Good show and plenty of laughs. (Laughs not because of Mr. Orbison, rest his soul.)

The next evening was the local chapter Free Masons annual ball. This required Ray and Eve to go off to the proceedings early and Ray could collect me later after the official (top secret) stuff was concluded.

About nine Ray arrived at the house and we set off for the Masonic hall. We arrived during a performance of some local classical instrumental trio who were wailing away on the stage. Apart from this very eerie sound the room was in silence as hundreds of blank faces stared at the spectacle on stage.

The bar was by the door as we came in so Uncle Ray and I began to pour ourselves a beer, with our backs to the performance. I have mentioned my propensity to giggle and Uncle Ray seemed to have the same problem. I noticed his shoulders starting to shudder; then he let a couple of chuckles slip. Next thing we are both chortling away like two school kids, much to the annoyance of the people near us who seemed to think the trio were good. It took several minutes of standing out in the hallway before we dare go back inside.

The next day Ray and Eve were throwing a Sunday afternoon party for their friends. As Ray was a Free Mason and was the manager of the local May & Hassell timber importers at the dock, quite a few of the Saturday crowd numbered in the Sunday guest list. This included the mayor and other town officials but also included the Harbor Master. The concept of a drinking party on Sunday afternoon was new to me but I was just happy to be there.

During the afternoon I got talking to the Harbor Master who, by then, was well on his way to a good hangover. He told me the weather was looking a bit dicey for the morning and we were due to sail in the forenoon. He asked me if I would like to stay another day because if I did he would tell my skipper he would not release the ship because it was too risky. I declined his kind offer but felt very powerful that I might have been instrumental in stopping a Royal Navy ship from sailing on time.

After a very good weekend we did sail the next day. The weather <u>was</u> bad and we came close to hitting the sea wall as we exited the harbor.

We arrived at HMS Lockinvar and tied up at the jetty. This was to be our base for a year. The base was literally right underneath the Fourth Road Bridge and only about ten miles north of the city of Edinburgh.

First job was to unload the skipper's mini. The Norton had to wait for a quiet moment when all the officers were otherwise engaged. Now we could head for Edinburgh on the motorbike. At the first chance Jan and I got dressed up in suit and tie, mounted the bike and off we went to explore the city.

Crash helmets were not mandatory at the time so we looked petty cool in our suits cruising into Princess Street on a Norton.

We found a place to park the bike and hit the pubs. Running parallel to Princess Street was the narrow Rose Street where many of the pubs were. This was quite a rough area in 1967 so one had to be a little careful.

Jan was a bit older than me but a less experienced drinker. Like Rodney, he tended to get intoxicated much faster than I did. This was not a problem till it was time to head back to the ship, some ten miles away.

We finally remembered where we had parked the bike and Jan swung his leg over to fire it up. He promptly tipped right over and fell on the ground the other side.

I was, by now, an accomplished car driver but other than the one-minute attempt to ride cycle master when I was about twelve—had no motorcycle skills.

Jan was in no condition to even start the bike and he sat on the ground just laughing. There was only one thing for it—I had to drive.

The bike was quite wide and heavy and had the traditional kick-start on the side of the engine. I fiddled around with the controls for a few seconds and gave it a kick. Sure enough it started first time. Now all I had to do was get Jan on board and figure out how to engage the gears and get going. Jan obliged by climbing on behind me and wrapping his arms around my waist.

I found a gear and gingerly edged forward. We stalled so I concluded it was too high a gear, so I tried another position and set off again. This time we started moving and I wobbled my way down a narrow alley to the main road. Jan was resting his head on my back and I was pretty sure he was

223

asleep. I was not going to get any technical directions from the back seat.

Once on the road I turned the throttle and we speeded up. I kicked up the gear lever and found another position that seemed to be going in the right direction. I wasn't sure how many gears it had and because of the low ratio box for the long departed sidecar the engine tone was not a good guide as to which gear I was in.

We made it out of the town center and I miraculously found the way to Queens Ferry Road, which would take us north and back to the ship. Once out of the city I opened the throttle wide and let the bike surge forward. By now I was getting the hang of it and my inhibitions were suppressed. (Probably aided by about eight pints of McEwans fine ales.) I did discover another higher gear and soon the speedometer was flickering on the eighty. At this point the dial behind the needle started to slowly rotate backwards caused by the vibration.

After that it was impossible to tell how fast we were going but I didn't care. Jan was still hanging on and silent so I assumed he was either still asleep or confident I could get us home without mishap. We arrived on the jetty without incident and I pulled over to the storage shed that we had commandeered to house the bike during the day; we stowed the bike. The watchkeeper on the gangway just shrugged as we came on board, so we went below to bed. It was probably one in the morning.

This routine continued every time we were able to go ashore. Jan would drive us into town and I would drive us home.

Responsibility is a funny thing; if I know that I have to be in charge of getting us home safely the alcohol seems to be less debilitating. If I know that someone else has the reins, then I go downhill much faster.

On one particularly liquid night we tottered back to the bike at some ungodly hour in the early morning. As usual it was me who tried to get the bike started. It was a bitingly cold night but we still only wore our suit and tie. I tried to kick the bike for what seemed like forever until I finally gave up and stepped off the thing.

Convinced it was a mechanical problem I dropped to my knees in the slush and tried to peer into the engine as if to diagnose the problem After a few minutes of peering, for what I had no idea, I suddenly noticed a rubber pipe that was hanging at the side of the engine, and not attached to anything at the bottom end. The pipe was cut at an angle as if someone had slit through it with a sharp knife. "Fucking hell, Jan, some bastard has cut the fuel pipe."

That was it; we had been vandalized. Even in my diminished condition I knew trying to fix the fuel pipe in the dark with no tools or tape was not going to happen. Only one thing for it, we would have to find somewhere to sleep for the rest of the night and try to make it back to the ship before 8:00 A.M.

We tottered off down the street and eventually came across a hostel that still had a light on. (Maybe the first Motel 6.) A scruffy-looking bloke with a strong resemblance to a Neanderthal was reading a paper in a booth at the front door. I enquired how much a room would be for the night (of which there was only about three hours left). "Five bob each and another five bob if you piss the bed."

The "room" was in fact the whole hostel, full of bunk beds, which in turn were full of infested stinking individuals who I was sure would all be paying the extra five bob in the morning. We paid our money and Neanderthal man pointed out two empty beds on one side of the aisle.

I let Jan take the bottom because if he was going to piss I wanted to be on the top. If I were going to piss he probably would not notice. In any case pissing in these beds would have improved the smell.

I asked Neanderthal man to make sure we were woken at 6:30 A.M. to which he replied, "I suppose you would like morning tea and the *Times* too, sir." Not to be provoked by his sarcasm I climbed onto the top bunk and fell asleep instantly.

I awoke with a start and as my eyes adjusted to the gloom I could see all manner of life's dregs shuffling about the room. I looked at my watch and saw it was nearly 7:30. Even if we could get the bike going it would take thirty minutes to get to the ship. We were AWOL for sure.

Neanderthal man was nowhere to be seen but the stench of urine and body odor was enough to remind me he would be at the door collecting five bob from nearly everyone. I dropped to the floor and tried to figure out where the toilet was. I made a guess and headed in that direction. A door at the end did in fact say Toilet and Shower. The description was accurate because there was one toilet and one shower, both of which held a urinating bundle of rags mumbling obscenities at no one in particular. I could not wait another second so I took the unofficial third option, which was a drain hole in the middle of the floor.

Once relieved I went back to find Jan. He was standing by the bunk with a bewildered look on his face and I invited him to use the facility PDQ as we needed to go. Once outside (now fairly sober) we realized just how cold it was. Further, we were not too sure where the bike was either.

After searching several streets we found the thing leaning over at an angle on its stand. I took another look at the cut pipe and instantly realized it was the oil vent pipe, not the fuel line. I straddled the bike and gave it a kick. It fired first time. Perhaps there is a God after all!

We arrived back at the jetty running about thirty minutes late. Fortunately the guy on gangway duty liked his rum so after a couple of finger gestures denoting the size of the measure he would get for not stopping us, we got to work before anyone in authority knew we were missing.

The sea was always rough once we got out of the shelter of the Firth so day trips to drop our dummy mines were always exciting. I really loved the rough sea and this boat moved about a lot. Much of the time it was necessary to have a lifeline attached to the rail that ran around the side of the superstructure so if you got hit by a wave you at least stayed on board (probably with a couple of broken bones but not drowned).

By now I was writing frequently to Sue, and Jan to his fiancée. One weekend sometime in the winter we decided to rent a car and drive to Lincolnshire. Jan's fiancée was to travel up from Devon to the farm and we would all have a weekend together in Lincolnshire. It was a little over three hundred miles from the base to the farm so we decided the bike was not an option.

We found a place in Edinburgh where we rented a Mark 1 Ford Cortina. This car was the first of a breed of very light and very fast economy middle size cars. It was so different to the heavyweight sluggish behemoths of the fifties, I thought it could fly.

We made the trip in just under five hours, most of the open road at over one hundred mph. At that time the A1 still had major sections of two-way traffic and many crossing points.

I leave it your imagination to determine if we acted responsibly!

We had a great weekend with the girls and I believe this was the weekend I proposed marriage. Based on the record trip time coming down, we departed about midnight on the Sunday night. This would give us enough time to get us back

227

to drop the car and collect the bike in Edinburgh and thus to the ship before 8:00 A.M.

At that time we never considered it important to have a night's sleep, so planning the trip with an overnight drive was the norm. Fifty miles into the trip we hit fog.

In the sixties we were still getting those pea-soup fogs that literally shut down the country for hours.

The A1 Ferry Bridge bypass in South Yorkshire was under construction at the time and we hit the fog as we approached that section. It got so thick that I was driving at five mph with my leg outstretched on the accelerator and my head out of the window to improve visibility.

It was impossible to see anything, even other tail lights. After about half an hour we trundled over a bump and I swerved to avoid a barrier in the road. We seemed to go down a little hill and I saw a light in front of the car. As I stopped I thought it looked like a red phone box. We got out of the car and went round to the front. Sure enough it was a phone box, in the middle of the A1?

No so, we were in some kind of parking area and obviously not still on the A1. After walking out in circles around the car we identified the entrance / exit back to a road. We set off with Jan walking in front till he yelled that he could see a sign to the A1. He jumped back in and I followed the signs as best as I could see. Sure enough we found our way back onto a dual carriageway. After a few minutes the fog lifted a little and we could speed up to about twenty mph. I caught sight of another sign with A1 at the top but could not read the rest. Gradually the fog began to lift and we were up to good speeds. We still had time to make it back as long as we did not have any more holdups.

Next sign we saw as the fog cleared said, "Newark fifteen miles." Bugger! We had gone about thirty miles back in the wrong direction!

We finally made it back at the ship at 10:00 A.M. and both lost two day's leave and two day's pay for being AWOL. Lucky for us we were not due to sail that day otherwise we would have prevented the ship from sailing, as we were sort of critical with such a small crew. After Christmas leave, back in Lincolnshire, and with an August date fixed for the nuptials I, once again, returned to Scotland.

Feb 1st came round being my 21st birthday. We were somewhere out in the Firth of Forth anchored off a little town. I was about to be Leading Hand of the afternoon watch but my mind was on 11:45 A.M. up spirits.

On your birthday the routine was for the other mess members to contribute part of their tot of rum to a glass (or glasses in this case) placed on the table for the birthday boy. I arrived in the mess to see two pint glasses of the amber liquid, one full to the brim, the other about half full (or is that half empty?)

All the lads were sat around waiting for me to partake. I managed to get it all down in about five minutes and felt an instant desire to love everyone, even Sub Lt. Bride. It was the most rapid descent into inebriation I have ever experienced. I could hear birds singing, girls whispering sweet nothings and I had not a care in the world.

I made it to the dining room as it was agreed some food would lessen the final impact of the dose.

The next impact was my face hitting the table as I fell flat out dead drunk.

I was finally brought back to consciousness sometime after 5 P.M. with several worried-looking mates standing by my bunk. Apparently it had been touch and go whether to call in a helicopter and fly me to Rosyth Hospital for a stomach pump.

I felt like shit for the next week and don't think I have ever got drunk on rum since.

The skipper kindly overlooked my absence from the day's affairs, fully expecting someone turning twenty-one to be shit-faced all day.

14

More Foreign Parts

Sometime in the summer we left our base in Scotland and headed for Amsterdam. Apparently the navy had been invited to participate in some celebration between the Dutch and the Brits. We didn't care why we were going just that we had the chance of a trip ashore in a new location.

We made our way right into the heart of the city, which is built around canals, so the *Abdiel* was an easy fit. After securing alongside we were all told to muster on deck to be briefed on our visit.

"This is an official visit and you are to be all on your best behavior." The Captain was in his full dress uniform and looked like he was off on some cocktail binge with the rest of the officers. "Shore leave will be in uniform only, so let's put on a good show, lads." That was it, we were so used to going ashore in civilian clothes it was a bit of a surprise to be restricted to uniform.

Nevertheless, we were in Amsterdam and we were not going to let the uniform spoil our fun. A couple of the old lags had told us to go window shopping on Canal Street but the significance of that was lost on we "skins." Jan and I left the ship at about noon and headed for the city center.

We were only about ten minutes walk from the city center so we ambled along looking for a nice bar to have our first refresher. We found a little café and walked in. It had half a dozen small tables and a short bar on one side. Other than a lone bar maid we had the place to ourselves.

I remembered the strange scotch ale I had discovered in Oostende and thought that would be a good place to start. Happy to be in new surroundings we sat and drank several brews and still had the place to ourselves. After a couple of hours (and brews) Jan stood up, a little unsteady on his feet, and looked around for a toilet. The bar maid gestured to a door at the other side of the bar and he headed through it. A few minutes later he returned and sat down and continued drinking his scotch ale.

A few minutes later the street door burst wide open and two large policemen came purposefully marching in. The bar maid pointed right at Jan. Without a word they hauled Jan to his feet and frog marched him to the door. Now I was a bit mellow though still sort of OK but I had no idea what was going on.

I stood up to chase after them when I realized the floor was covered with a couple of inches of water. Still confused I rushed through the door to see Jan being unceremoniously pushed into the back of VW van. One cop had gone round to the driver's door and the other was climbing in the passenger side. Intent on saving my friend from this manic assault I ran to the van as it started to pull away. The sliding passenger door, which served the right rear side, was still being pulled shut as I grabbed at the handle.

The van left but the door stayed. I found myself lying on the pavement with the VW door across my chest. The van stopped with a screech of brakes and the cops came running back and hauled me to my feet. Now I was thrown in the van and an irate cop was trying to fit the door back on its runners. After a couple of minutes he managed to secure the door and we set off with the siren screaming.

We arrived at the police station and still without a word

spoken were marched down some steps into a dingy office. After a confusing twenty minutes trying to understand what the problem was and filling in our names on a form, we were pushed into a dingy cell.

After a couple of minutes our eyes adjusted to the low light and we could see all manner of weird individuals sitting around on wooden benches.

Some were obviously so drunk they didn't stir at all. Others gave us a passing glance but took little further interest.

In all there were probably twenty men of different ages sitting around with nowhere to go. The place stank of urine and vomit and it was not long before the aroma got to me. I managed to prevent most of my vomit from hitting anyone who looked big enough to tear my head off but alas, not my white shirt.

Jan had slumped into a corner and sat with his head in his hands, now showing the dangerous signs of sobering up and realizing the deep shit we were in. I had lost my hat and one shoe and now had a nice dark vomit stain down my white front to complete the ensemble.

The skipper's words flooded back with alarming clarity as I tried to reason what had happened to incur the wrath of the Amsterdam police. Then I remembered the water on the bar floor. It transpired (when the police finally informed my superiors of the offense) that Jan had broken the little sink and plumbing in the toilet and caused the flood. The bar maid, believing we were English sailors on a drunken binge, assumed that it was intentional and called the cops.

Jan did not have a vandalistic bone in his body; he even picked up other people's litter, so I knew he did not do this intentionally.

Anyway, here we were sitting in a jail, uniforms a mess, no idea what we had done and surrounded by drunks, thieves and drug addicts. After what seemed like hours the door slid back and one of our escorts called my name. I walked to the door and he grabbed my arm. I thought I was going to be interrogated so I shuffled along (with one shoe) as best I could. Gripping my arm like a vice he hauled me up the steps to the front door and pushed me out into the street.

After yelling something at me in Dutch and waving his arm in a get lost manner, he slammed the door in my face.

OK, I'm in the street but my best buddy is still in jail. I was always told that if you get into trouble in a foreign land you get help from the British Consul. Without another thought I looked around for a taxi. The driver gave me some strange looks but decided I was harmless enough; with only one shoe he could have outrun me anyway.

"Take me to the British Consul."

We arrived at the consulate in a very short time, so I suspect it was just round the corner but he made a few guilders on the deal. I jumped out and purposefully marched up the steps to the front door to be met by two uniformed sailors barring my way.

I didn't recognize them so they were obviously not from the *Abdiel*. I demanded to see the British consul on an urgent matter. One of the guards stood in my way but the other opened the door and stepped inside.

As the door opened I could see a big crowd of uniforms and other people dressed in their finery. Now I knew where the skipper was going in his dress uniform. Fuck. Before I could retreat I was grabbed by two MPs, courtesy of the Dutch Navy. They had mysteriously appeared behind me. I was invited to join them in their Land Rover and they drove me to the ship.

It was pointless trying to explain to them what had happened so I sat silent till they marched me onboard. I felt sure the Skipper had caught a glimpse of me, vomit-stained and hatless, on the steps of the Consulate so I knew I was in for the high jump.

Sub Lt. Bride was the unfortunate officer who was left onboard as officer of the watch and he had been waiting to get his own back after the tanker incident in the channel. I did my best to mitigate the horror of the afternoon but he seemed somewhat skeptical about my story.

I did manage to make him understand that Jan was probably having his feet thrashed with canes in the jailhouse and being forced to confess to murder. I spent an uncomfortable night in a four ft. by six ft. steel locker equipped with a bunk and a bucket.

Next morning I was invited to join the skipper for morning tea on the quarterdeck. I think his hangover was worse than mine because he forgot the tea. Jan, having been returned to the ship by the police just a few minutes before, was standing at attention with his hat behind his back.

"You horrible imbecile. Have you any idea how embarrassing it was to see you in that state at an official function, the Mayor, the Ambassador. As for you, Craven, you are a disgrace. Neither of you will ever come to anything in this man's navy with that kind of behavior."

The tirade went on for some time as we stood as still as we could. Our pathetic attempt to explain did nothing to reduce the Skipper's anger so we decided it was better to get it over and take our medicine. Five days leave and five days loss of say seemed to do the trick. At this rate I would be working for nothing.

As for the Skipper's prediction about our worthlessness, I heard several years later that Jan had made it to the rank of Master at Arms, the highest non-commissioned rank in the navy, and basically a ship's Chief of Police!

As for me, well you will have to judge for yourself.

We had to endure the next several days sitting out our time in Amsterdam on board as our leave had been revoked. We were pleased to get back to the routine of Lockinvar and mostly day trips out at sea to drop our dummy mines.

My next assignment (if I chose to accept it) was to join HMS *Fife* a new County class destroyer. But before that, I was transferred to Portsmouth for the summer of 1968 to wait until my embarkation date on the *Fife*, of January 2nd.

When I arrived in Portsmouth I was billeted on HMS *Belfast*, which at the time was mothballed in the Naval Dockyard and used as an accommodation ship. It now helps deposit rust in the Thames in London and cracks old ladies' shins with its steel ladders. While in Portsmouth I volunteered to train as ship's diver. I passed the aptitude test in a large tank wearing bottles and fins (scuba gear). I was sent to Plymouth to start the training course and mustered on the first day with about twenty other volunteers.

The first day was in the classroom where we learned about all the things that can kill you whilst diving. No air, too much air, air in your bloodstream (the bends), crushing by big ships, propeller blades, sharks, eels, etc., etc.

I was not too sure I wanted to do the second day but I turned up anyway. After half an hour in a decompression chamber, where the pressure makes you talk like Donald Duck, we were introduced to the proper stuff in the shape of a deep-sea suit, helmet and lead boots.

The idea was for us to don the suits and be lowered twenty feet into the water off the jetty and chop a piece of chain in half with a hammer and chisel. I was fine till they put my feet into the lead boots. It was like someone gripped my throat, I couldn't breathe.

Ten minutes with the medical officer later I was diagnosed as having acute claustrophobia brought on by the immobility of my feet. I always thought this condition was something to do with being in an enclosed space but he was the doctor and I was an Able Seaman. In this case an unable seaman, when it came to diving.

Back in Portsmouth I spent most of the time playing field hockey and worrying about getting married. I remember one game where my team played an all female Wrens team. Getting a hockey stick hooked up your crotch from behind, ten seconds into the match introduced an element of fear that forced you to get rid of the ball instantly. Thankfully I resisted resorting to the tactics of a teammate who suffered the same provocation, by head-butting their captain in a tackle. He got sent off, the girls won by an embarrassingly wide margin and I gave up field hockey.

Sue and I got married on August 30th 1968. I was twenty-one and Sue was seventeen and one day.

We borrowed my family's MG Magnette and honeymooned in Norfolk and went to see the *Jungle Book* after nearly getting killed by an oncoming Jag as we were on the way down to Oulton Broad.

After the honeymoon we found a furnished flat in Portsmouth and moved in for the remainder of the year, waiting for the transfer to Chatham.

I now needed another car so we could travel home to see family and friends. I found a Renault Dauphine going for twelve pounds. I still have the little paper receipt that the garage owner gave me. It didn't start but other than that it had most of the bits required to go once I had figured out how to make it start.

I found a little back street garage who advertised cheap repairs. After the massive investment in the vehicle I had little money for repairs. The mechanic soon identified the trouble. The wiring loom around the side of the engine (in the rear of the car) was burned through. By some miracle he happened to have another Dauphine on the blocks under piles of other junk cars in the backyard.

He pulled out the required bits and had it running in about half an hour. The cost, one pound, ten shillings. I now had a running vehicle for an investment of thirteen pounds, ten shillings. It still had road tax and I had some credit from my previous insurance on the Triumph so we were off.

Once married I became eligible for married quarters so we applied for a quarter in Chatham ready to move into after Christmas. Little did we know that the army had moved their people out because it was an awful slum. The army had kindly signed it over to the navy.

We went home to Lincolnshire for the Christmas holiday and headed to Chatham after Christmas. On the way down, with all our worldly possessions crammed into every piece of available space, we hit a Dalmatian on the A15 near Yaxley, just south of Peterborough. The dog rolled over a few times in the road and then jumped up and ran off at lightning speed. Obviously the pride of the French automobile industry was not heavy enough to kill a Dalmatian whilst doing fifty mph. (The car not the dog.)

I got out and surveyed the damage. The left front wing, already well rusted and patched with masking tape, had completely peeled back converting the left front half on my car to an open wheel racer.

The impact had also fractured the part of the frame that supported the shock absorber inside the wheel mounting. That also exhibited some advanced corrosion. It still looked like it was holding together so I pulled the flapping metal work away from the car and dumped it in the hedgerow.

By the time we arrived in Chatham the left front side was curtseying to the onlookers and let out a piercing squeal if the steering was turned too hard to the left. We managed to find our quarter and went inside to survey our new home.

It stank of damp, or piss or both. The Spartan furniture was shit brown and had all manner of stains in different colors. The bed sagged in the middle and the floors, apart from a filthy rug in the sitting area, were vinyl.

This same flooring in the bathroom was split and curled up around the bath and toilet and it smelled awful. My bride sat down on the sofa and wept. This place made Rackman look like a philanthropist.

We spent a miserable half hour carting in our limited possessions, mostly household type wedding gifts. Two toasters; a furry, hot water bottle; polyester sheets; and a few other items that probably eventually ended up at a jumble sale.

The next morning I left Sue sobbing at the front door and went to the dockyard to find HMS *Fife*. The *Fife*, a County Class Destroyer, was a fairly new ship and was equipped with sea slug and sea cat missile systems.

As a gunner, my job, apart from regular seagoing stuff, was to handle missile movement in the magazines. We had six months to train up to full operational readiness and then we were off to South America, through the Panama Canal and up the west coast of the USA, finally ending up in Vancouver, Canada.

The next several weeks were a blur of new experiences. I had never even seen these missile systems but in less than six months I was supposed to be able to deliver a three-ton Sea Slug to the launcher on the stern without setting off the one ton of TNT that lurked inside.

The magazine was like a mini railway shunting yard. Each missile was on a trolley that could be wheeled along on narrow gage tracks using sophisticated hydraulic control systems. My job was to move them about, as they were made ready to be poked up into the launcher.

All this time, life at home was getting worse. The place

was so bad and the neighbors even worse, that it was soon clear we could not live in this place. I complained to my divisional officer but got nowhere. At the same time I was having problems with my left knee. I had injured it by falling on a concrete floor a couple of years before and it would often lock or let me down at a crucial moment. It was a good job, we didn't have to carry the missiles like the old shells of the four-inch guns

I had had several examinations by the ship's doctor and even been sent to the Queen's own Orthopedic surgeon in Portsmouth.

They claimed there was nothing wrong and thought I was trying to "work my ticket," a term used to describe sailors who wanted out but had no valid reason to dump Her Majesty before our time was up.

However, my knee was a real problem. All navy ships have steep steel ladders and when we were required to move fast in drills I would always manage to clout my knee at least once a day.

After two miserable months I agreed to take Sue home to her mother's and abandon the married quarter. We had also decided that we would have a baby, not the most sensible strategy in our current circumstances but that was the plan. By moving onto the ship it did enable me to get back on the rum issue, so it wasn't all bad!

In any case we were due to depart in a couple of months and be gone for almost a year. That prospect did not sit well with either of us but much less so with Sue. At least I got the rum! Subconsciously I decided that I had to get out of the navy before the departure date. I knew once we sailed I would have to do the full trip, as they were not too keen on retraining people halfway into a commission.

Several weekends I traveled home and fell back into the routine of spending most of it covered in grease trying to keep my rapidly disintegrating Renault from falling apart. I fitted a wooden block into the frame on the front nearside wheel arch and bolted it together to hold the shock absorber up. It worked like that until I finally got rid of it several months later. I had also found a replacement wing and headlight unit and hoped I would not encounter any more flying Dalmatians.

I deliberately started going back late and getting hauled up in front of the Captain. I tried to convince my divisional officer my knee was causing me to be dangerous but to no avail. After several weeks of deliberate rule breaking, and about fourteen days before we were due to leave for the other side of the Atlantic, I was finally granted a compassionate discharge from the navy.

However, I had to stay on for another six weeks so they could train a replacement TNT jockey. Now I did not do well in math at school but even I could figure out that there are forty-eight days in six weeks and only fourteen of them were to be in Chatham. Or was that forty-two?

I told my divisional officer I had to go home before the ship sailed or I would be walking back from Panama. I thought I had permission to leave so that I could spend the remaining six weeks of my naval career at home but somehow with lack of communication it got a bit screwed up. So after waiting over a week with the departure day looming with incredible menace, I loaded up my Renault with everything I was allowed to keep, the rest I dropped off at the Master at Arms office in the dockyard.

I drove to the gates and after giving the finger to the sentry for good measure, I headed for home. It was June 6th, two days before the *Fife* was due to sail. Officially I was AWOL as I did not have permission to leave at that juncture, however, my paperwork showing I was a civilian showed up two weeks later, but I knew if I was on that ship when it left the dock I was gone for nine months.

After winding my way out of Chatham and heading north in the direction of Lincolnshire I had plenty of time to reflect on my naval career and the position I was in. Seven years had passed in a flash and I had gone from a boy who knew nothing of the real world to a man who knew a lot, with a wife and child on the way.

15

Civvy Street Here I Come

Once home in Lincolnshire, living with the in-laws, no civilian qualifications, just married and pregnant, no money, no prospects and a sick Renault things looked bad. Because I left school at fifteen I had not taken any academic tests that conferred the slightest indication that I was even literate. The prospect of landing a job that did not require some amount of heavy lifting was remote to say the least.

As Winston said in 1940, "This is our darkest hour." Anyway, things were a bit tricky. Fortunately the economy was in fair shape so there were jobs around, they were just not quite what I had in mind. In fact I didn't have anything in mind, I had not a clue how the hell I was going to support my new family or secure a home of our own.

As usual, when impending disaster is looming the pub proves to be a good place to regroup. One evening, just a few days into my civilian career (joke), I was sipping a freebee pint and talking to a casual acquaintance in the Fortesque Arms. He told me that his employer, the Amey Sand and Gravel Company, were looking for lorry drivers. Well, I could drive a car, and a tractor, how difficult could it be to drive a lorry? He gave me the number of the works foreman and told me to call him the next day. The following Monday I am sitting in the site hut at Amey Sand and Gravel at Baston Pit near Peterbourough.

The foreman interviewed me for a little while asking about my experience as a lorry driver. In those days the HGV (heavy goods vehicle) license rules had not yet been established, so all you needed was a basic car driver's license. I told the foremen I had been driving navy heavy good vehicles in the Far East for several years and had plenty of experience. Well, a ship is a heavy good vehicle, I just forgot to mention it was a ship, that's all.

To try me out he agreed to let me start the following Monday by driving one of their 6-wheel delivery bulk vehicles to some local customers. I arrived at the site in good time and the foreman gave me a once over on the various controls in the lorry. He stood and watched me as I tried to reverse the 6-wheeler under a loading shoot. After about three attempts, I got the lorry under the shoot and felt the 16-ton load drop into the back in just a few seconds. The foreman climbed in the cab and told me to head out of the gate and to then turn left. We set off in the direction of Spalding where the load was to be delivered. Things were fine until we came into a little village where cars were parked along the street, making the way through, very narrow.

I had never driven a vehicle of this size (other than the aircraft carrier) so it was a bit daunting trying to judge the gap. I managed to miss the cars but mounted the pavement (sidewalk to our American cousins) and bounced back down on the road a little heavy. My instructor grumbled something under his breath and gestured for me to carry on. We found the building site where the load was destined for and tipped it out on the ground. We drove in silence back to the base and got out of the cab. I thought I had done quite well but he didn't. "Too heavy on the vehicle," he said, "you need some more practice before I can let you on the road."

I wondered how I could practice without *being* on the road.

244

He solved the mystery by walking me over to a giant Volvo dump truck parked on the site. These trucks were used to transport the gravel from the pits to the processing plant, which separated out the various grades of sand and gravel. The pit, where the dragline was dredging, was a couple of miles from the plant so the dump trucks trundled down some dirt roads to load up with thirty odd tons, and then came back and tipped the load into the giant hopper at the processing plant. This seemed easy enough and it did not require me to venture onto public roads.

Once again the foreman showed me the controls and pointed in the direction of the quarry where I would receive my first load. The dumper was huge and bounced around like crazy while it was empty. I managed to find my way to the quarry and saw where the other dumpers were turning to wait for the dragline to fill the back. I must have waited about ten or fifteen minutes as the previous truck was loaded. There were three in all and we rotated all day filling, driving back to the plant and tipping, then back to the quarry for more.

By the second day I realized that if one dumper was left at the quarry for filling, the driver could take an already loaded truck back to the plant. In the meantime the next truck would be back and that driver could then take the now filled second vehicle and leave the third for loading. What a brilliant plan. This meant that the company could achieve the same output using two drivers instead of three.

I couldn't wait to share my cunning plan with the Foreman. He listened with interest as I explained my theory. This was to be my first lesson in trade union economics. I spent the remaining two days of that week mowing the grass at the front of the plant and received my pink slip on Friday afternoon. I later learned from my causal friend at the pub that they thought I was a Time and Motion Study spy put in to

245

the job by the management to thwart the union's hold on how many employees they needed to run the plant. I was determined not to sign on for unemployment benefit so I scanned the local paper for job offers. I saw an advertisement for a *low loader* driver, good pay, plenty of over time, experience needed. Well, I had experience driving Naval heavy goods vehicles, dump trucks and 6-wheeler's. I was made for the part. I was not too sure what a low loader was for, but I thought it was worth a try. I phoned the owner of the business and was invited to go to his yard at Kirkby Underwood, only about six miles from our temporary lodgings.

I turned up at seven in the morning as requested. Nelson Green was a large man of few words. After a very brief discussion he invited me to get in his car and we headed off to another yard in Morton village a couple of miles away. We drove into an old railway yard, no longer threatened by the 8 A.M. express. The place was full of all manner of partly dismantled vehicles. Tractors, some with wheels, some on tracks, lorries, earth graders, road rollers and dozens of Thames Trader army trucks.

I later discovered that Nelson's father had made a fortune by buying up army surplus vehicles after the war and turning them into fertilizer spreaders or salvaging them for parts to repair others. This was at a time when vehicle manufacturers had very little inventory of spare parts. He then graduated to other types of machinery including giant caterpillar tractors, and the like. Nelson had taken over the family business and carried on in similar vein.

Standing menacingly across the yard was a huge low loader tractor unit and trailer. Now I knew what the job was. The whole thing was fifty-five feet long and was designed to carry oversized equipment, some over forty tons in weight.

Nelson introduced me to the yard foreman who turned

out to be his brother-in-law. With that he jumped back in his car and was gone. Geoff, the brother-in-law took me over to the low loader and we climbed up into the cab. It was an AEC Mandator with an 11-3 engine designed specifically for oversize and overweight loads. He ran through some of the controls and then asked me if I was familiar with this type of unit.

"Oh yes, no problem, drove them all the time in Singers."

"OK, well today's delivery is Liverpool docks." We climbed down and he pointed to a little Ford Major tractor fitted with tracks. The tractor was quite old but had a new coat of paint and looked like it was complete. The job was to collect the ones they purchased and deliver the refurbished machines, once they had re-sold them. This one had already had the once over and had been sold to an Irishman who was eagerly waiting delivery in County Cork. It was to be shipped from the docks at Liverpool, my first assignment.

Geoff climbed on the Ford and started it up. He swung it round and drove it straight up the side of the loader and spun it fore and aft in one simple move. That looked so easy I was sure I could do it in reverse to get it off once I reached the docks. He showed me how to chain it down and then went into the office and reappeared with the paperwork.

"Do you know where Liverpool is?"

"Oh yeah, that's where the Beatles come from."

"OK, this needs to go to gate eight at the docks, see you tonight." With that he turned round and walked back into the office. I climbed back into the cab and sat looking at the array of intimidating controls.

After a couple of minutes I switched on the ignition and pressed the starter button. The massive engine burst into life and I nearly jumped through the roof. The tone settled down to a low uneven throb as the cab shuddered with the vi-

247

bration. I slowly put my hand over one of the two gear levers and depressed the clutch. I had no idea which position the lowest gear was as the schematic had long worn off the gear knobs. I pulled the gear into a slot and eased out the clutch. The engine tone lowered and the whole cab started to shudder a little more but did not make any effort to move forward. I quickly depressed the clutch again and decided to try the other gear lever. This time nothing happened. Ah, that means the second lever must be the high and low and the longer of the two was the main set. Now I was in business, all I had to do was figure which side of the gate to start.

Geoff had told me it had twelve gear ratios so if some where on the high low stick there were probably six on the main shift. I tried a position on the opposite side of the gate and slowly let the clutch up. We were off, very slowly. I pointed the cab at the entrance leading on to the public road and headed towards it at about two miles per hour.

I didn't want to attempt another gear in earshot of Geoff so I pulled out into the road in whatever gear I was in. I forgot that the back wheels were some fifty feet behind me and watched helplessly in the mirror as the rear wheels butted against the gatepost and left it leaning at an angle. I caught a glimpse of Geoff scratching his head as I headed up Morton High Street toward the A15.

With new confidence I pushed the clutch down and pulled the gear lever back toward my left knee. I must have got a much higher ratio as the engine tone dipped but the rig started to accelerate quite quickly. The load I was carrying was only a fraction of what it was equipped to haul so I had lots of power to spare. I made it through the village without killing a child and then turned north on the A15 with the intention of heading for Nottingham. Liverpool was northwest of Lincolnshire so I had to go across country to get there.

In 1969 no direct Motorway routes were built linking east to west so the trip required passing through quite a few towns on the way. I had an old highway map that seemed to indicate that Nottingham, Derby, Stoke on Trent was the most direct route to Liverpool. I soon found out that this lorry could get up to seventy mph in a hurry. With so little weight to haul it was very responsive and it was soon clear I only needed two or three of the higher gears unless I had to slow right down or stop. After a few miles my confidence built up and I was able to roll along at fifty to sixty without fear.

All was well as I found my way round Nottingham and Derby. On approaching Stoke on Trent I got confused by some of the road signs and found myself heading into the town center. *No problem,* I thought, *I will just go through and come out the other side.*

The next thing I know I am in a very narrow street heading toward a shopping area with large signs saying, "No Lorries." I pulled up at the curb to try to figure out what to do. As I sat peering around for divine intervention, a policeman rode up on his bike. "Can't take that bloody great thing down here lad, you're in a one way system."

"Well, what should I do then?"

"You will have to back up to the corner and take a left out to the ring road." He propped his bike up on my trailer and walked to the back of the rig waving his arm as he went. Only problem was I had no idea which was reverse, as I had not tried going backwards before.

The policeman stood patiently waiting for me to respond to his arm gestures a few yards behind my rig. I tried a couple of positions before I found reverse. Now all I had to do was keep it straight and not run over the policeman. After a few embarrassing twists and turns I managed to get it past the point where I could pull forward and head for the ring road. I waved a thank you and started speeding up to find my way out of town.

I took one last look in the mirror to see the policeman running down the road behind me waving like crazy. I suddenly realized his bike was still on my trailer. I pulled up and let him catch up. He gave me a dirty look and shrugged his shoulders before pulling his bike off the trailer. After re-adjusting his cycle clips he swung his leg over the seat and peddled off in the direction of the shops no doubt in search of a donut.

Back on route I hoped I would avoid any more town centers. After a total trip time of about five hours I finally arrived at the docks. By now it was early afternoon and I still had to go all the way back to the depot after unloading my cargo. I pulled up to the gate and passed my paperwork to the face peering out of a wooden box. He yelled something about pulling over near the crane. I looked across the yard to see several ships alongside the jetty and a huge crane mounted on tracks that ran the full length of the dockside. He handed me a sheet of paper and gestured me to go on in. I pulled over by the dock and climbed out of the cab. I had been driving for about five hours without a break and was ready for a drink and something to eat. I stood around for about fifteen minutes and no one came to see me.

I was not sure what the next step was at the gate man had not told me to report to anyone. After half an hour I thought I might as well unload the tractor, then, when and if someone turned up I was ready to go. Big mistake! After unchaining the tractor I climbed up on top and started it up, ready to drive it off the side of the trailer.

From nowhere, two obviously irate dockworkers were climbing up on the trailer yelling at me to cut the engine. I obliged so I could hear what they were saying. Every other word was fuck or bollocks or bastard. I formed an opinion that they were upset about something.

Trying to understand the Scouse (Liverpool) accent was bad enough but with them both yelling at the same time it was very difficult to figure out what the issue was. Finally it become clear that the load had to be lifted off by the crane, why, I had no idea. My attempt to unload the tractor had apparently cut across union rules. They made me wait two hours before a crane operator wandered over and slowly climbed up into his machine. Three other, equally speed challenged individuals slothed their way onto the trailer and fixed lifting chains to the tractor.

After what seemed like an hour one of the trailer sloth's waved his arm to signal the crane driver to lift. In about ten seconds the tractor was on the dock and I was being stared at in silence by all three of the offended union casualties. One of them pushed his hand out for the paperwork. Without a word he scribbled his name at the bottom and rammed it back into my hand. I made a feeble attempt to apologize but they were having nothing of it. In strong language and almost impossible to understand Scouser English he told me to fuck off back to the bosses and tell them to stick their fucking games up their fucking arses. From that I deduced I had been singled out as some kind of management mark yet again. Not a good start to my civilian career.

Helpless to change anything, I decided retreat was the best strategy, before I got to look at the underside of the freighter for the rest of my life. I jumped into the cab and set off with as much noise and dust as I could muster. Several fists were raised in the air as I exited the dock in search of a sandwich and pint of beer. Having decided my new friends in the union might not give me the best advice I decided to take my chances potluck style. I managed to find a roadside café and get some sustenance. Despite the rather unpleasant encounter with the lads at the dock I was feeling rather bullish having accomplished the task in hand. Now I was heading out of Liverpool on a dual carriageway in the direction of home.

The rig felt even more loose now I had no weight on the back. I was in the right lane of a two lane road, passing a couple of cars that were indicating to turn left, and doing about forty when a traffic light just ahead went amber. A mini in front of me right on the light had plenty of time to continue through but hit the brakes just a few yards short of the line. I had not had to stop this rig quickly and was also blissfully unaware of the dead man brake that was a separate lever on the dash. I just hit the foot brake. The dead man brake was a device that locked the four rear wheels, to be applied before the foot brake that worked the others. The idea was to hold the trailer straight in an emergency stop and prevent a jackknife.

With an enormous squeal of tires and lots of bouncing, I managed to halt the rig without hitting the mini. When I looked through the back window my trailer was missing. Well, not exactly missing but jutting out to the left at ninety degrees with the back wheels up on the pavement. Miraculously I had not hit anything or anybody, nor done any damage to Liverpool's municipal property.

Several cars were backed up behind me but no one had shunted anyone else. I jumped out to give my opinion to the old dear in the mini but as I made it to her window the light changed and she drove off, probably totally unaware she had nearly caused a multiple pile up.

I now had a new respect for the outfit I was driving, if I had hit that mini I doubt the old lady would ever have played bingo again. After a grueling four more hours I arrived at Nelson Green's yard where my car was parked. It was about eight in the evening. As I drove in Nelson appeared from his house on the other side of the road.

"Did you get the delivery to the dock?"

"Yes sir."

"Did you break anything?"

"No sir."

"It's seven and six an hour and ten-bob for overtime and there will be plenty of that. Do you want the job?"

"Yes sir."

"Right, be here at seven tomorrow." With that, he turned round and went back to his house. I had a job, paying at least twenty pounds a week. That was nearly twice what the navy had been paying me. I was rich!

I couldn't wait to get home and report my success on the job front. When I arrived I got a bit of a cold reception as I had only gone off for a couple of hours for the interview. I had no idea I would actually be sent on a job on the same day. Nevertheless, my newfound employment had relieved our immediate fiscal difficulty and we expected that we could now try to find a place of our own before the baby came. Oh yes, I think I mentioned that by then we were pregnant.

A lady my mother-in-law knew had a small house available for rent and it was just down the road about half a mile from the village. We phoned and made an appointment to see it at the weekend. Next day I was at work by seven looking forward to whatever the schedule was to bring. The business had several other lorries of varying size that were used to transport parts or pieces of equipment that did not warrant the big rig. I never knew from day to day what I would be doing as Nelson was not given to much forward planning. Now that I had a new job I decided I needed a more reliable car to get to work.

The Renault was just about on its last legs when I took it

to a local dealer who had another Wolsley for sale for sixty pounds. This was a 1956 model 444, a smaller version of the previous 690 I had before, and sporting a 1250 cc engine. It was in very clean condition and ran well so I asked how much he would give me on the Renault. He looked it over for a few minutes and turned round and said, "It's not worth much, boy. I can only allow you fifty pounds." Fifty pounds, I couldn't believe it, I only paid twelve for it and had put 25,000 miles on the clock in less than a year. I handed over a crisp ten-pound note and consummated the best car deal in the history of motoring.

The 444 was a smooth car that glided along very quietly. However, with a 1250 cc engine in a two-ton car it accelerated about as fast as a three-wheel bike. The manufacturer had anticipated this small flaw by ensuring that the speedometer read ninety when the car was probably doing fifty. Zero to sixty only if a down gradient was available!

Despite its tortoise-like characteristics, I liked that car. It was good-looking, solid and comfortable, and best of all it started up every morning.

Over the next few weeks I carted all manner of strange items, some coming in to be refurbished, some on their way to a new home. One of the most memorable trips involved a delivery and collection to Port Talbot in South Wales. I was to load a large international tracked monster and take it to a site just outside of Port Talbot. Then, once unloaded I was to go to the harbor front where they would show me a damaged caterpillar tractor to return to base. I had the contact phone number of the business owner I was to call when I got to the outskirts of Port Talbot.

The trip was uneventful and I arrived in the early afternoon. I pulled into a lay-by that had a phone booth. After calling the number I had to wait about half an hour for the guy to arrive in his Land Rover. Once he arrived I was instructed to follow him and he would lead me to the drop off sight of the first tractor. We set off and followed several twists and turns and then started to climb. The gradient continued to get steeper and steeper until he suddenly turned into a gate taking us over a cattle grid and onto a dirt road. We were way out of town and high in the hills. Without stopping he headed up the dirt road, which continued to get even more steep.

By now my rig was starting to feel the gradient as I had about thirty tons on the back. Finally he crossed over another cattle grid and disappeared out of sight over the hillcrest. I was down to first gear and creeping very slowly with full revs. As my drive wheels crossed the cattle grid they started to spin and the rig began to bounce and slide from side to side, but did not move forward. Then I started to lose ground and slip back. On a hill this steep I knew if the rig started to roll back off the dirt road and onto the wet grass I would not be able to stop it.

It took all of my four weeks of experience to hold the thing steady and I gradually managed to stop the slide and lock on the brakes. I was in all kinds of trouble because there was no way I could make a start over the cattle grid and if I tried to roll back to take another shot I ran the risk of losing the whole thing and ending up a the bottom of the hill in a pile of twisted metal. As I contemplated my incredible short career as a lorry drier and wondered how much it would hurt to be squashed in the cab, the Welshman appeared over the hill driving a wheeled, Ford tractor. He positioned the tractor in front of my rig and jumped off pulling a huge chain behind him.

After some arm waving and yelling he then hooked me up to the back of the tractor. He jumped back up and gradually tensioned the chain. At the agreed signal I rammed the rig in gear and slammed my foot hard on the accelerator. In a series of screaming tires and spinning wheels we managed to make it over the grid and keep going to the crest of the hill. I was somewhat relieved to be on level ground at the top and not mashed into a pulp at the bottom.

I was shaking like a leaf and it was obvious to him the whole experience had been a bit scary. The next problem was to get the tractor off the back. Unlike most of the equipment I delivered, this one had one track that was still broken. Consequently it would only turn one way.

After my pathetic attempts to maneuver it off the back, the agitated Welshman climbed back on his wheeled tractor and, in a series of pushing motions using the weight tray on the front he managed to force the load half off the side of the trailer. We then chained the two together and I pulled the rig forward while he pulled in the other direction. Finally we managed to drag it all the way off my trailer. How he intended to fix the track on top of this mountain I had no idea.

The next part was to follow him back down the hill right to the harbor front to collect the other vehicle. Going down was almost as scary as going up but we made it safely out of the field and onto the road.

When we arrived at the shore I noted the other tractor looked quite normal, both tracks in place and no obvious defects. Not so, apparently the clutch was burned out so once started in gear, it could only be stopped by killing the engine. The Welshman said he would drive it onto the trailer for me, as he knew "how the bugger thinks." Until that point I was unaware that tractors had minds of their own but I was new to the job, so what did I know?

He climbed on board and pressed the starter. The machine was in gear because without the clutch it was impossible to select a gear once the engine was running. The thing lurched forward as the starter growled and then suddenly burst into life. We had removed the four large wheels at the back of the trailer to enable the tractor to be driven straight up the back with no need to turn. The thing clanked up the back and onto the flat bed of the trailer. I could see him frantically trying to pull the engine stop but it kept going forward. It climbed up the front ramp to the high level of the trailer and came to a stop, only inches from crushing the back of my cab.

"Bugger Boyo, we nearly buggered yer lorry." I had had enough excitement for one day so I declined to not say anything.

Once the engine had stopped, he somehow managed to pull it out of gear and, with the help of gravity, the thing clanked backwards till it settled on the level part of the trailer. After bidding my farewell, with damp shorts and chains taught I headed for Kirkby Underwood.

By now I was driving anything up to seventy hours a week. This was before the tachometer was introduced and the logbook system was virtually ignored. On several occasions I drove round trips of twenty-four hours only stopping for food and relief for less than two hours in the day. While this was good for the overtime money it was not doing my knee much good. The clutch on this rig was so heavy and because of the tremendous weights I hauled I was always changing gear. I decided that I needed a job with less heavy lifting, but how was I going to do that? Other than reading the local paper for other job options I was resigned to keep on trucking till something came along.

One Monday I was dispatched to somewhere in Nottinghamshire to pick up a six-wheel earth grader and take it about forty miles to a village in South Yorkshire. I arrived at the collection site and took a look at the grader. Now I was still pretty green but it seemed obvious to me this bloody great thing was not going to fit on the back of my rig.

After all kinds of attempts to get it to fit I gave up trying and phoned Nelson.

"If you can't get it on you will have to drive it there on the road and get the foreman to pick you up and take you back for the lorry." I had spent over an hour getting to know this strange machine trying to load it so I knew this was no simple task.

The machine had a huge blade that hung under its belly and everything was controlled by a series of hydraulic levers in the cab. Problem was, as with my lorry, all the diagrams had long worn off the knobs and this time there were six different ones. One pair controlled the four back wheels that could turn almost at right angles, one set controlled the two front wheels and another set controlled the blade. Not to be beaten I took my map from the lorry and pinpointed where I had to go The foreman at the site agreed to fetch me back in a couple of hours because it would likely take me several hours to get there on this thing. It was not too bad to go straight but turning was really weird because it had no steering wheel.

To turn required a steady pull on one of the levers, but if you were not quick enough it would oversteer and try to go in a circle. The other problem was that all the levers were in a cluster and it was hard to look down to see which one to pull while trying to keep my eye on where I was going. I managed to get about half way to my destination without taking a layer off the A164 when I found myself heading into a small village.

In the middle of the village, the road took a sharp right and was divided by some keep left bollards right on the bend. I had to stop because some idiot had parked a car partly blocking the road so it was clear this thing would not go through the gap without some careful manipulation. I had been running with the blade turned almost fore and aft to narrow the unit as much as I could but in that position the rear wheels could not be angled to help swing the back out to take the narrow turn. All this required the blade to be turned out at about forty-five degrees to clear it and allow a turn on the rear wheels. I was looking at the back wheels as I pulled the blade control to see how much more was needed.

At the same time I was easing the machine forward to start the turn round the bend. As soon as I thought I had swung it enough I grabbed the lever for the rear wheels and pulled it enough to swing the back out after I was sure I had cleared the car. While all this was going on a small crowd was gathering on the side of the road and a surprising number of vehicles was backing up behind me on the A164.

This all added to the pressure as I gingerly moved forward. Sods law had to set in and just as I thought I had it all together I pulled the blade lever to turn it fore and aft again but it went the opposite way. I had a sickening feeling as it swung out to full width and with absolute precision cleaned the keep left bollards right off their mountings. Before I could do anymore I had made the turn and was bouncing along away from the village. I had no hope of parking this thing off the road and now with several dozen irritated motorists behind me I decided to keep going. To my knowledge we never heard from the council about replacing their bollards.

Hopefully, by the time this is published, the borough surveyor will have passed away.

My next interesting trip involved a JCB digger. This machine was a large tracked vehicle with a huge hydraulic arm and bucket that, when bent double in the resting position, was still about twenty-five feet high. It was easy enough to load on the trailer and secure for the trip but became a very high load.

259

The next problem was I had to take it to Rugby and that mean going through quite a few towns and villages. Somewhere near Husbands Bosworth I entered a village and, on rounding a bend was confronted with a low railway bridge. The clearance was about thirteen feet and my total height was about twenty-six feet. The prospect of reversing back to a place I could turn and try another route was immediately removed as the inevitable traffic build up started behind me. To further the embarrassment I had positioned myself such that anything bigger than a mini coming from the opposite direction could not squeeze by either. The situation required some quick thinking as not to completely paralyze the whole East Midland traffic system.

I decided I had only one option and that was to start up the digger and lower the hydraulic arm and bucket behind my back wheels. Then get back in the rig and drive it through the bridge before stopping again and putting it all back as it was. I had never operated this beast so it took me several minutes to figure out what levers moved what parts. I also had to ask the cars right behind me to shove back a little lest I should place the digger bucket through the leading car's windshield. I finally figured out how to shift the arm and brought it thumping down on the road just inches from the very wary chap in the nearest car.

I could not make the arm stay in one place so the only option was to let it rest on the road and drag it through the bridge behind me. I jumped back in the lorry cab and started to pull forward, at the same time taking quick glances behind me to see if I was bringing half the road surface too. I was. Well, some of it. But I was too far under the bridge to change tactics. Once the bucket was cleared I stopped and surveyed the damage. I had rolled up about 100 pounds of tarmac in several quite neat strips. The rips in the road were not too deep so once I had sheepishly thrown the tarmac on the trailer I restowed the digger and set off for Rugby with as much speed as I could muster.

Because of the fifteen minutes wait at the bridge a huge convoy of vehicles had built up behind me, and most of them had to follow me all the way to Rugby. I could feel hundreds of angry eyes piercing my back as I drove. I found my drop-off address and was pleased to be relieved of the digger. Before heading back I found a transport café and went in for my all day breakfast and mug of tea. As I pulled in only one other lorry was in the parking area. It was a much more modern low loader rig about the same size as mine. After bellying up to the counter and getting my bacon, eggs, sausage, fried bread, baked beans, black pudding, tea and toast I went over to where the other driver was tucking into an identical gourmet feast.

"Your rig?" I said to break the ice. The other driver looked around the otherwise empty café and then back at me.

"Guess it must be, mate, there's no other bugger in ere."

"Hard job, isn't it?"

"It's not so bad, especially the money."

"Yeh, I get about forty quid a week driving seventy hours."

"You must be crackers mate, I get seventy quid for about fifty hours." It was the final insult, I had been killing myself for weeks driving every hour possible and was getting about a third of the going rate for this type of vehicle.

All the way home I planned how I would approach Nelson to have my wages adjusted to equal the going rate. By the time I got back that day it was too late to bring up the subject, and I made the mental excuse that I was too tired to do it justice. The next morning I was terrified of addressing the issue but knew if I did not do it right away I would chicken out and the moment would be lost.

"Er, Mr. Green, yesterday I met this bloke and he told me he was, er well er um, you know, like he's getting seventy quid a week and he's driving a lot less hours than me, er, and I thought . . ."

I stopped to test the reaction of Nelson who did not appear to be even paying attention to what I was saying. He finally raised his eyes to look me straight in the face and said, "It's seven and six an hour and ten-bob for overtime and there will be plenty of that, do you want the job."

"Er, yes Sir."

"Right, let's have a look where you're going today." That concluded the wage negotiations for the year. I wondered briefly if I should contemplate looking up some of my union friends but decided I might get murdered before I could convince them I was changing sides.

Today's job turned out to be another trip to Wales, only this time in the flat bed Thames Trader to collect a pile of spare parts Nelson had bought at a Forestry auction somewhere deep in Dean Forest. Riding empty this old lorry could do about seventy as long as the road was straight enough to build up the speed so I made it to the collection site in record time. When I arrived I saw dozens of different piles of all manner of equipment lying around on the ground.

After searching for a few minutes I identified a huge pile of mainly caterpillar tracks and mounting wheels (the bits the tracks fit on) plus an assortment of other heavy metal lumps that had a sign, lying on top. Green. The lorry had a hydraulic lift fitted behind the cab so I began to load the various bits and pieces as best as I could fit them.

The total load capacity of this Thames Trader was only ten tons and I had no way of measuring how much weight I was putting on at a time. I finally managed to get it all on and chained securely in place. It was quite obviously well overloaded but I had no way to call Nelson, nor did I expect him to be sympathetic to the problem. So, with no other option I started up the forest road back to the highway. Now the old Thames started to show its age. With probably double my load limit I headed slowly in the direction of Lincolnshire. Every hill was a trial as I gradually dropped down the gears to first on almost every, even modest incline.

By the time I was half way home the engine cover inside the cab as so hot I could not let my left knee rest against it. But she kept going until, on a bit of downhill doing about fifty, one of the right side double rear tires blew out with a mighty bang. I brought the lorry to rest half on the grass and half on the road. I was miles from anywhere and it was already after six in the evening. I wouldn't mind betting that the guy who thought up the cell phone used to drive a lorry! Eventually another knight of the road pulled over and he took Nelson's number and my position and promised to call for help. About 9 P.M. a tire truck finally arrived and proceeded to change my flat. I still had at least three more hours to get home and I had been on the road since seven that morning.

I set off again and made very slow progress. I was nearly home when a tire on the other rear blew out. It was after midnight and I was two miles from home. I left the lorry on the road and walked home. Next day my father-in-law took me out to the lorry after I had called Nelson for another tire repair service. When I finally got to the depot and unloaded I was sent off South down the A1 to collect some other small parts in the same Thames Trader.

Now, without twenty tons to hold me up I was able to get up to seventy again. Well, for a couple of miles anyway. There was a brief grinding sound and then an almighty crack and clatter and the engine cover in the cab lifted off its mounting. I jammed on the brakes but very little happened.

This vehicle had hydraulic brakes that took pressure from the engine, only now I didn't have an engine. Bits of the crankcase were scattered in the passenger side and there was oil splattered up the windows. Of course I did not know what had actually happened until after the fact but that was the problem.

I finally managed to stop the thing after frightening several day-trippers in a mini bus, on their way to London. Yet another distress call to base and I am once again sitting by the roadside waiting for help. Help arrived in the guise of Geoff, the brother-in-law. He turned up in an identical Thames Trader with a very short length of chain, ready to tow me home. One look under the oily mess in the cab confirmed that a piston had broken and several large parts of metal had smashed through the left side of the engine block.

I wondered what might have happened if the piston had come through the other side! With the very short chain between us we set off down the A1 to try to find a place where we could turn back, to go north. Geoff had done his driver training in a Demolition Derby and had no regard for me in the brakeless wreck behind him.

He saw a gap in the middle and swerved over to the center. It was all I could do to stop hitting the back of his lorry, as I yanked on the hand brake and jumped hard on the foot pedal. He just swung round in a U-turn and off we went again.

After several very scary miles we arrive back at the Morton depot. Nelson was standing by his Rover looking very stern. We climbed down from our respective vehicles and walked over to where he was standing. "What's wrong with it?"

"Engine's buggered."

"Right, show him where he can get another and get it

in." The conversation was limited to the bare essentials. Nelson got back in his Rover and drove out of the yard.

"What's he mean, get it put in?" I asked, as if I really did not know the answer.

"We have about fifteen more Traders down the line, we need to try a few to find a runner then you can get it fitted." Right enough, the depot ran way back down the side of the old railway and it was littered with dozens of other vehicles, with plenty of Traders to choose from. Apparently, many of them had been driven there over ten years before and never moved since.

Geoff climbed on a Ford major tractor that had a lift mounted on the front. He went over to a shed and came out with a cart holding two gas cylinders and a blowtorch. He hooked the cart on the front of the tractor and climbed back on board. "Follow me," he said heading off in the direction of the graveyard for Thames Traders.

He pulled up by one and told me to get in the cab. He ran some jump wires to the battery location and yelled OK. I turned on the key and he yelled again for me to press the manual starter button. The engine turned over for a little while but showed no signs of continuing without life support. We tried about five more before we finally got one to run unassisted.

"OK, this one will do it. Get the torch and burn off all the rods and mountings so you can lift it out." I had no idea how to use the blowtorch or which bits I was supposed to burn off without rendering this engine useless as well.

With that he strode off back to his hut in the main yard. I realized I needed to rig chains from the tractor lift around the engine before cutting it loose from its mountings. So with that done I slid underneath among the nettles to see what had to be done to free it.

I determined that several steering rods were in the way

265

of getting to the mounting bolts so they had to go. Then I could get a straight shot with the socket wrenches to undo the nuts. It took me several attempts to get the gas mix right and generate a flame that could actually cut metal. I made a few fancy cuts in the front bumper to make sure I had everything set. I shuffled back under the front of the engine and lay on my back to angle the flame at one of the steering arms. I soon realized that I needed some goggles as the sparks shot all over the place. Once goggled, I resumed cutting. After a couple of minutes I managed to cut through one of the smaller rods. I then tackled a much bigger one that seemed to be taking far too long to succumb.

All of a sudden there was a bang and a screech of metal on metal. I stopped cutting and crawled out of the nettles to see if I could figure out what had made the noise. It transpired that this steering arm had a ball joint on the end packed with grease. I must have heated it so much the outer part blew off the ball and swung the now-loose steering rod, smashing it up into the bodywork, just inches from my head.

I used a great deal more caution for the rest of the cutting jobs. Eventually I had the engine free of its mountings and loaded onto the lift on the tractor. It took me most of the next day to remove the broken engine still in the other lorry, and a third day to fit the new one. When it was all done I jumped into the cab and pressed the starter. It fired up immediately and ran without a hitch.

I don't know why it is that now I freak out if I have to change a wall plug in the house. Maybe all my fixing skills were used up too soon?

16
Sell, Sell, Sell

All the time I was driving the lorry I was keeping my eyes open for a job opportunity that did not demand lots of qualifications. Furthermore, the heavy weight duty was killing my damaged knee. By now I had moved my wife and I into the little rental cottage so at least we had our own place while we waited for the baby to arrive, due early the next year.

Then it happened, one Saturday the local paper ran an advertisement. Salesmen Wanted, Training Given, Generous Commission, No Qualifications or Experience Needed, Must Have Own Transport.

Well, I had no qualifications, and no experience, and I had a car, so I could meet the criteria. I phoned the number in the ad and spoke to a man who I later found out was the Sales Director for the company in question. After asking me a few questions about myself he said he would send an application form for me to fill in. The job as selling double-glazing for Everest. I watched the mail every day and had just about given up when the envelope arrived. I filled in the forms and discovered that selected applicants would be invited to attend a two-day training seminar in Warwick, coming up in a couple of week's time. It would mean taking two days off work as the course was on the Thursday and Friday. I thought I could feign sickness. A week went by and I heard nothing. Again, I had given up on the opportunity when, on arriving home from work, I found out Everest had phoned and invited me to the training course and a formal interview.

The next Thursday, in my wedding suit and scrubbed clean of as much oil and grease as I could remove without my epidermis, I headed for Warwick (the town, not Dionne). I arrived at the designated hotel and checked in with the receptionist, who was sitting under a giant sign reading, "Everest, The Peak of Perfection." To my horror there must have been fifty or more people standing around in the foyer, all in their wedding suits and all scrubbed clean. Nevertheless I still thought I had a shot, and I was there anyway. The process started when a smartly dressed guy wearing glasses announced that he was the Sales Director and that we would all be interviewed during the morning. This would be done by several sales managers, who were mingling with the group. A show of hands identified his accomplices and the show began. We were ushered into groups of six or eight and separated into different rooms. One by one each person was called by name to disappear into another adjacent room. Some came out looking very glum and headed straight outside to the car park. A couple of others sat back down with a smile on their faces.

It was not difficult to figure out what was happening. My turn came and I went in to meet the Sales Manager who was responsible for the East Midland area where I lived. He asked me a few simple questions but nothing really difficult. It seemed he was more interested that I had not had a DUI or was on probation for theft. After about five minutes he told me I was selected to meet the Sales Director and could wait outside for the next call. Now I sat back in the chair with a big smile on *my* face.

My imagination started to run away, sales job, lots of

money, promotion, wear a suit to work instead of oily over-alls. It was all I could do not to shout out loud.

Eventually I was ushered in to meet the Sales Director, Mr. Bingham. He told me that I had been highly recommended from my first interview and he was keen to see if I was the stuff Everest needed to expand sales by 100 percent. I have no idea what I told him but it seemed to work because after about five questions he announced I had been selected to stay for the training program and could select one of several sales territories that were vacant. It was soon to become obvious why they were able to hire on such limited information. Their risk zero, my risk 100 percent.

I was told to report to the secretary under the sign and tell her I was selected. She took down my details and told me that lunch would be served in a private room and after that the training would commence at one-thirty P.M. Only about twelve of us had been singled out from the fifty or sixty hopeful's. Mr. Bingham gave a little welcome speech before we sat down for lunch and then we ate. I was more used to my all day breakfast than the rather skimpy hotel fare but I was not complaining, after all I was now a salesman. The training turned out to be how to fill in order forms and send in commission claim forms. Then we were introduced to the sample box. This was a mini set of windows about twenty-four inches long and fifteen inches high.

A perfect little sliding set of double glazed windows.

We were entertained to a nice evening meal, again in the hotel and then shared a few stories at the bar before turning in. The other participants seemed to come from all walks of life. Some had been in the air force, others had already tried sales jobs but were looking for a new challenge. I, on the other hand was just trying to get a job that didn't hurt. The next day was much of the same, all about forms and measuring windows and how to follow up on orders. It was only toward the end that Mr. Bingham got down to the nitty, gritty. The way it worked was that each sales person had a territory, as agreed by the various Sales Managers in the room. There were no expenses covered by the company, the salesman used his own car and own phone and own everything. The commission was 15 percent of the gross sales value of the orders taken.

At that time a typical order might range from one hundred and fifty pounds for a couple of windows right up to several thousand pounds if you happened to get the full house at the local plastic surgeon. No sales, no income. If you ran up lots of travel expenses and still made no sales then you were in the hole on your own. Nevertheless, it was a foot in the selling door, if I could only hold out for a few months I might be able to move on to something with a bit more security. The very last hour was spent talking to my new Sales Manager. He was a scruffy looking individual who was 50 percent overweight and smelled like he needed a bath. He lived near Lincoln and he told me the area South of Sleaford down to Peterborough was open. This included the town of Stamford but not Peterborough itself. There were a couple of decent sized villages plus two other small towns but not much more. Mr. Bingham came by and wished me every success and expected me to be top salesman by Christmas, just four months away (Christmas 2000 I thought).

Armed with forty pounds of glossy brochures and my mini window set I loaded up the car and headed back to Billingborough. My mind was in a whirl, what should I tell Nelson on Monday, did I have enough sense to actually sell these windows? All the way home I was torn between the safe bet driving the lorry, even though it was hard work, and taking a chance on this opportunity. I decided the best thing to do was sleep on it and then go out the next morning and give it a try.

Bright and early on Saturday morning, in my wedding suit again, I headed toward Stamford, which was about eighteen miles away. Passing through a little village not more than six miles down the road, I saw a man and woman working in their front garden outside a modern bungalow with big picture windows. Why not? I reversed back to their garden gate and climbed out with my folder of brochures and my mini windows.

"Er, good morning. I'm from Everest Double Glazing. Er, do you need some double glazing? Er, er." The lady looked at me for a moment and turned to her husband.

"You know, George, we have been talking about doing those two big windows at the front." She gestured toward the two windows in question. George grunted something and lay his shovel down on the ground. "I'll make some tea while you tell George all about your windows." George was not too keen on parting with any money but the wife kept chipping in with comments and it did not take me long to figure out that the problem was drafts around the frames.

Like a ferret down a rabbit hole, I found the bit in the brochure that talked about 100 percent draft proof frames. George was toast. I measured up the two windows and filled in the order form. The total came to 150 pounds. The order was only good once the engineer came by the following week to take very accurate measurements that the windows would be manufactured to. But as long as their roof didn't come off over the weekend I had made my first sale and earned twenty-two pounds and fifty pence. Bingo, I was going to make a fortune. Twenty-two pounds in just one hour, this was going to be easy! I loaded up the car and decided I had made enough for today, after all I was going to be raking it in as soon as I started full time. I went home to report the news.

Monday morning came round and I drove in to work

extra early. I wanted to catch Nelson before he went out so I could hand in my notice.

Nelson was not pleased but told me I had to work to Friday or else. I didn't want to find out what else was so I agreed Friday would be my last day. I blew out another Thames Trader engine on Friday but managed to limp back to the yard. I parked the lorry as far back as I could and hoped no one would need to drive it for a few days after I had gone. With my severance package in hand (a large bottle of brown ale from Geoff) I headed home to start my new career.

It took me two weeks before I even got into another home, let alone to make a sale. But I persevered and managed to make several sales totaling about one thousand pounds in commission for the month. Not too bad but I had not anticipated the cost of the petrol and saving to pay my taxes and eating out and the telephone bills.

After the first month I began to develop a technique. It was obvious the women wanted the new windows but always the men tried to talk them out of it. I would cold call during the day and "sell" the woman of the house and then make an appointment to come by in the evening when hubby was home.

If I timed it just before he normally ate then I would either rush through the presentation or agree to come back after dinner, at great inconvenience to me. If we rushed I could often get him to sign on without too many questions and if I had to come back he was tired and feeling a bit guilty because I had had to reorganize my appointments.

October and half of November was great. The windows took about six weeks to have made and installed and they all wanted them in for Christmas. After all, little Jimmy would be able to sit right by the windows in his pajamas to unwrap his gifts without getting cold. All was fine till I reached the day when the expected deliver date was in January. After that sales dried up completely.

I had made quite a bit of commission in the good times but we were facing several weeks with no new sales. The money ran out by early January and it was time to re-think strategy. No one was interested in buying double-glazing after Christmas because they had spent all their money on little Jimmy. After that it was summer on the way so the need to double glaze would be delayed for a time.

I decided on Plan B, which was not to tell Everest I was giving up but to find another job to tide me over and just keep the double glazing pot boiling at weekends. I began to scour the paper again for driving jobs and eventually saw one for Modd's Transport. They were looking for a driver for a flatbed-six-wheeler for local deliveries. I called for an interview and was all but offered the job on the phone as long as I had a license. Modd's were based at Colsterworth right by the A1 highway. I went over to meet the Transport Manager and was hired to start as soon as I could.

That was the next day. The pay was about the same as the previous driving job so I was at least able to make ends meet for the time being. Modd's had a contract with ICI Fertilizers and many of the deliveries were bagged fertilizers delivered to farms around the East Midlands. Other cargos included sacks of grain that some of the smaller farms had to use if they had no bulk storage. These were sold and transported to grain merchants. My lorry was an aging six-wheel Dodge that had almost non-existent brakes. My first introduction to the grain sacks was on my second day. Another driver and I were dispatched to a farm where we were to load our two flat beds with about twenty-five tons of grain between us.

I was up first, waiting at the top of the elevator as the first sack menacingly approached. I turned to take it over my shoulder and felt the weight transfer. It almost crushed me into the floor. I staggered forward and managed to tip it at the front of the lorry. I later discovered that the bags averaged about fourteen stones (196 pounds). Once I knew what was coming I was able to anticipate the weight.

Between us we handled all twenty-five tons onto the lorries. My mate was physically sick before we drove out of the yard. After just two days I had made my mind up that I was going to be in selling, not in lifting heavy weights.

A couple of days later, I was sent to Liverpool to collect a load of animal feed that had been salvaged from a ship fire. This stuff was in Hessian sacks and was still wet, presumably from the firemen's efforts to put the fire out. The feed meal was to be taken to a mill near Gainsborough in North Lincolnshire. I waited by the dock as the lorry was loaded. (This time by my union friends whom I did not offer to help.) They kept throwing it on till the load looked very high and I called a halt.

I knew I was way over the weight limit of sixteen tons but the prospect of asking them if they minded taking a few off did not seem like a good idea. I set off in the direction of Gainsborough and hoped for the best. Apart from being very slow it all went well until I was pulled into a Ministry of Transport Weigh Station on the Derby ring road. The inspector started to do his inspection, crawling about underneath. He periodically came up for air and wrote notes on his clipboard. I knew it was not going well as every time he resurfaced he gave me a scowl and purposefully dived back under for another look.

Finally he told me to get in the cab and drive the lorry up a steep concrete ramp at the end of the yard and lock on the brakes and hold it in position. I drove up and rolled straight back. No matter what I did, with the foot and hand brakes I could not make this thing stay on the ramp. He then made me go on the weighbridge. I was 25 percent over-loaded. That did it, the inspector told me to park the lorry and come into the office. I went in and he handed me a notice that had large red letters on the top telling me my lorry was impounded for defective brakes, broken springs, overloading and bald tires. I thought of mentioning the hole in the exhaust but thought better of it.

I called the depot and they told me they would talk to the inspector. After some heated words on the phone the inspector told me he had agreed that the company could send another lorry to take the load and he would let me drive home empty. It took a couple of hours for my mate to arrive and start transferring the load. About half way through, the inspector came over and said he wanted to test the other lorry before we put any more weight on it. That one failed too. It took several more phone calls before the inspector reluctantly agreed to allow both to go half loaded but Modds would have to have both lorries repaired before they could go back on the road. By the time I finally got home I had been on the go for eighteen hours.

Another reason to favor selling versus heavy lifting. The weather was nasty by early February and I was miserable out in all weathers humping all kinds of wet slippery bags. One of the things I noticed was the name of the agricultural merchant who was selling the fertilizer to the farmers. It was called Barker and Lee Smith of Lincoln. As luck would have it I was scanning the local paper job section at the weekend when I saw an advertisement by Barkers who were looking for a trainee chemical salesman.

Well, I was a salesman, and I was very familiar with chemicals, and I needed training, once again I thought I met the criteria, well sort of! Another plus was the fact that my father's boss, Mr. Proctor, was a very good customer of the same company. One phone call to him ensured a letter of reference for me to take if I could secure an interview. I phoned the company on the Monday and was put through to the department manager, Mr. Meldrum. He asked me the usual questions and finally invited me to send in a letter of application and he would consider me for an interview. Within two weeks I had my interview planned, to take place at their mill and office in Lincoln. The day before the interview I was driving home from work when my Wolsley decided to give out. The engine just stopped working, no sound, no fuss, no go. I managed to get it towed to the local garage where my pal, Blondie, worked. It took him about ten minutes to determine that the most likely problem was that the crankshaft had broken. A later strip down inspection proved his theory. She was very sick.

Not to be put off, I borrowed my parents' car and headed for Lincoln the next morning. I met Mr. Meldrum and we spent some time talking about my experience and he told me what the job would entail. Barkers were prepared to provide training in agronomy and pesticide use to the lucky candidate. It would also cover crop nutrition and soil testing. The training would mainly be provided by the various suppliers of chemicals, such as ICI, Fison's, Shell and others. The job was to provide chemical sales support to twenty-five animal-feed salesmen that covered the whole East Midlands for Barkers. I would get a company car, an expense account and a base salary. After we had exhausted all the questions he invited me to wait a few minutes while he went off to see the Managing Director. I could hardly sit still thinking about prospect of having a job like this which was everything I could hope for.

I came close to prayer. (Close.) After what seemed like forever, he returned and beckoned me to follow him. I was ushered into the MD's office and introduced to Mr. Bartlett. He was a fairly elderly man in a dark suit and sitting behind a huge wooden desk. He rose to shake my hand and I tried to give as firm a grip as I could without crushing his fingers. I had become extremely strong over the past few months with all the heavy lifting and sometimes forgot how strong.

Mr. Bartlett smiled and gave me a long handshake. "Bruce tells me you were in the Navy."

That was an invitation to explain what a worldly wise traveler I was, although I had to be careful not to lapse into some of the experiences that would have curled his hair. He held up the letter from Mr. Proctor and commented that he was a fine gentleman and that he seemed to have a high regard for me. Phew!

We went over all the same questions again until he finally rose from his chair and invited me to take a tour of their facilities. As the three of us walked along the corridor he turned to me and said, "By the way, how much do you know about fertilizers?"

I was a little taken aback for a moment then said, "I know how much the bags weigh because I have been lifting the damn things for the last few months."

Mr. Bartlett just roared with laughter and said to Bruce, "That's the sort of humor we need round here." I was in.

Before I left, Mr. Meldrum (Bruce) said that I would be offered the job in a letter, which would outline the salary and terms of employment. The relief was incredible. After seven months of trying to find a job that had any kind of training and future potential here I was being told I had succeeded. I drove home like a maniac (usual speed) and blurted out the good news. As our son, Wayne, was due to drop by in two weeks, the timing could not have been better.

The offer arrived a couple of days later and explained that I would be placed on a training salary of eight hundred pounds a year but would have a fully funded company car and out of pocket expenses provided. The salary was about

277

half what I was earning on the lorries but with the car and prospects it was a no-brain decision. My start date was to be March 10 (1970). I had just turned twenty-three.

I continued to drive the lorry for Modds, having handed in my notice, waiting for my first day at Barker's. On the morning of March 2 I left for work as usual, getting home at about five-thirty P.M. Sue was not at home and before I could call anyone I got a call from my mother to tell me Sue had gone into labor and was in Grantham hospital.

I got cleaned up and had my dinner before heading off to Grantham for visiting time. Nothing had happened yet, so I sat and chatted to Sue as she periodically squirmed as she had the occasional contraction which did seem to be coming more quickly.

At 8 P.M. the nurse came round the ward telling us it was the end of visiting and to come back tomorrow. I was not invited to stay, even though it was clear the baby was imminent. I drove home and watched a little TV before going to bed. The program was "Doom Watch." And the episode was all about intelligent rats eating people.

I got up the next day and went to work. After work, I phoned the hospital to discover I was a father. Wayne had been born during "Doom Watch" the night before. It seemed odd now that it was all so matter of fact, with no expectation for the father to be involved in the process at all. (Other than the obvious bit early on.)

The other strange thing that happened was that Sue's grandfather, in a ward in the same hospital, died within hours of Wayne being born. We did not know he was there until several days later. Mother and son stayed in the hospital for several days before moving back to the cottage.

Lincoln was over thirty miles from my home so it would require moving a little closer in due course. The first few weeks would involve very intensive training, as I knew absolutely nothing (other than the fact that fertilizer came in eight stone bags). My next problem was to fix the Wolsley so I could sell it as I now had a company car. Blondie told me I might be able to get a crankshaft at a dealer in Boston. I called the dealer and they told me they did have one in stock but it might take some time to find it. I was intrigued by this comment but I borrowed my mum's car and drove over to Boston to fetch it.

When I arrived, the parts manager invited me into the storeroom to collect the item in question. I thought this was a bit strange but followed him anyway. He pointed to an object lying on a rack that was wrapped in an oily canvas coating. A dirty crumpled label displayed a part number and the word Crankshaft, and was dated 1935. He explained that the engine in my 1956 Wolsley had the same engine block that was first used in the Austin 10 in the 1930s. It was indeed the correct part and Blondie had it all back together in a couple of days.

I sold the car for sixty pounds, exactly the amount I had paid for it, taking into account the credit on the Renault. I just wish I could still make car deals like that today.

That was the last car deal I had to do for many years as now I had made it to the illustrious ranks of those who enjoyed the benefits of company cars, usually a source of extreme envy by the neighbors who don't get one.

I had made it, survived seven years in the navy, got a salaried job with a company car, and, above all, training for a real job in Civvy Street. What more could a man ask?

Little did I know just how interesting life could get on the outside, but that's probably a story all on its own.